A Transaction of Free Men

DAVID HAWKE

❈ ❈ ❈ ❈ ❈ ❈ ❈ ❈

A TRANSACTION
OF FREE MEN

The Birth and Course
of the Declaration of Independence

As there is not a more distinguished Event in the History of America, than the Declaration of her Independence—nor any, that in all probability, will so much excite the Attention of future Ages, it is highly proper, that the Memory of that Transaction, together with the Causes that gave Rise to it, should be preserved in the most careful Manner that can be devised.

JOHN HANCOCK—1777

Charles Scribner's Sons
NEW YORK

TO *Anne*

Contents

❁ ❁ ❁ ❁ ❁ ❁ ❁ ❁ ❁

A Transaction of Free Men

Chapter 1

The Course of Events

❋ ❋ ❋ ❋ ❋ ❋ ❋ ❋ ❋

But America is a great, unwieldy body. Its progress must
be slow. It is like a large fleet sailing under convoy. The
fleetest sailers must wait for the dullest and slowest. Like a
coach and six, the swiftest horses must be slackened, and
the slowest quickened, that all may keep an even pace.

JOHN ADAMS—1775

IT HAS been remarked that the Declaration of Independence
distilled in a few lines over a century and a half of American
experience. Jefferson himself agreed. "It was intended to be an
expression of the American mind," he once wrote. His endorsement makes the observation, a half-truth at best, doubly hard to
fend off. The Declaration could have been written only in
eighteenth century America and only by an American; to that
extent it distilled American experience. But more to the point, it
distilled Jefferson's conception of that experience. He evoked
a private vision of America's past and present, and he anticipated
a future that would have unsettled most leaders of the day if they
had comprehended his vision. He did more than summarize ideas
accepted by all thoughtful Americans of the time. He inten-
tionally gave new implications to old terms.

Jefferson created so well that his ideas slipped through Congress with few essential changes, despite heavy trimming by the
delegates. How he managed this feat is an intriguing part of the
Declaration's story. Jefferson's agreeable, circumspect character
and his aristocratic Virginia background figure prominently in

3

that story. A Declaration by Tom Paine, for instance, would have received brutal treatment. Also involved are the varied personalities of the delegates in Congress, along with the confusion of the times and the need for haste. Above all, Jefferson's literary skill contributed. Wright Morris has written, and his words surely apply to Jefferson's Declaration, that the great artist will manage "to displace an old god with a new one—but the new one will bear an astonishing resemblance to the one it displaced." So much of a resemblance, it might be added, that years would pass before America saw clearly what Jefferson had been up to.

When Jefferson snapped shut the portable desk on which he had written the Declaration and carried the finished paper from his second-floor apartment on the outskirts of Philadelphia down to the State House, he had, knowingly or not, cleared the way for the shaping of a new pattern of thought in America. He had taken such words as "liberty" and "equality" and "happiness" and projected his experience with these words in a way that his experience was to become *the* American experience. He had crystallized one version of that experience into a creed that has yet to cease influencing the American mind.

But there was another version. John Adams of Massachusetts, a man of greater repute and power in the Second Continental Congress than Jefferson, would spend a good part of his political life in the remainder of the eighteenth century battling many of the ideas his friend embedded in the Declaration. (For a time the battle would become so warm that the friendship would wane, then break off completely for a number of years.) Adams, curiously, came closer than Jefferson to reflecting the more accepted, respected version of the American experience among the leaders of 1776. When he eventually saw what Jefferson had been up to, he spent a good many hours fuming in print and in private over what "equality" and "liberty" and "happiness" meant. They meant, of course, something entirely different to this man of New England.

The urge to focus on Jefferson intrudes too often in most accounts of the Declaration. It is the hope in the pages that follow to recapture something of the shape and complexity of thought in eighteenth century America by not centering solely on Jefferson but including also the contrasting ideas of John Adams. The delegates of Congress, too, as they fretted and argued their way toward independence through the summer of 1776, must have their say if the full story of the Declaration is to be told. The task itself has sufficient fascination to need no further justification. Further justification, however, does exist. If, as has been said, it is necessary for Americans to be wiser than their creed if they would survive the twentieth century, then they must know clearly what that creed is, how it came about, what its flaws might be, and how it has been used and misused throughout the nineteenth and into the twentieth century.

This, then, is not Thomas Jefferson's story alone. He remains, however, a central character, and for that reason it seems sensible to begin with him. Moreover, the record should show, if only for those intrigued by the part chance plays in history, that Jefferson returned to Philadelphia on May 14, 1776, determined to depart again from the city and from his seat in the Second Continental Congress as swiftly as possible.

Nothing occurred the first day back to change his mind. Sometime around ten in the morning he stepped beneath the King's arms that hung over the main entrance to the State House and turned into the first-floor chamber that the Pennsylvania Assembly had loaned to Congress. (Some in Congress wanted to "purchase a handsome Time Piece...as a Present for the Use of the Room" but the Pennsylvania delegation refused even to consider the gift.) No doubt at once he became involved in greeting old acquaintances, for he had been absent for some time. He had left Congress late the previous December for a supposedly brief visit to his ailing wife in Virginia. The trip home had been prolonged by the death of his mother in March, then by the recurrence of one of his "violent head aches"—this one lasting six weeks.

The greetings over, he found an empty chair and slumped into it—"he sits in a lounging manner," said a later observer, "on one hip commonly, and with one of his shoulders elevated much above the other." He was ready, for the time being at least, to assume again a share of what even in his short previous tours of duty had become an increasingly heavy burden. Congress, with little power and less money, had the job of directing a war for thirteen self-centered colonies against the world's greatest military and naval power, a task John Adams had described this way: "When fifty or sixty men have a constitution to form for a great empire, at the same time they have a country of fifteen hundred miles extent to fortify, millions to arm and train, a naval power to begin, an extensive commerce to regulate, numerous tribes of Indians to negotiate with, a standing army of 27,000 men to raise, pay, victual, and officer, I shall really pity those fifty or sixty men."

Shortly after the bell in the State House tower had rung the hour of ten, John Hancock, president of Congress, prepared to rap the delegates to order. Though these fifty or sixty men were on the whole hard-working, punctuality did not number among their virtues. As a rule they straggled in slowly to the meeting room throughout the morning, many of them delayed by committee meetings often held before Congress convened. On days when important matters were to be debated, Hancock had to plead, as one member noted in his diary, for "the Delegates to be upon Honor to meet punctually at 10 oCloc."

Once Hancock had judged a quorum present, the doorkeeper, Andrew MacNair, closed the large paneled doors and took up his post outside, where he would bar all but tardy delegates from joining the secret discussions within. Hancock this particular morning opened the session with the customary reading aloud of letters from George Washington and other military commanders that had arrived since yesterday. The custom bored many delegates—one insisted he "never knew a General Quillman good for anything"—but it served so well to brief all Congress at once on affairs, and at the same time bring returning delegates like Jefferson quickly up to date, that no one seriously considered ending the routine.

Hancock led off with a letter from Washington. It was already being said of Washington, with less than a year as commander-in-chief of the continental army behind him, that "his late generalship in driving Howe and the British from Boston will immortalize his name," an opinion most of Congress appeared to share. The General had recently moved his army from Boston to New York, where any moment he expected an invasion by the British. His latest report, however, dealt with other matters. Problems of discipline still harassed him, and he spoke of a colonel who had refused to make the move from his native Massachusetts to New York because "it did not suit his convenience." Washington wished to have the colonel cashiered from the service, and he hoped Congress would understand why he meted out this severe sentence at the same time he handed only mild rebukes to several ex-farm boys whose mutinous acts by normal military standards warranted the death penalty. "I have found it of importance and highly expedient to yield many points in fact without seeming to have done it," he explained. "Time only can eradicate and overcome customs and prejudices of long standing. They must be got the better of by slow and gradual advances."

Washington went on to request advice on exchanging prisoners-of-war. The British maintained they were putting down a rebellion and thus the rebels they captured should be treated as common criminals, not by the standard rules of war. Washington had failed to budge the British military from this attitude, and he now wanted Congress to suggest the next move. Having served up this sticky problem, he went on to comment on the latest rumors that England had dispatched Hessian mercenaries to the colonies. ("...lest the account of coming should be true, may it not be adviseable and good policy to raise some companies of our Germans to send among them when they arrive, for exciting a spirit of disaffection and desertion?") And toward the end of his letter he asked, almost incidentally, for "the appointment of some brigadier-generals, not having more here." He had none because Congress had ordered all those available to Canada.

The second letter Hancock read—from General Philip Schuyler, commanding the Canadian invasion from a post in upper New York—made clear at once that affairs in that area verged on disaster. The Americans had invaded Canada a year ago, and all went well at the start. Montreal had fallen quickly into American hands and the army had moved on to Quebec, expecting that within a few weeks Canada would become America's fourteenth colony. Early success had soon faded. Word reached Congress in mid-December that Benedict Arnold was "near Quebec but has not Men enough to surround it and his Powder so damaged, that he has only 5 Round apiece." When Jefferson soon after had left for home, it was apparent the American invasion of Canada had settled down to a stalemate for the winter. To make matters worse, French civilian resistance had in the meantime stiffened. Farmers and merchants began to demand payment in gold for supplies when there was little or no gold to pay out; priests proceeded to spread the tale, fundamentally true, that Americans distrusted Catholics. Congress had dispatched Benjamin Franklin, now seventy, and Samuel Chase, with two Maryland Catholics, to do what they could to soften the anti-American feeling among the French Canadians. All the while, English troops comfortably entrenched in the rock fortress of Quebec had watched the sieging Americans suffer through a Canadian winter on short rations. With the approach of spring the Americans found they had endured the winter only to be struck by an epidemic of smallpox. Meanwhile, news came that

British re-enforcements were sailing up the St. Lawrence to raise the siege of Quebec. Schuyler had told most of this story in earlier reports. His latest only continued the dreary tale. Everything occurring or about to occur in Canada, he said, "are so many sources of inexpressible distress to me."

Strangely, the unrelieved gloom of the morning mail provoked no talk among the delegates about the hopelessness of the American cause. Clearly, the coming summer would be the testing time for America. Equally clearly, America was in no position to be tested. Yet few men in or out of Congress faced the future with fear. The country overflowed with confidence.

The roots of this confidence lay deep. Shortly after Braddock's defeat in western Pennsylvania in 1755, the then young John Adams had written: "...if we can remove the turbulent Gallicks ...the only way to keep us from setting up for ourselves is to disunite us." Others of the day shared Adam's prescience. Braddock's defeat and the colonists' subsequent role in the French and Indian War convinced many that British soldiers were incompetent and cowardly and this eventually led to the belief that Americans equalled if they did not excel the British in all ways. Even Benjamin Franklin, slow to rash predictions, could write in 1760: "I have long been of the opinion that the *foundations of the future grandeur and stability of the British Empire lie in America;* and though, like other foundations, they are low and little now, they are, nevertheless, broad and strong enough to support the greatest political structure that human wisdom ever yet erected."

A sounder basis for confidence than the superiority of American character or her political structure existed in 1776, one that failure in Canada or even the capture of New York, Boston, and Philadelphia would not undermine. Late in 1775 a farmer named Aaron Leaming traveled to Philadelphia to find out what informed people thought about the war. He ran across a soldier who had been in Boston and he spent sometime asking this man questions, carefully noting down the answers in a pocket diary.

Toward the end of the conversation Leaming recorded this exchange between himself and the soldier:

Q. What is the worst the British forces, if made ever so strong, can do?

A. Knock down the Seaports as at Boston but not March into the Country.

Q. Will that reduce America?

A. No.

Others, too, saw that the European system of warfare, where capture of a key city meant defeat, would not work in America. About the time of this exchange a lad named Alexander Hamilton, still in his teens, phrased the soldier's sentiments this way: "The circumstances of our country put it in our power to evade a pitched battle. It will be better policy to harass and exhaust the soldiery by frequent skirmishes and incursions than to take the open field with them...."

Jefferson was another who clearly saw the land as America's silent ally. "Our idea is that every place is secure except those which lie immediately on the water edge; and these we are prepared to give up," he wrote soon after returning to Philadelphia. Indeed, he went on, the loss of the seaports would encourage the kind of society he envisaged for the future of America. "...I can easily conceive the situation of a farmer, depending on none but the soil and seasons, preferable to the precarious tho' more enlarged prospects of trade."

Congress, of course, knew confidence alone could not win a war, that it could in fact, when blended with apathy, defeat America as effectively as it had the fabled hare. Many of those in Congress strong for independence felt that the people already resembled too much the gentleman from the Pennsylvania backcountry who, because he "loved ease and Madeira, much better than liberty and strife, declared for neutrality, saying that *let who*

would be king, he well knew that he should be subject." How
were men like these to be stirred into fighting for their liberties?
Sam Adams of Massachusetts, the supreme politician of the day,
answered that events alone would provoke the people to demand
independence. "One Battle would do more towards a Declaration
of Independencey than a long chain of conclusive Arguments
in a provincial Convention or the Continental Congress." But, he
added, Congress cannot make events. "Our business is wisely to
improve them." As events did materialize—an exchange of shots
at Lexington and Concord, occupation of Boston, the burning
of Norfolk, a landing of troops in North Carolina—Congress did
the best it could to stir up the people with "animated addresses"
and continental fast days. One fast day, or "Congress Sunday"
as the people called it, had been tried, and on the strength of that
experiment another was scheduled for May 17. On that day
preachers in all the colonies would work to arouse their congrega-
tions. Possibly an animated address of some sort from Congress
would also be needed to excite concern over affairs in Canada.
Promptly after John Hancock finished the morning mail, Congress chose a committee of three to study the correspondence
and draw up recommendations for the delegates to act upon at
a later date.

Congress turned next to the embarrassing problem of Dr.
Benjamin Church. Months earlier Dr. Church had been appointed
by Congress as chief physician of the army hospital in Boston,
having been urged for the job by his friends John and Sam
Adams. He had been an early and eminent patriot whose loyalty
to the rebellion had never been questioned; not long after receiving the appointment, Dr. Church had been caught passing
military information to General Howe. The people of Boston,
understandably vexed, promptly labeled Dr. Church a traitor
and tried to lynch him. Congress, which was a nest of lawyers,
saw the problem as something more involved. Dr. Church might
be a traitor but against whom? Massachusetts, technically at

least, still professed loyalty to England. The doctor may have
been indiscreet but legally he had been exceedingly loyal. What,
then, should Congress recommend be done with him? The people
must be appeased or respect for Congress along with enthusiasm
for the war might diminsh. Yet the law, too, must be respected.
Congress had mulled over this dilemma for many weeks, and the
delegates rehearsed again all its subtleties the day of Jefferson's
return. After long debate, in which someone must have suggested
that the confusion stemming from affairs like this and the issue
over prisoners-of-war offered one more argument for a prompt
declaration of independence, Congress eased out of the predic-
ament by resolving that Dr. Church be allowed to post bail of
"not less than one thousand pounds" and be set at liberty to stand
trial at a later date. Behind this recommendation lay the unex-
pressed hope that Dr. Church, now old and ill, would either
gracefully die or silently slip away to British protection. (He
chose to escape and disappeared months later at sea in an attempt
to reach the British West Indies.)

The lengthy wrangle over Dr. Church ended, and Congress
pushed on to other business without pause for a noon meal. (In
accord with the custom of the day, the delegates arrived at the
State House nourished by a hearty breakfast that sufficed to keep
them going until mid-afternoon. Those with a strong need for
refreshment, liquid or otherwise, could step across Chestnut
Street to a convenient tavern. Bored delegates could slip out for
a stroll or smoke in the State House yard where, surrounded by
a seven-foot wall of brick, their privacy for discussion remained
preserved.) William Ellery, newly arrived from Rhode Island,
now presented his credentials and the latest instructions his government had drawn up to guide its two-man delegation in Congress. The instructions disappointed those like Jefferson who
longed for independence. They authorized Ellery and his colleague Stephen Hopkins to work for all measures "for promoting
and confirming the strictest Union and Confederation between

the said United Colonies," and to exert their "utmost Abilities in carrying on this just and necessary War, in which we are engaged against cruel and unnatural Enemies, in the most vigorous Manner, until Peace shall be restored to the said Colonies, and their Rights and Liberties secured upon a solid and permanent Basis." They neither mentioned independence nor indicated the Rhode Island delegation had permission to vote for it, though a private covering letter from the Governor to the delegation made clear that he, the Governor, saw no reason why Rhode Island could not vote for independence if the issue arose. Generally, the instructions accorded with the accepted view in Congress that independence was not to be considered until a confederation of some sort had been worked out by Congress. All agreed the problem of union must be solved before the United Colonies, so called, dared declare independence.

The problem of how to hold together thirteen diverse, contentious colonies, each determined that none of its customs, laws, or rights should be infringed upon by outside authority, had dominated nearly every day of Congress's existence. "We had much conversation upon the practice of law in our different Provinces," John Adams wrote soon after he reached Philadelphia in 1774. "Mr. Allen [of Pennsylvania] asks me, from whence do you derive your laws? How do you entitle yourselves to English privileges? Is it not Lord Mansfield on the side of power?" Adams, like so many delegates, had never strayed from his native region until chosen to serve in Congress, and his attempts to comprehend traditions flourishing in other colonies typify the efforts of most delegates.

When these fifty-odd strangers settled down to petition the King, they spent much time trying to agree on the basic rights. The city librarian reported that in their search for common ground Vattel, Burlamaqui, Locke, and Montesquieu seemed to be "the standard to which they refer either when settling the rights of the Colonies or when a dispute arises on the Justice or

propriety of a measure." In time the delegates found they shared
more than they first suspected. All admitted they sought only to
preserve old values and rights which England seemed bent on
revoking. They showed no urge to effect a real revolution, to
wipe away past customs and traditions and build anew, for they
believed, rightly, that America was already the freest society in
the world.

Despite basic agreement, divisive forces kept cutting through
the thin threads of unity. Sometimes nothing more than the eccentric views of an individual could disrupt a placid session of
Congress. One morning when a letter from General Washington
was being read aloud, Edward Rutledge of South Carolina
jumped up and, reports one delegate, "moved that the Gen. shall
discharge all the Negroes as well Slaves as Freemen in his Army."
The New England and Middle Colonies sat silent as the South
exploded at the suggestion: "he (Rutledge) was strongly supported by many of the Southern Delegates but so powerfully
opposed that he lost the Point." Another day it had been Benjamin Harrison of Virginia who broke the calm. On hearing of
Washington's complaint that New England soldiers resisted
enlisting for more than a one-year term and that they refused
to serve under any officers but those of their own choosing, Harrison had "proposed that 3 Millions of Dollars shall be given
Annually to the 4 New England Governments and they to carry
on the War their own Way...." No record survives of the New
England reply provoked by Harrison's sarcasm.

Personal enmities were bound to erupt under the pressure of
the confinement Congress endured. Harrison's taunts stemmed
in part, no doubt, from his distaste for the prim ways of several
New England delegates. John Adams could, in turn, be roused
to near fury when he contemplated the indolent ways of Harrison, who enjoyed conviviality more than work. But the sectional distinctions among New England, the Middle Colonies,
and the South, which stood out so sharply at the early sessions of

Congress, continued to split the delegates apart more often than personalities. Something supposedly so trivial as the pay of officers in the continental army could balloon into a major policy decision. The South wanted officer pay raised because, said John Adams, "These gentlemen are accustomed, habituated to higher notions of themselves, and the distinction between them and the common people, than we are...." The pay was pushed up to appease the South, and Adams warned his friends at home to swallow the concession: "For God's sake ... reconcile our people to what has been done, for you may depend upon it that nothing more can be done here...."

A new divisive threat had insinuated itself into discussion as the question of American independence gradually moved to the front. At first the issue of separation had remained essentially a sectional matter agitated mainly by New England men, John and Sam Adams in particular. After the fighting began at Lexington and Concord, they advanced the idea steadily but always cautiously, fearful that excessive boldness might splinter the fragile ties of union.

By early 1776 the idea of independence began to attract interest outside the New England delegations. The pamphlet *Common Sense* came out in early January, and along with it came word that the King had declared the colonies in a state of rebellion. When George III denounced the colonists as rebels, he convinced many they must finish what they had started. Since they risked hanging for what they had done, they might as well risk it for something worthwhile—independence.

The King's pronouncement carried an implied determination to crush the pretensions of unruly America and to abandon all pretense at reconciliation. Rumors bearing out that implication followed quickly. From the backcountry came amplifying details to the old story that British emissaries were stirring up the Indians to make war on the colonies. And ships in from Europe brought a steady flow of rumors that the King planned to send Hessian mercenaries to fight in America. This last galled Congress. Not only did it confirm suspicion that England meant to fight the war to the end; it convinced many America would be ravaged by soldiers who made it their business to profit from war.

While Jefferson had waited down in Virginia for the pain of his "violent head ache" to subside, he had heard of the King's pronouncement and had also received from a friend in Philadelphia a copy of *Common Sense*. Soon after reading the pamphlet he had ridden about the neighboring countryside sounding out the people's sentiments on the idea of independence. "In the upper counties I think I may safely say nine out of ten are for it," he reported after his survey.

Now, Jefferson's thoughts and hopes for the future were oriented—in mid-1776 at least—more toward his "country" of Virginia, as he called it, than toward the continental scene. He viewed independence first as it would affect his "country" and saw that it would bring in its wake, among other things, the need for a new government to replace the royal government that had ruled Virginia for over a century and a half. Jefferson desired to help create the constitution for that new government, and it distressed him to learn as he prepared to return to Philadelphia and Congress that a convention of Virginia's leading politicians was assembling at home for that purpose. "It is a work of the most interesting nature and such as every individual would wish to have his voice in," he said. "In truth, it is the whole subject of the present controversy."

Jefferson had thus set out for Philadelphia determined somehow to escape as promptly as possible from his duties in Congress. His chances were obviously slim; Virginia's rotation system for its delegation meant he would be the last to return home again. By the time he had arrived in Philadelphia and settled into a seat in Congress, he had devised a stratagem he hoped would sidestep this objection. He explained the plan to a friend this way: "In other colonies who have instituted governments they recalled their delegates leaving only one or two to give information to Congress of matters which might relate to their country particularly, and giving them a vote during the interval of absence."

Possibly Jefferson would have been less eager to escape back to Virginia if he had spotted some sign on the day of his return to Congress that the colonies verged on a declaration of independence. Obviously, strong sentiment favoring a break had built up in Congress since Jefferson's departure in late December. It had begun almost before he had cleared from the city. On January 9, the day *Common Sense* appeared, James Wilson of Pennsylvania had tried without success to persuade Congress to go on record as opposed to the idea of independence. In mid-February, Jefferson's old mentor and friend George Wythe had suggested that since the King had declared the colonies in rebellion they now had the right to make foreign alliances. Promptly, "an Objection being offered that this was Independence [,] there ensued much Argument upon that Ground...." The subject intruded on the most innocent resolutions. One day William Livingston of New Jersey rose to offer a routine resolution of thanks for Dr. William Smith's funeral oration on General Richard Montgomery, who had died recently in Canada. The resolution led to a bitter debate, for in his sermon "the Dr. declared the Sentiments of the Congress to continue in a Dependency on G Britain which Doctrine this Congress cannot now approve." The main speakers for the resolution had been James Duane of New York and James Wilson and Thomas Willing of Pennsylvania. These men and their colonies represented the nub of resistance to independence. So long as Pennsylvania—the richest, most powerful, and, by her central location, the keystone colony—balked at the idea of a permanent break with Great Britain, there was little chance of driving such a resolution through Congress. While Pennsylvania held off, the four other Middle Colonies—New York, New Jersey, Delaware, and Maryland—would follow her lead. With five of the thirteen colonies still opposed to independence, any chance of it must have seemed a distant dream to Jefferson on May 14. Even if the thirteen clocks could be timed to strike as one, as John Adams put it, the work of securing foreign alliances and of forming a confederation still took precedence in the minds of most delegates over a declaration of independence. Tangible evidence of colonial unity must be given to the world before the final bold step was taken. It seemed senseless to Jefferson to waste time in Philadelphia when events he viewed of greater importance were coming to a head in Virginia. For a young man eager to put his stamp on the future, there, obviously, was the place to be.

Chapter 2

A Mind in the Making

❊ ❊ ❊ ❊ ❊ ❊ ❊ ❊ ❊

We have two or three great moving experiences in our lives
—experiences so great and moving that it doesn't seem at
the time that anyone else has been caught up and pounded
and dazzled and astonished and beaten and broken and res-
cued and illuminated and rewarded and humbled in just
that way ever before.

F. Scott Fitzgerald

CONGRESS, unaware of the short stay Jefferson had planned
for himself, had welcomed him back in the best way it
knew—by putting him to work within an hour after he had
settled in his seat. John Hancock had no sooner finished droning
out the morning mail than the delegates chose Jefferson to head
a committee of three to study the correspondence and draw up
recommendations for Congress to act upon at a later date.

This was Jefferson's third trip to Congress. He had first arrived
in late June of 1775 and remained for a month; he returned in
October of that year and stayed through December. In these four
months of Congressional duty his colleagues had sized him up as
a hard-working, pleasant young man. Even John Adams liked
him, and Adams rarely missed the blemish in any man. At one
time or another he had lined out caustic remarks about most of
the delegates. (James Duane had "a very effeminate, weak voice,
a sly surveying eye"; Benjamin Harrison was "an indolent and
luxurious heavy gentleman of no use in Congress or committee";

19

Caesar Rodney was "the oddest looking man in the world";
Francis Hopkinson's head "is not bigger than a large apple.")
When Jefferson first arrived in Congress, Adams only noted he
had heard the young Virginian was a great "rubber off of dust,"
having taught himself several foreign languages. Later, Adams
recalled that Jefferson had impressed him as "prompt, frank,
explicit, and decisive upon committees and in conversation," so
much so "that he soon seized upon my heart."

Jefferson's height alone should have given the truculent, stumpy
John Adams instant grounds for dislike. Jefferson stood six feet
two and a half inches—a good six inches taller than John Adams.
A slave of Jefferson's named Isaac once described him as "as neat
a built man as ever was seen in Vaginny, I reckon, or any place—
a straight-up man, long face, high nose." A less generous observer, noting the long arms and legs, large wrists, the jutting
chin, sand-colored hair, and brick-red face flecked with freckles,
said his features blended in a way that gave him an appearance
"much like that of a tall large-boned farmer."

Contemporaries, for some reason, never remarked on the sim-
ilarities between Washington and Jefferson, though they were
of almost identical height, weight, and general build. Washington's physical presence left an indelible impression on those who
met him where Jefferson's did not. Something about Washington
forced men to note his "towering" height, his "majestic walk,"
his "commanding countenance." Once, when asked to explain
the General's eminence, John Adams had replied he owed it
mainly to a handsome face and to his height, "like the Hebrew
sovereign chosen because he was taller by the head than the
other Jews." Jefferson, equally tall, impressed few as imposing.
His height generally passed unnoticed, his walk was "easy and
swinging" and he went about with "a loose shackling air...a
rambling vacant look." Perhaps a strong personality can accent-
uate a man's physical presence—Louis XIV, who stood five feet
five inches, was once described as "a very tall man...six feet

tall as near as makes no matter"—as a bland personality can obscure it.

Bland seems an odd word for Jefferson, yet one contemporaries would have found appropriate. To them Jefferson was, as has been said of another, almost "forgettably pleasant," an amiable young man who rarely if ever lost his temper, never swore, never argued in public or private; who shunned gossip and spoke "only of the good qualities of men"; who drank sparingly in a day of hard drinkers, watering his wine to the point where no one, as old Isaac put it, ever saw Jefferson "disguised in drink." Strangers found him grave at first—"nay, even cold," said one. "But the chilled feeling was only momentary," a lady reported of her first meeting, "for after taking the chair I offered him in a free and easy manner, and carelessly throwing his arm on the table near which he sat, he turned towards me a countenance beaming with an expression of benevolence and with a manner and voice almost femininely soft and gentle, entered into conversation on the commonplace topics of the day...." His reserve seemed to melt so fully that one visitor found that "before I had been two hours with him we were as intimate as if we had passed our whole lives together."

Jefferson invariably left behind the illusion of intimacy. He had an extraordinary capacity for friendship that stemmed from and blended with a deep desire to be liked. The perceptive visitor noticed how deftly he turned the conversation from himself "to subjects most familiar to those with whom he conversed, whether laborer, mechanic or other." His reticence about personal affairs and opinions stood out even in an age that respected privacy. Only occasionally, and then on trivial matters, was the façade penetrated. Once, for instance, he let slip the fact he had the habit on rising of dipping his feet into a tub of cold water—a habit, incidentally, deplored by Philadelphia's Dr. Benjamin Rush, who said that "the bowels sympathize with the feet above any other external part of the body, and suffer in a peculiar manner from the effects of cold upon them."

Jefferson's public character, the one Congress knew in 1776, served as protective coloration for an elusive, complex personality which, had the delegates even partially comprehended it, would have roused suspicion of the Declaration of Independence when it came up for discussion in Congress. Jefferson lived both within and without the design of his times, accepting most of the eighteenth century pattern of life in America at the same time he had set his mind to reshape parts of that pattern. Edmund Randolph, a Virginia friend who saw this wayward streak, once said that "it constituted a part of Mr. Jefferson's pride to run before the times in which he lived." There was more to it than that, for other men have run before their times and achieved little. Jefferson's genuis was to travel only slightly ahead. He managed to remain unique without being ostracized, an art of living that developed out of his youth in Virginia.

Whatever forces shaped Jefferson's character, adversity cannot be numbered among them. The major event that marred an otherwise placid boyhood was the death of his father when Jefferson was fourteen. The available facts make it clear Peter Jefferson lived long enough to shape his boy to a remarkable degree. Father and son shared similar temperaments, talents, and appearances—even their handwriting was alike—and a deep attachment clearly existed between the two. The lack of a father's advice through adolescence perhaps made Jefferson less sure of himself and more dependent on guidance from older men in his youth. The loss of an affectionate confidant possibly made the boy shyer, more reserved than he might otherwise have been. Jefferson summed up the situation accurately when he remarked that with the death of his father "the whole care and direction of myself was thrown on myself entirely." The care and direction of his mother and sisters were not among his worries. Peter Jefferson left the family comfortably fixed, and with the management of family lands in the hands of overseers his son remained free of financial hardship and able to spend his time pretty much as he wished.

The wealth and position Peter Jefferson passed on to his son had been achieved largely by his own energy and talent, both of which he had in high degree and also handed on to his son in full measure. Peter Jefferson came of a respected but undistinguished family of farmers. Since formal education was not to be wasted on plain people, and since he was a third son with little hope of a decent inheritance, he turned to surveying for a livelihood. His father, however, proved more provident than expected and passed on a parcel of land in the sparsely settled western part of Virginia, well up the James River in Goochland County. Peter Jefferson promptly began to farm the inheritance, at the same time continuing his surveying. Ability, ambition, and a genial temperament soon forced him into public life, and he became a justice of peace of the county when he was twenty-seven and sheriff at thirty.

Peter Jefferson avoided rash gambles, preferring to blend caution with boldness, another trait he passed on to his son. The year he became sheriff he added to his holdings by purchasing land some thirty miles upstream along the Rivanna River, in what was to be Albemarle County. The land here, though wild and empty of people, was cheap, fertile, and, with the Indians retreated over the mountains to "a retired part of the country," safe for settlement. The purchase increased Peter Jefferson's chances for prosperity without endangering what little he already had.

Those chances further increased in 1739, two years after the Albemarle purchase, for in that year he married his friend William Randolph's sister Jane, then a girl of nineteen. He married at thirty-two, late for the times; but he married well. The Randolphs counted among Virginia's eminent families, and Jane brought to the marriage both a handsome dowry of land and slaves and a secure position among the elite of the colony. Peter Jefferson soon built a house for his bride on the Albemarle tract and, being a man with no background to speak of and thus impressed by his wife's, thin as it was, called it Shadwell, after the London parish where she had been christened. Here on April 13, 1743, his third child and first son, Thomas, was born.

Life continued full for Peter Jefferson. A steward and several overseers managed his now considerable lands, leaving him time to help survey the Fairfax Line in northern Virginia, the Virginia-North Carolina boundary line, and to share in making the first accurate map of Virginia. He found time, too, to serve as an Albemarle justice of peace, county surveyor, county lieutenant—this last entitled him to the title of "colonel"—and eventually as a member of the House of Burgesses.

Peter Jefferson died at the age of forty-nine, not long after he had been elected to the House. At his death, the name Jefferson, once largely unknown, was respected throughout Virginia. He left a family fixed among the elite and passed on to his son, exclusive of other bequests, some twenty-seven hundred acres of land, sixty slaves, twenty-five horses, two hundred hogs, and seventy head of cattle. Clearly, the son, who had held all the public offices his father had held, including a seat in the Houses of Burgesses, while still in his twenties, rose to early eminence on the shoulders of his father.

Peter Jefferson also provided for his son in less material ways. He saw to it the boy was reared properly for his role in the Virginia elite. The fact that Shadwell lay near the frontier and that Indians were frequent visitors to the house had not hindered the task. The Three Notch'd Road passed close by and overnight guests—so many that Jefferson once complained their numbers kept him from his studies—held the plantation in touch with tidewater society. An itinerant dancing master was hired to instruct the children in something more sedate than a backcountry reel. The boy learned to read music and play the violin. He learned, of course, to ride well—"uncommonly well," an overseer once remarked. He knew sufficient Latin, Greek, and French to scatter foreign phrases through his conversation and letters, for his father, sensitive to his own lack of a formal education, had placed his son "at the English school at five years of age; and at the Latin at nine," and won a promise on his deathbed, tradition has it, that the boy would continue his classical education.

After his father's death, Jefferson studied for two years with the Reverend Mr. James Maury, "a correct classical scholar," according to Jefferson, and also something of a gadfly who eventually tangled in court with that "little pettyfogging attorney" Patrick Henry, to use Maury's phrase. He once advanced some sarcastic observations on Virginia's attempt to ape the English gentlemen that did little to endear himself or the Church of England to the Virginia elite. A thorough training in Latin and Greek seemed sensible to Maury for a British nobleman, whose vast incomes "warrant his indulging himself in the Enjoyment of that calm Retreat from the Bustle of the World." A Virginian, to Maury little more than a glorified farmer forced to spend the days managing his lands, had no need for this sort of education. Maury advised first a sound grounding in the English language and its literature, then in practical subjects like geography, history, and mathematics.

A glimmer of Jefferson's character in these years with Maury shines through the ancedotes of his classmates. His practical jokes were clever rather than boisterous. Once he agreed to race his slow pony against the swifter horse of a classmate, provided the race occurred on February 30, and none of the boys suspected the hoax till the last day of the month. He favored the oblique approach to a goal, putting the other boys up to asking for a holiday to go hunting rather than advancing the suggestion himself, then dutifully finishing his lesson before taking off.

Neither the diligence nor deviousness irritated his companions, several of whom remained life-long friends.

In 1760 Jefferson rode down from the backcountry to begin life at William and Mary College. He left Shadwell with the outward appearance of a Virginia gentleman, although he had probably not wandered much beyond twenty miles from his birthplace. The seventeen-year-old lad took with him a set of preconceptions that would shape judgments about the world around him throughout life. A backcountry upbringing had made him especially aware he lived in an unformed society, one in the making, not made. From any mountain top near Shadwell he looked out on a countryside still largely empty of settlers. Nearby Charlottesville, a village of only a few houses and the inevitable tavern of all colonial villages, still lacked a courthouse in which to conduct county business. In time, the boy knew, the forests would be leveled, the land cleared, houses built, and the rivers made navigable. His aspirations conditioned him to strive to duplicate the British nobleman's way of life; his intuitions told him Maury was right: knowledge must somehow be practical, helpful in making the world, the Virginian's world at least, a better place to live. Poetry, music, painting all enriched one's life, but they must always be subordinated to useful knowledge.

Life at Shadwell had also shaped Jefferson's ideas on government. The Virginia plantation resembled the self-contained manor of medieval times; slavery had in a sense created an extreme form of feudal society. Shadwell housed as many people as Charlottesville, if not more, among them carpenters, coopers, blacksmiths, tanners, curriers, shoemakers, spinners, weavers, sawyers, and probably even a distiller. The plantation owner had the problems and duties of a feudal lord. Ties with the outside world were thin. When bridges needed to be built roads improved, rivers deepened, slaves hunted, or the poor cared for, the local gentry handled the matter without assistance from the government at Williamsburg. While the colonial government could not be dismissed from mind, its most important functions were confined largely to rebuffing attempts by the Crown to increase control over Virginia affairs, to conducting foreign affairs—these included dealings with other colonies as well as with England—and to waging war. On internal matters it did little more than see that no part of the colony acted against the welfare of the whole, leaving direct action always to the gentry on the local level, who worked either through the county government, through the parish, or informally among themselves.

Jefferson also carried down to Williamsburg an orthodox Christian view of life and the world around him. Possibly his parents, certainly the Reverend Mr. Maury, had seen to that. He knew the Bible well, he accepted the validity of miracles, the Noachian Deluge, the expulsions of man from the Garden of Eden, the existence of heaven and hell, and a personal God who controlled directly all men and events in the world. His was a benevolent God. ("I can never join Calvin in addressing *his god*," he told John Adams late in life. "He was indeed an Atheist, which I can never be; or rather his religion was Daemonism.") His orthodoxy had not made him fond of formal religion. Maury once remarked that the clergy in Virginia led "the Life of Postboys" and were denied all the rights and privileges that "first tempted Mankind to quit a State of Nature for the social & civil Life." Jefferson shared the average planter's low view of church and clergy, possibly because he resented the quality of the clergy foisted on Virginians by a bishop three thousand miles distant. Indignation over outside control of a local institution may have been increased by the obvious inappropriateness of a ritualistic church in a backcountry setting.

Along with these preconceptions, Jefferson carried to Williamsburg an abundance of optimism that deserted him only for brief periods during his life. Possibly optimists are born, not made, and robust health accounts for their outlook. Certainly Jefferson rarely knew the sick bed in an age filled with disease and was annoyed in a long life only by his "violent" headaches. Perhaps, too, the Virginia environment explains his buoyant attitude. Little in Jefferson's youth gave him reason to think man naturally prone to evil. He knew nothing of cities where the gin-soaked poor battled for survival. He had never smelled the stench of an alleyway, never watched a mob gaily turn out for a public hanging, never endured the sight of beggars pleading for food. He lived in a world dominated by the land, where, it has been said, "the aggressive energies of the American farmer were directed primarily against nature, not against other human beings." Such an environment might well lead a man to expect well of the future.

Jefferson liked to look back on the years at Williamsburg as ones in which he sowed many wild oats and came close, as he once said of another young man, to running "wild after the tinsel of life." When he recollected "the various sorts of bad company with which I associated from time to time, I am astonished I did not turn off with some of them, and become as worthless to society as they were." He may have lingered at a cockfight once or twice, lost a few shillings at cards or on a horse race, he may even have reeled home occasionally after a dipper too many of punch; his indiscretions hardly exceeded these. Once he had settled in at the college he worked out a schedule that left little time for frivolity. A typical day began at sun-up. (Jefferson rose early all his life, remarking once he could hardly recall a time when the sun had caught him in bed.) If later habits prevailed at this time, he put in an hour or two of work before breakfast. An afternoon of study followed on the heels of a full morning of classes. Often in the twilight he jogged a mile or so out into the countryside to clear the brain for an evening of further study. Occasionally, he may have taken an hour or two in the afternoon to listen to debates in the House of Burgesses.

Jefferson and his times flowed together at Williamsburg. Until

then the boy's intellectual life had strayed barely beyond the
sixteenth century. Now he was pulled forward swiftly. However, moving into the eighteenth century did not rip apart all
the values he had been reared to respect. William and Mary was
no nursery for radical ideas. Neither the Virginia planters, who
kept a watchful eye on the college, nor the Bishop of London,
under whose aegis it operated, would have tolerated such nonsense. The college sought only to nourish traditional values. It
was essentially a finishing school for gentlemen. Since the intellectual standards of gentlemen rarely prove hard to meet, the
students, who numbered less than a hundred, found sufficient
time to enliven the night life of Williamsburg.

The quality of work demanded of the students reflected the
quality of the professors. The school's president was a drunkard.
The professor of moral philosophy, equally fond of the bottle,
was relieved of his duties soon after Jefferson's arrival for leading the students in a drunken town and gown brawl. All save
one of the faculty were Anglican clergymen, ineffectual men
for the most part who had found it difficult to obtain a decent
"living" from the church and so had drifted into teaching. The
only requirements for a post in the college were orthodox religious views and a knowledge of Latin and Greek, the two
languages that dominated the curriculum. Commercial courses,
classes in agriculture, or in modern languages like French or Italian were ignored as beneath a gentleman's attention, and anyone
who suggested introducing them, like the Reverend Mr. Maury,
was dismissed as a radical. The single concession to modern
tastes was a course called natural philosophy.

By 1760 not only William and Mary but most colonial colleges—Harvard, the College of New Jersey (Princeton), King's
College (Columbia), and Queen's College (Rutgers)—had
bowed to the spirit of the eighteenth century by hiring a professor of natural philosophy, whose field of study embraced what
today is lumped under the heading of science. The innovation in

time jolted American education out of a well-worn routine. The professor of natural philosophy was usually the first layman added to the faculty, for few clerics were well grounded in mathematics. The novelty and complexity of the subject forced out old methods of rote learning and led to the introduction of the lecture system. And what was even more momentous, these men brought to college education for the first time the idea that, as one historian puts it, "it was the business of the mind to discover things hitherto unknown."

The first class in natural philosophy at William and Mary was taught in 1758 by a young Scotsman of twenty-four named William Small. He seems to have been an effective teacher. A classmate of Jefferson's once said that until he listened to Dr. Small, as he was called in later life, "History and particularly Naval and Military history, attracted my attention. But afterwards natural and Experimental Philosophy...." And Jefferson, on one of the few occasions he admitted a large intellectual debt to another, said Dr. Small "probably fixed the destinies of my life." He went on to describe the teacher as "a man profound in most of the useful branches of science, with a happy talent of communication, correct and gentlemanly manners, and an enlarged and liberal mind. He, most happily for me, became soon attached to me, and made me his daily companion when not engaged in school; and from his conversation I got my first views of the expansion of science, and of the system of things in which we are placed."

The new subject created little fuss when it was slipped into the William and Mary curriculum. No doubt Dr. Small, with his "correct and gentlemanly manners," helped to ease suspicion about it. But even Small could not have prevented the dust flying if natural philosophy had not by now become sufficiently bland pablum for young gentlemen-to-be. It had taken well over a century of controversy and intellectual adjustment to make science palatable. The sixteenth and seventeenth centuries had fought the battles and the eighteenth century enjoyed the victory.

Men of western civilization have always searched for laws that governed nature, for a universal scheme of order underlying the universe. In the Middle Ages those laws of nature were identified with the law of God. Men looked at nature mainly to throw light on some theological problem. By the sixteenth century a few had begun to examine nature not necessarily as it illuminated religion but as it provided a sufficiently satisfying study in itself. But more than their attitude toward nature had changed. They now searched for laws governing the universe by asking questions that could be answered by experiments based on observation. They then attempted to express the results of their observations in mathematical abstractions. Each of these abstractions became for them a law of nature.

The church did not object to, in fact it encouraged, this new approach to the study of nature. Galileo met trouble only when he began to insist that Copernicus's theory that the earth revolved about the sun as well as rotating on its axis was true. The church had willingly accepted the theory as a convenient fiction for making calculations, such as those on which the Gregorian calendar was based. It refused to accept the theory as fact; this would put fact in conflict with revelation. Did not Psalm Ninety-three say: "The world also is established, that it cannot be moved?" Did not proof that the sun moves appear in Joshua's command on the evening of the battle of Gibeon: "Sun, stand thou still upon Gibeon; and thou, Moon, in the valley of Ajalon; and the sun stood still, and the moon stayed, until the people had avenged themselves upon their enemies?" The church demanded that, unless science absolutely proved the Scriptures wrong, reason must give way to revelation. Galileo eventually endured a humiliating retreat in which he publicly accepted the Copernican theory as "a poetical conceit," to use his own bitter phrase.

Galileo's mortification did not stem the rise of natural philosophy. Tycho Brahe produced a compromise theory of Copernicus's which said the sun and moon revolved around the earth and the five planets revolved around the sun. Johann Kepler's observations revealed that the planets moved in ellipses, not the perfect circles theologians had assumed, and that they moved at varying rates of speed through their orbits. Kepler said the universe was "something like a clock work in which a single weight drives all the gears." Isaac Newton found the single weight. He capped a multitude of seventeenth century observations by explaining the movements of *all* celestial bodies by means of the laws of gravitation. He had used the tools of natural philosophy to find what men had always assumed—complete order in God's universe—and as quickly as his ideas could be popularized they became accepted.

Newtonianism, as it came to be called, "substituted a natural for a supernatural explanation of phenomena." Even Christianity now became "reasonable." John Locke, a young English physician who was a friend of Newton and had been trained in the methods of experimental science by the chemist Robert Boyle, "proved" that God existed in his book *The Reasonableness of Christianity*. Newton and Locke faced none of Galileo's troubles because the slow accretion of scientific findings through the sixteenth and seventeenth centuries had given devout men time to adjust. Moreover, any divergence between the world of Biblical tradition and the world of science was not even dreamt of at the time. Newton himself believed his findings re-enforced rather than destroyed the foundations of Christianity, for "the most beautiful system of sun, planets and comets could only proceed from the counsel and dominion of an intelligent Being." Not only did his findings verify assumptions once taken on faith, but they undermined *none* of the old beliefs. The Scriptures taught that God had created the universe in six days, and nothing Newton discovered destroyed that truth. Indeed, his findings verified the Biblical picture of a static world completely made and not still in the making. Nor did his laws undercut the view of a personal God, for as Newton saw it God could still step in any time He wished to work a miracle. (A miracle now became something that momentarily defied natural law.) The universe might be a Great Machine, a clock, but the operator remained God, a personal God who kept His hand on the throttle.

With Newton's discoveries, natural philosophy—that is, a philosophy derived from a study of nature—superceded religion in prestige. A new vocabulary began to dominate men's thoughts. The fashionable words—nature, natural law, balance, machine, engine, and, above all, reason—now were drawn from science. Locke was only one of many to lift the new vocabulary out of context and—as Spencer, a lesser Locke of his day, would do with Darwin's ideas—apply it first to religion, then to government, to philosophy, and eventually to the concept of man himself. If natural philosophers could use reason to uncover the scheme of the universe, surely reason applied to the affairs of men would expose similar laws. Once the rules of the game had been revealed, what could block man from perfectability? Pope expressed the confidence of the age in a couplet that quickly became the cliché of the eighteenth century:

> Nature and Nature's laws lay hid in night.
> God said, *Let Newton be*! and all was light.

Confidence that man verged on solving all God's riddles was the keynote of the age. The eighteenth century came to believe, with the arrogance of the innocent, not only that it was enlightened compared with past epochs, but that it verged on complete enlightenment.

William Small specialized in mathematics, but like most eighteenth century intellectuals who saw science as an integral part of life, he went beyond his speciality. When the professor of moral philosophy was sacked for leading a student riot, Dr.

Small accepted an interim appointment to fill the vacant chair. Jefferson never commented on the content of Small's classes, except to remark he had discarded the rote method of teaching and become the first "who ever gave in that college, regular lectures in Ethics, Rhetoric, and Belles Lettres." Since Dr. Small had "an enlarged and liberal mind," Jefferson possibly first heard of novelists like Fielding, Richardson, and Sterne, of poets like William Shenstone and Pope in these lectures. Small may also have explained how Newtonian ideas influenced the views on government of Locke, Montesquieu, Burlamaqui, and Bolingbroke, but the subject if touched was touched lightly, for this was a halcyon period in Virginia politics that produced little talk or thought about the theory of government.

Dr. Small may also have expounded on Locke's *Essay on Human Understanding*. (Locke here argues that God had stamped no truths, no innate ideas on men's minds. He had furnished men only with the ability to know; knowledge itself emerged from experience. All start life with equal desires, an equal capacity for good and evil, and whichever road a man chooses, his environment, not God's will, starts him down it. Men's actions are not pre-determined by God nor handicapped by the blot of original sin. If men use their minds, apply reason to life, they are capable of perfecting their lives and making the world a better place to live.) If Small exposed Jefferson to this Lockean doctrine of free will, the boy failed to absorb it, for he left the classroom with his old religious views intact. He still believed a year after college that, as he put it, "man proposes and God disposes," that God determined all events, and that "whatever does happen, must happen." He told a friend that a man must go through life "with a pious and unshaken resignation till we arrive at our journey's end, and where we may deliver up our trust into the hands of him who gave it, and receive such reward as to him shall seem proportioned to our merit."

Jefferson emerged from the classroom of Dr. Small with past

beliefs intact but with a new touchstone—natural philosophy—for judging and viewing the world around. Throughout life Jefferson would try to cram everything he observed and experienced into an orderly system whose core was natural philosophy. The dazzling experience of Dr. Small's classroom would illuminate his life to the end.

Now, natural philosophy provided the intellectual touchstone for most thinking men of the eighteenth century in America, but not all these men found what Jefferson did. Tom Paine immersed himself and came up a radical in politics and religion. John Adams, about Paine's age, followed a similar intellectual trail, reading the same books, using the same vocabulary; he emerged, so far as labels can be accurately applied, a conservative. Jefferson, coming along a few years later but exposed to the same books and ideas, came out somewhere between his two friends. Just as the men of genius of the seventeenth century had built on a foundation of medieval conceptions, so Jefferson would use natural philosophy to build on beliefs that stemmed out of his Virginia background. He would use it to clarify vague ruminations about the world around him, to justify a mode of action, to explain an intuitive belief—but always in relation to experience in his "country" of Virginia. What might seem natural and reasonable to an Englishman like Paine, who had known hardship and failure most of his adult life, or to a New Englander like John Adams, would often seem unnatural to Thomas Jefferson.

In 1762 Jefferson left William and Mary but not Williamsburg. He would have Dr. Small's companionship for two more years, then his mentor would return to Scotland to become a doctor of medicine. Before departing, Small "filled up the measure of his goodness to me," Jefferson said, "by procuring for me, from his most intimate friend, George Wythe, a reception as a student of law, under his direction, and introduced me to the acquaintance and familiar table of Governor [Francis] Fauquier, the

ablest man who had ever filled that office. With him, and at his
table, Dr. Small and Mr. Wythe, his *amici omnium horarum*
[friend of all hours], and myself, formed a *partie quarée*, and
to the habitual conversations on these occasions I owed much
instruction."

Jefferson remained a law student for the next four years. Because affairs of the planation were largely in the hands of overseers, he had nearly all his time free for private interests. The Virginia of those days gave a gentleman leisure and time to mature.
Jefferson's interests steadily widened and deepened. He spent the
time from dawn until eight o'clock, if he followed his own advice,
reading "Ethics, religion, natural and sectarian, and natural law."
The rest of the mornings went to learning law from the books
in Wythe's office, and the afternoons to casual reading in politics
and history. He gave much attention to Greek, for Wythe was
one of the ablest classicists in Virginia, and Small was equally
proficient. He also found time for poetry and novels. (And how
did a lad bent on acquiring only useful knowledge justify poetry
and fiction? "I answer," Jefferson said, "every thing is useful
which contributes to fix us in the principles and practice of
virtue." The "murther" of Duncan by Macbeth excites "a great
horror of villainy," and "a lively and lasting sense of filial duty
is more effectively impressed on the mind of a son or daughter
by reading King Lear, than by all the dry volumes of ethics
and divinity that ever were written.") From "Dark to Bedtime"
was best to ponder "belles lettres, criticism, rhetoric, and oratory."

Then there were the evenings at the Governor's Palace. Fauquier, an easy-going, genial gentleman, filled the night with
good talk. He had been a friend of Admiral George Anson,
whose *Voyage Round the World* had been among the books
Jefferson had inherited from his father. Anson's death in 1762
must have sparked a variety of anecdotes from the Governor
during Jefferson's visits Fauquier's father had worked under

Newton in the mint, and that, too, undoubtedly produced stories about the "incomparable Mr. Newton." Jefferson once said that during those evenings in the Palace he had "heard more good sense, more rational and philosophic conversation, than in all my life besides. They were truly Attic societies." There was music, too, for the Governor was fond of it "and associated me with two or three other amateurs in his weekly concerts."

It remains open to speculation who gained more from these genial evenings at the Palace. Jefferson, though still in his teens, obviously had already revealed something of his abilities to attract three of the liveliest intellects in Virginia, and it must have pleased his companions to share in shaping that mind. On the other hand, Jefferson obtained intellectual companionship and something more. He still felt the lack of a father's guidance and had yet to gain confidence in his own judgments. Wythe and Small—not Fauquier, who liked to gamble heavily and thus verged too close to the rake to serve as a moral mentor—in a sense served as stand-ins for Peter Jefferson. Jefferson once remarked that when faced with temptations and difficulties he would ask himself what Small and Wythe, who always pursued an "even and dignified line," would do in the situation. Assurance came slowly to Jefferson, and the lack of it would sometimes cause him to disguise his true sentiments in clichés of the day.

Jefferson from the vantage point of old age viewed the Williamsburg years as among the happiest of his life; they were in fact among the most miserable. His trip into manhood proved as unpleasant for him as for most young men. Williamsburg in his letters became "Devilsburgh." The books he read for law, like *Coke upon Littleton*, oppressed him. ("Well, Page, I do wish the Devil had old Cooke, for I am sure I never was so tired of an old dull scoundrel in my life.") The life of the mind bored him, or so he said. ("But the old-fellows say we must read to gain knowledge; and gain knowledge to make us happy and be admired. Mere jargon! Is there any such thing as happiness in this world?")

Jefferson endured the miseries of love during this "happy" period. His affections centered on a handsome girl named Rebecca Burwell, and she seemed attracted to him. Jefferson, however, tarried in asking for her hand, and by the time he found the courage to act she had chosen another. He tried to dismiss the rejection lightly by remarking that "Many and great are the comforts of a single state...." Hard upon this setback came "a violent head ach," the first of many to plague him during emotional crises.

It has been said young men are full of themselves, and Jefferson proved no exception. The shock of rejection turned him more inward than ever. He began to keep a Literary Bible, as he called it, filling it with excerpts from his voluminous reading. Naturally, he favored derogatory comments about women. From Euripides he culled a lamentation that described their sex as "a curse deceiving men" and the suggestion that "Mortals should beget children from some other source and there should be no womankind; thus there would be no ill for men." A couplet copied from Pope's *Iliad*—"To labour is the lot of man below/ And when Jove gave us life, he gave us woe"—verified the fact life was a depressing affair. Evil, too, abounded, and Jefferson noted Cicero's comment that "as soon as we are born and received into the world, we are instantly familiarized with all kinds of depravity and perversity of opinions; so that we may be said almost to suck in error with our nurse's milk."

Many of the selections indicate Jefferson's concern with the way he should shape his life. He saw a duty to his aristocratic background. (Euripides: "To be of the noble born gives a peculiar distinction clearly marked among men, and the noble name increases in lustre in those who are worthy.") He must be a moderate man. (Euripides: "Moderation everywhere is beautiful and assures good repute among men.") And he must be a reasonable man. (Cicero: "...there is present to every man reason, which presides over and gives laws to all; which by improving itself and making continual advances, becomes perfect virtue. It behooves a man, then to take care that reason shall have the command over that part which is bound to practice obedience.")

It has been remarked that, with Locke, a break occurs in the traditional conception of natural right that had been rooted in classical and medieval thought. "The pre-modern natural law doctrines taught the duties of man," says Leo Strauss; "if they paid any attention at all to his rights, they conceived of them as essentially derivative from his duties. There was, in short, a shift of emphasis from natural duties to natural rights." Professor Strauss regards the shift as unfortunate. "Rights express what everyone desires. Men can more safely be depended upon to fight for their rights than to fulfil their duties." These observations hold for the natural rights doctrine as it was used in the nineteenth century; they fail to hold for eighteenth century America. Professor Strauss overlooks the fact that the minds of most eighteenth century American intellectuals were rooted in classical thought. Jefferson, like the classical philosophers Strauss speaks of, "regarded the best regime as that regime whose aim is virtue." His own ideas of happiness—that it resulted from virtuous activity—came from ancient writers. The concern with men's duties, the deep belief that any solid reform in society must start with the individual emerged from the same source. The emphasis on the virtues of reason stemmed as much from the Greeks and Romans as from natural philosophy. Natural philosophy, as interpreted by Jefferson, only lent new power to the ideas of the classical authors. It reinforced, clarified, and strengthened them.

None of the early entries in the Literary Bible indicated much influence of natural philosophy on Jefferson's ideas nor an original slant to his thinking. But midway in the notebooks he veered from the well-worn trail. The new route, while not especially daring, marked the first steps outside the pattern of his times, and also indicated how he would manage to blend classical thought with natural philosophy. About 1764 he began to read deeply in the works of Bolingbroke, an English philosopher who questioned the Bible as an historical document and used natural law to undermine orthodox Christianity. "I say that the law of nature is the law of god," began one of the sections Jefferson copied from Bolingbroke. "Of this I have the same demonstrative knowledge, that I have of the existence of god, the all-perfect being. I say that the all-perfect being cannot contradict himself; that he would contradict himself; that he would contradict himself if the laws contained in the thirteenth chapter of Deuteronomy, to mention no others here, were his laws, since they contradict those of nature; and therefore that they are not his law." Bolingbroke goes on to question the Bible as a source of ethics. He said, Jefferson noted, that "it is not true that Christ revealed an entire body of ethics, proved to be the law of nature." Where, then, if not the Bible, did men find a source for ethics? In the writings of the Greek and Roman sages.

By the time the years at Williamsburg ended Jefferson had accepted most of Bolingbroke's deistic ideas, yet he never publicly strayed far from religious orthodoxy. He remained all his life good friends with clergymen, for he rarely confused a man's beliefs for the man. When he returned to Shadwell to practice law, he was elected a vestryman of Fredericksville parish, and, when that was formed into a new parish, he continued to serve until 1785. Even as an old man he would ride down the hill from Monticello to church services in Charlottesville courthouse's, bringing his own seat, "some light machinery which folded up, was carried under his arm, and, when unfolded, served for a chair on the floor of the courthouse."

Jefferson's religious views—public and private—fit a pattern followed through life. The breaks he made with the past remained private and were rarely aired in public. Perhaps James Byrnes's perception about Franklin Roosevelt—"that within him there must have been continuous conflict, with his vivid imagination and unbounded curiosity prompting him to embrace new ideas, and a conservative streak restraining him all the while"—applies equally well to Thomas Jefferson.

Once Jefferson had worked out in the Literary Bible his hatred of women and had reasoned his way into deism, he applied his mind to other topics. Some idea of the depth and variety of his interests appears in the orders for books he placed at the office of the *Virginia Gazette* for the year 1764:

February 4
> Joseph Baretti, *A Dictionary of the English and Italian Languages*
> Francesco Guicciardini, *Della Istoria d'Italia*—two volumes
> *Opere di Niccolò Macchiavelli*—two volumes
> *Scapulae Lexicon*
> Henri Louis Duhamel du Monceau, *A Practical Treatise of Husbandry*

February 10
> Milton's *Works*—bound in "gilt"

February 14
> Robert Richardson, *The Attorney's practice in the Court of Common Pleas* and *The Attorney's practice in the Court of King's Bench*
> Joseph Harrison, *The Practice of the Court of Chancery*

February 20
> *The Attorney's Pocket Companion*

February 22
> "Death of Abell"

March 2
> David Hume, *History of England*—six volumes
> William Robertson, *History of Scotland*

March 28
    William Stith, *History of the First Discovery and Settlement
    of Virginia*
April 9
    Abbe d'Olivet's *Thoughts of Cicero*
October 3
    William Rastell, *Collection in English of the statutes now in
    force*
October 18
    "had the poet Akenside's works bound"

The year 1765, Jefferson's fifth as a student, saw no diminu-
tion in either his reading or book-buying habits. He had, nonetheless, begun to abandon the role of full-time student. He now
spent much time at Shadwell, coming down to Williamsburg at
court time and occasionally to socialize with friends. He was on
hand when Patrick Henry rose in the House of Burgesses to
denounce the Stamp Act. Henry, a new member of the House
and still young, was opposed by his elders—"not from any questions of our rights," as Jefferson remembered it, "but on the
ground that the same sentiments had been at their preceding
session expressed in a more conciliatory form to which the
answers were not yet received." Among those who attacked
Henry's fiery sentiments was Richard Bland, a cousin of Jefferson's but who in 1765 left no lasting impression on him. Jefferson
long after could recall that there were "torrents of sublime
eloquence from mr. Henry," and that the debate that afternoon
had been "most bloody," but he could remember little that had
been said nor who said it.

Jefferson's interests began to expand even further in 1765. He
escaped from law books long enough to undertake his first public project. The preceding year, when twenty-one, he had taken
a trip up the Rivanna to see if there was any chance to make it
navigable. He found only one spot where rapids blocked the
stream. Remove the loose rock in that spot and the river would

be open to sizable boats, and planters along the banks—among them Jefferson—could float their tobacco all the way down to wharves where sea-going ships for England tied up. The rocks that blocked the Rivanna had also blocked the development of Albemarle County since Peter Jefferson had moved into the area. Here a perfect project—useful and with little in it to stir up ill-feeling—offered itself for an ambitious young man eager to make his mark. It required energy, confidence, and persistence. It also required the backing of other landowners along the river, who would share the expense, for it was assumed that local initiative and money would do the job without aid from the colonial government. Their willingness to go along with the idea would be a measure of their judgment of Jefferson. He risked little and stood to gain much. If he succeeded, he won the praise of the country; if he failed, he received understanding, for no one had even bothered to try before. Late in the year, after sounding out neighbors, "I set on foot a subscription and obtained £200."

While he organized the Rivanna project, Jefferson also concentrated on his imminent bar examinations. These intimidated few young Virginians—Patrick Henry had taken them with almost no preparation and passed apparently with ease—but for the less assured and more thorough Jefferson they meant one of his hardest years of study. His legal notebook—Commonplace Book he called it—is crammed with extracts from his reading. Lord Kames's *Historical Law Tracts,* a book which among other things applied natural law to the legal profession, made a deep impression, to judge by the number of entries. These are of more interest than the many others made strictly for legal information. They mark, as Gilbert Chinard has said, "the beginning of Jefferson's interest in more general questions." Kames's comments on a variety of topics intrigued Jefferson: on property ("Property gives life to industry, and enables us to gratify the most dignified natural affections."); on entails ("They are a

snare to the thoughtless proprietor...”); on balanced government (“...the safety of a free government depends on balancing its several powers . . .”); on strong governments (“. . . unnatural and uncomfortable, because destructive of liberty and
independence.”); on society and the individual (“The perfection
of human society consists in that just degree of union among the
individuals, which to each reserves freedom and independency,
as far as is consistent with peace and good order.”). Clearly,
Kames clarified sentiments already fixed in Jefferson’s mind from
his years as a Virginia youth.

Jefferson was admitted to the bar in 1767. He opened an office
in Albemarle County at once. The morose student of Williamsburg began to fade, and the amiable man of later years emerged
—at least to a middle-aged female acquaintance who referred to
him in a letter as “Thou wonderful Young Man, so piously
entertaining. . . .” He was, of course, something more than
“piously entertaining.” His efforts in 1770 to help a young man
named Oglivie make that clear. Oglivie yearned to become a
clergyman in the Church of England but found himself blocked
by church politics. He turned to Jefferson for assistance. Jefferson’s attitude toward the Anglican Church was such that, as he
explained it, “any application if known to come from me would
rather be of disservice.” He therefore asked a more influential
friend to aid Oglivie “merely on the principles of common humanity to which his situation seems to recommend him....”
Aside from revealing something of Jefferson’s generosity, the
incident indicates his already deep distrust of any man-made
institution that tended to stunt the free development of an individual. His animus in 1770 was directed against the church because it alone then interfered with men’s liberties. Later, and for
the same reason, his anger would be turned against government.

Jefferson’s character exposed itself clearly in the home he
began to build in 1768. The house that eventually resulted has
been praised as among America’s most magnificent mansions. It

has also been censured. "With its excessive elaboration, its echoes of European models, and its somewhat chilly magnificence, it lacked both the charm and the comfort of the more simple and less self-conscious buildings of earlier periods, such as George Washington's Mount Vernon," writes one historian. The impulse behind this urge for magnificence provokes curiosity. Did Jefferson simply wish to give his aristocratic background full display? Possibly, for about the time he began to build, he inquired in London about the family coat of arms. Or did it merely reflect the confidence and pride of a young man who had already exceeded his father's achievements and now wished to create the brilliance of Europe in the near-wilderness of Virginia?

Whatever his reasons for splendor, the house Jefferson built reflected his character in all its complexity. For one thing, it is obviously the house of an eclectic who blended the borrowed into something original. The plans at first called for no castle, as Jefferson assured a friend, but "only a small house...." Those plans died possibly in 1765 when he purchased the works of William Shenstone, an English poet famous for the lavish development of his estate and gardens. Jefferson in the beginning decided to call his home the Hermitage, no doubt after the hermit Polydore who is described in Shenstone's works. ("Polydore, a new inhabitant in a sort of wild uninhabited country, was now ascended to the top of a mountain, and in the full enjoyment of a very extensive prospect. Before him a broad and winding valley, variegated with all the charms of landskip. Fertile meadows, glittering streams, pendent rocks, and nodding ruins...distant hills almost concealed by one undistinguished azure.") The view from Polydore's mountain top resembled that from the hill where Jefferson built.

Shenstone influenced the setting and Palladio the architecture of Jefferson's house. A generation earlier Palladian architecture had been the rage in England. The style called for immense

buildings of classical design that were a harmony of proportion
and balance—all appealing features to a Newtonian and an ad-
mirer of the ancients—and for gardens of clipped hedges, contrived waterfalls, twisting secluded paths. The grandeur of the
buildings and the artificial attempts to heighten the effects of
nature did not escape censure. William Hogarth satirized the
fad in a print called "The Taste of the Town." A huge semi-
circular colonnade, exactly the sort Jefferson favored, dominated
the print. Taste for Palladian architecture had soon died in England, and homes designed for comfortable, less pretentious living
became the accepted thing once again. The new mode slipped in
about the time Jefferson fell for the old one.

He may have lagged behind English styles, but even so Monticello, as he called the place, was for an American the house of a
man whose pride was "to run before the times in which he
lived." Most Virginia homes of the day were set in the elbow of
a hill, sheltered from winter winds and driving rain squalls,
and close to a river or road. Jefferson ignored tradition and,
like the hermit Polydore, built away from river and road on an
inaccessible hill fully exposed to all weather. Impractical, of
course, but old Isaac sensed the reason behind his master's decision: "From there you can see mountains all round as far as
the eye can reach."

Monticello is the house of a reflective man; it reveals also a
pretentious man eager to display his learning and to attract attention. Jefferson could have chosen no name more apt or
lovely than Monticello, the Italian word for "little mountain,"
for his mansion, but something ostentatious emerges when the
garlic in the garden becomes *Aglio di Toscania*, the beans
Fagiuoli d'Augusta, the wild endive *Radicchio di Pistoia*. Something equally pretentious appears, too, in the gadgets Jefferson
devised for his home. (Gadgets had intrigued him since youth.
"You know I had a waggon which moved itself," he wrote a
friend in 1770. "Cannot we construct a boat then which shall

row itself?") Some, like the storm windows he invented to ward off winter winds, served a practical use. Some, like the hidden passageways that allowed slaves to move about the house unseen by guests, smack of the devious. Most of the others—the dumb waiter, concealed in a side panel of the fireplace, which brought wine up from the cellar; French doors that swung open together with a light touch to the handle of one; living room windows that became passageways to the outdoors when the lower sash was raised; a weather vane that could be read from the porch ceiling—were no more than clever attention-getters.

And, finally, Monticello discloses the character of a man willing, eager even, to change his mind, of a man constantly open to new ideas. "They was forty years at work on that house before Mr. Jefferson stopped building," old Isaac said. Monticello, which, with its balanced wings and its appendages that always harmonized with the whole, revealed the influence of ideas drawn from natural philosophy, remained the same for Jefferson all the while he expanded, refined, and altered his ideas. He aspired to an ideal—vague, changing, but slowly becoming clarified—and as with a man who writes and rewrites attempting to achieve the exact expression, he worked to realize his ideal perfectly. The ideal of a highly civilized house may have been ludicrous in the backcountry of Virginia, but at least Jefferson had the tenacity and boldness to persist in the attempt to realize it. This discounts much that is chilly and pretentious about the building.

Jefferson broke free from Williamsburg in 1766 and treated himself to a trimmed down version of a once contemplated grand tour of Europe—a visit to Philadelphia and New York. In Philadelphia he was innoculated against smallpox, an act that suited his cautiously bold character, for many of the day viewed innoculation with live smallpox germs a needless risk, except when an epidemic was upon them. Jefferson was admitted to the Virginia bar in 1767 and then returned to Albemarle County, where he began to practice law shortly before his twenty-fourth birthday. He continued to practice for seven years, ceasing finally and perhaps gladly in 1774 to give full time to private affairs and to politics. During those seven years the honors that came slowly to his father—appointments as the county's chief military officer and as its surveyor and election to the Assembly —came swiftly to the son. And Jefferson, as if emulating his father in all ways, took his time marrying. Not until January 1, 1772, only a few months before his twenty-ninth birthday, did he wed Martha Wayles Skelton, a wealthy widow, whose estate when joined to her new husband's made Jefferson one of the largest landowners in the county.

Jefferson had already made his mark in politics and law by the time of his marriage. His success as a lawyer was considerable. He was involved in as many as four hundred and thirty cases in one year. The effort produced only modest financial returns—in 1770, his best year, he collected £213—but he profited in other ways from the work. Court day provided one of the grand events of a Virginia year, with the cases on the docket only the main event amid many side shows. Most of the surrounding countryside turned out to trade horses, sell Negroes, collect debts, make contracts, and, of course, to drink and gossip. Jefferson's practice forced him to travel regularly through his own and neighboring counties, and by the end of a circuit or two of court days he had met the worthy and worthless of the entire backcountry.

After two years of practice, Jefferson at twenty-six felt confident enough, or was made to feel so by unknown advisers, to run for one of Albemarle County's two seats in the House of Burgesses. He faced a less arduous campaign than a modern politician, but he nonetheless had to court the voters to a painful degree for a shy man. (A candidate in 1776 remarked bitterly he had "kissed the —————— of the people and very seriously ac-

comodated himself to others" and still he lost.) James Madison
later deplored "the corrupting influence of spirituous liquors
and other treats" on elections. He felt it was "inconsistent with
the purity of moral and republican principles" and in his first
campaign refused to provide refreshment. He lost. Jefferson,
more accomodating, accepted custom without complaint. He
won.

The result was not necessarily assured from the start. Virginia elections exceeded even court day for excitement, especially
when a candidate had entered the field for the first time. They
were generally held at the courthouse and an unwritten rule
required all candidates and their advisers to be on the scene.
Virginia favored voting by voice, and when a voter stepped
forward from the crowd an exchange similar to this one occurred:

Sheriff: "Mr. Blair, who do you vote for?"

Blair: "John Marshall."

Marshall: "Your vote is appreciated, Mr. Blair."

Sheriff: "Who do you vote for, Mr. Buchanan?"

Buchanan: "For John Clopton."

Clopton: "Mr. Buchanan, I shall treasure that vote in my
            memory. It will be regarded as a feather in my cap
            forever."

Having survived the obloquy of his first campaign, Jefferson
took his seat in the House of Burgesses in early May, 1769. His
first session lasted only ten days. This probably pleased Jefferson, for he now had time to prepare for his new career in the
same thorough way he had studied for the law. In the summer
of 1769, shortly after the legislature had adjourned, he ordered
a small library of books on government. They arrived in September, and among them were John Locke's *Treatise on Govern-*

ment, Jean Jacque Burlamaqui's *Le Droit Naturel*, Ferdinand Warner's *History of Ireland* and *History of Civil Wars*, Thomas Petty's *Survey of Ireland*, Montesquieu's complete works, Adam Ferguson's *An Essay on the History of Civil Society*, and Sir James Stewart's *Political Oeconomy*.

Jefferson eventually became familiar with the contents of all these volumes, but to judge by his writings he apparently read Locke earlier and more attentively than the others. Jefferson found that when Locke looked at government he asked: what is government's right to authority? Divine right, answered some; God had given the king the right to rule and the people must accept God's dictum. What resources do the people have if the ruler turns out to be bad? God would punish him, went the litany. What would the people do in the meantime? Suffer, unless someone dreamed up an acceptable way to dispose of the king. Locke set out to devise a way out of the impasse. He developed a "right of rebellion" theory based on the law of nature. Men were born free, unhampered by government, and with certain "self-evident" natural rights, among which were the rights to life, liberty, and property. Now, the state of nature is difficult to maintain, for evil exists in the world and there are times when the individual cannot cope with it successfully. To protect their rights, men voluntarily band together and make a compact whereby one of their own is chosen to rule over them. This ruler and the government he creates exist only to protect men's natural rights. If the original compact is broken, the people then have the right to rebel, for they, not God, have chosen him and can depose him.

Locke's "right of rebellion" theory held little interest for Jefferson in 1769, when Virginia's relations with England drifted along tranquilly. Other sides of Locke's political ideas appealed more strongly because, with only slight trimming, they clarified and justified views Jefferson already held about government. Locke invited men to test all their institutions by the yardstick of reason. For Locke such institutions as primogeniture, entail, the established church, British regulations of trade, met the test. But it was the principle, not the specific applications, that mattered. Jefferson, of a different century and a different country, might find his own answers of what met the test of reason. Locke favored and was the first to advance the idea of a minimal state, though his seventeenth century conception of what was the least government also differed from Jefferson's. Again, it was the principle and not the details that jibed neatly with Jefferson's view. Locke said government should be based on the consent of the people—propertied people, of course—and this rule fit the situation in Virginia, where only those with land could vote. Locke said that the "great and chief end...of men's uniting into commonwealths and putting themselves under governments is the preservation of property." The Virginia government sought the same end. It interfered in the affairs of men only when men's property was endangered by aggression.

It has been argued by Leo Strauss that Locke unleashed the acquisitive instinct in western society. He says: "The burden of Locke's chapter on property is that covetousness and concupiscence, far from being essentially evil or foolish, are, if properly channeled, eminently beneficial and reasonable.... By building civil society on 'the low but solid ground' of selfishness or of certain 'private vices,' one will achieve much greater 'public benefits' than by futilely appealing to virtue, which is by nature 'unendowed.' One must take one's bearings not by how men should live but by how they do live." No doubt Locke was thus read by many of Jefferson's contemporaries—John Adams perhaps?—but he was not so read by Jefferson. Long acquaintance with the classics had, if nothing else, taught Jefferson that liberty with a reasonable man is held in check by his sense of duty to himself and to society, that happiness came not with the satisfaction of animal or material desires but was the ultimate result of moral virtue. Jefferson never judged the acquisitive instinct as beneficial to society. Jefferson always took his bearing by how men should live. It was this quality that made him seem to run ahead of his times. Moral virtue was the goal of all men. Locke appealed to him, among other reasons, because the sort of government he propounded seemed the best likely to permit man to achieve moral virtue.

The aspect of Locke's ideas highlighted by Professor Strauss probably slipped by Jefferson completely, for as a young politician he mainly wanted clarification of his thoughts on government. Even in this restricted field Jefferson surely missed many of Locke's implications on first reading. Whatever may have slipped past, however, he could have picked up from his cousin Richard Bland when the House reconvened in November of 1769. Bland and Jefferson had been thrown together at once on one of the House's many committees, and it was possibly the older, experienced politician, one of the ablest and most widely read members of the House, who had worked up the elaborate reading list for Albemarle County's new member. Bland was now nearly fifty, "a learned, bookish man" who, perhaps because of that failing, had let his estates run down to the point where he was by a neighbor's lights "in needy circumstances." He was also known to be "staunch & tough as Whitleather," and something of a maverick, speaking out so bluntly on public matters that his loyalty was questioned. (He would soon be called "an enemy of his country," and in 1775, while serving as a Virginia delegate in Congress, the false rumor floated down from Philadelphia that he "has turned traitor.") He despised entails and primogeniture as well as slavery; he was deeply concerned with human rights; and "he attacked with boldness every assumption of power...." Clearly, he would have served as an excellent mentor for any young politician.

Bland had made one of the abler retorts to Patrick Henry in 1765, though it had apparently escaped Jefferson's memory. A year after the debate, still rankling over Henry's hazy thinking and emotional approach to a serious matter, he had published *An Inquiry into the Rights of the British Colonies*. Bland developed his own variation of Locke's argument: Men are in nature absolutely free and independent so far as sovereignty is concerned. When they enter into society, they agree to submit to society's laws as long as "it will conduce to their Happiness, which they have a natural Right to promote." There are two ways, Bland said, of abrogating the old contract—by rebellion or by migration. Americans chose "to retire from the Society, to renounce the Benefits of it...and to settle in another Country." When they reached America, they made a new compact in the form of a charter; they made it with the King, not with Parliament. Bland went on to state American rights and to undercut at length the argument that Parliament had power over the colonies. He shunned rash talk about revolution. His tone resembled that of a wise son attempting to set an erring parent straight.

The mechanics of government attracted Bland hardly at all. For him, the least government the best. He fought every assumption of power that infringed on rather than protected the rights of individuals. Long use of power did not necessarily justify it for Bland, and for years he carried on what must have seemed a petty fight to many against "a very ancient usage of the secretary of Virginia, to appoint the clerks of the county courts." The custom angered Bland because it deprived the people of a right that belonged to them and to their representatives and not to the government.

Bland's concern for the individual overrode all other interests. Anything that divested a man of liberty defied natural law. He did not shirk from carrying this view to its logical conclusion. He never tired of denouncing slavery. Here he proved a warm and useful friend of Jefferson, who had entered politics determined to do something to improve the lot of the Negro in Virginia. Jefferson set about this provocative project in much the manner he had long ago wangled a holiday for hunting in the Reverend Mr. Maury's school. "I drew to this subject the attention of Col. Bland, one of the oldest, ablest, & most respected members, and he undertook to move for certain moderate extensions of the protection of the laws to these people," Jefferson remembered. "I seconded his motion, and, as a younger member, was more spared in the debate; but he was denounced as an enemy of his country, & was treated with the grossest indecorum."

The reasoning behind Jefferson's urge to improve the Negro's lot turns up in 1770, when he argued in court against the enslavement of the mulatto grandchild of a white woman and a Negro man. "I suppose it will not be pretended that the mother being a servant, the child would be a servant also under the law of nature,..." he told the court. "Under the law of nature all men are born free, every one comes into the world with a right to his own person, which includes the liberty of moving and using it at his own will. This is what is called personal liberty, and is given him by the author of nature, because necessary for his own sustenance. The reducing of the mother to servitude was a violation of the law of nature: surely then the same law cannot prescribe a continuance of the violation to her issue, and that too without end, for if it extends to any, it must to every degree of descendants." Jefferson noted in his brief that Pufendorf "supports this doctrine"; the court dismissed the argument as worthless.

No one apparently regarded Jefferson as a radical to be ignored because of the way he used the concept of natural law. Other Virginians shared his concern for the individual, his distrust of the established church, his distaste for slavery and for such feudal heritages as entail and primogeniture. Most young men desire to clear away the rubbish of the past and remake the world along modern lines. Jefferson must have seemed less rash to his elders than most his age. They saw to it that his duties and responsibilities in the House continued to increase. Peyton Randolph, Speaker of the House and the most patient of men—Jefferson included him with Small and Wythe as a model on which to pattern his own conduct—took a special interest in the young man and saw to it he began to appear on the most important House committees. By 1774 Jefferson had spent six full years in politics. He had learned the mechanics of law-making and the art of parliamentary procedure. Past failures had taught him to sense the sentiments of his colleagues, and perhaps it was Peyton Randolph who warned him that if he must travel ahead of the crowd never to travel too far or too obviously ahead.

Jefferson appeared to forget the admonition and to toss caution to the winds when in 1774 he turned out an essay that reached print under the title of *A Summary View of the Rights of British America*. The pamphlet struck many of the day as a bold attack on the crown, yet a review of its argument uncovers little to explain that judgment. Jefferson regards the King as "no more than the chief officer of the people, appointed by the laws, and circumscribed with definite powers, to assist in working the great machine of government erected for their use...." He takes Bland's view that out of love for the mother country the colonies did submit "themselves to the same common sovereign, who was thereby made the central link connecting the several parts of the empire thus newly multiplied." Obviously, Parliament "has no right to exercise authority over us," yet it clearly seems bent upon "a deliberate, systematical plan of reducing us to slavery." If the King expects things to calm down in America, he must make Parliament change its ways. He would do well also to mend his own ways, which have become exceedingly oppressive. He has, for instance, forced slavery on the colonies, an evil which insults "the rights of human nature." He has also delayed consideration of our laws; endeavored to take from the people the right of representation; dissolved representative bodies doing their duty; delayed the issue of writs for choice of new representatives; perpetuated feudal landholding practices; and sent troops among us. Jefferson ends with advice to the King: "The whole art of government consists in the art of being honest. Only aim to do your duty, and mankind will give you credit where you fail."

Jefferson offers little new here—unless it be the wild charge that the King foisted slavery on the colonies. The essay, like Monticello, presents an eclectic collection of ideas long in the air. But also like Monticello, old ideas reassembled acquire a new sheen. The impression of boldness and originality the pamphlet left with contemporaries stems mainly from its vivid style and admonitory tone. (There exists a striking similarity in tone, style, argument, and even in phraseology between *A Summary View* and Tom Paine's *Common Sense*, which also gave the air of originality to ideas long abroad.) A good deal of its forcefulness arises from the moral fervor that pervades the essay. It sounds in spots like a religious tract rather than a political pamphlet. Substitute the word God for natural right, devil for King, and it resembles the rumblings of a New England divine. By centering on the evil of the King, Jefferson dramatized and simplified the story as effectively as a backwoods preacher telling a tale of battle between the devil and one of God's people. The fervor that Jefferson, born in another time, might have directed into religion he now directed into politics, and it was this, the passion rather than the logic or originality of his argument, that left its imprint on men of the time.

The effect *A Summary View* had on pushing America closer to independence cannot be estimated. The effect it had on Jefferson's career is clear. It gave him fame outside his "country," and won him a seat in Congress. He was elected by the Virginia Convention in May, 1775, and left promptly for Philadelphia, traveling northward as a southern gentleman should, with four horses and two slaves to attend his wants. He arrived in Philadelphia on June 21. With Lexington and Concord still a fresh memory, there was already some talk about independence, although few in Congress aside from Sam and John Adams had definitely made up their minds. Benjamin Franklin, only recently returned from a long sojourn in England, had refused as yet to take a stand, and among some of the Virginia delegation gossip had it he was acting as a British spy. Two days after Jefferson's arrival Congress assembled to escort George Washington, recently chosen commander-in-chief of the army, out of the city and on his way to beleaguered Boston. He had hardly departed when news arrived of the Battle of Bunker Hill.

Jefferson arrived something of a celebrity, for most of Congress had read his pamphlet. Five days after he had slumped for the first time into a seat in the State House chamber, a committee reported out a Declaration of the Causes and Necessity for Taking up Arms. Congress disliked the report and decided a fresh approach was needed. Jefferson, along with John Dickinson, was added to the committee with the expectation that both men, known for their literary skill, would rewrite the document into something more acceptable.

Jefferson made the first try, but not until he had graciously offered the opportunity to William Livingston, another member of the committee. Livingston refused the offer and suggested in turn that Jefferson must draw up the paper. When Jefferson again urged him, Livingston became ruffled.

"We are as yet but new acquaintances, sir," he said; "why are you so earnest for my doing it?"

"Because," said Jefferson ingratiatingly, "I have been informed that you drew the Address to the people of Great Britain, a production, certainly, of the finest pen in America."

The tribute missed the mark, for Livingston had not drawn the document Jefferson mentioned. A courteous gesture had backfired, but the incident pointed up Jefferson's friendly, likeable nature as well as the cautious manner he adopted to advance his own star.

Jefferson's share in framing the Declaration of Causes—which was considerable—together with an answer to Lord North's conciliatory proposals he drew up for Congress a month later, constituted his main contributions this first brief trip to Philadelphia. The summer heat of the city soon began to enervate the delegates and Congress adjourned on August 2. "We are all exhausted," one delegate said, "sitting so long at this place and being so long confined together that we feel pretty much as a Number of passengers confined together on board ship in a long Voyage."

Jefferson returned to Congress in October, having been reelected with the highest number of votes among the Virginia delegation. The compliment had nothing to do with his effectiveness on the floor of Congress. "During the time while I sat with him in Congress," John Adams recalled in old age, "I never heard him utter three sentences together," and if the month of December in 1775 was typical—a month, incidentally, in which Adams was absent—he understated the case only slightly. On December 16 a delegate noted "Jefferson moved that no new Motion shall be offered after 12 oCloc without special Permission till Order of the day is satisfyed...." A week later "Jefferson from the Com.ee brought in a List of Business before Us," and three days later "Instructions to Col. Irwin [were] brought in by Jefferson and passed."

Throughout this second tour of duty Jefferson remained in constant worry about the health of his wife. "The suspense under which I am is too terrible to be endured," he finally wrote. "If any thing has happened, for god's sake let me know it." Finally, the strain became unendurable, and in late December he headed for home.

As the expected brief visit home stretched from weeks into months, Jefferson found himself with a great deal of time to write and read. Perhaps his ability only a few weeks after returning to Philadelphia to compose, almost effortlessly, his statement of American political beliefs owed much to this period of forced retirement. He must have spent a good deal of time in his library during the four and a half month "vacation" at Monticello, and a fair share of that time must have gone to working out and clarifying his own political ideas. At least two great issues, aside from the question of separation from Great Britain, demanded attention. There was first the problem of a confederation of the colonies. Shortly before leaving Philadelphia, Benjamin Franklin had handed Jefferson a copy of his ideas on a confederation. This perhaps spurred Jefferson to study the constitutions of other nations. Possibly the lengthy remarks in the undated Commonplace Book on the Union of Utrecht, the constitutions of Switzerland, Denmark, Sweden, and Poland were made during this holiday from public affairs.

The second issue that undoubtedly drew Jefferson's attention was a constitution for Virginia. Quite possibly this matter led him at this time to read with care and take detailed notes on Montesquieu's *Esprit des Lois* and Cesare Beccaria's *On Crimes and Punishments*. Montesquieu, whom Jefferson later held little respect for, at this time seemed the source of many ideas, if the mass of notes he made are any indication. Beccaria interested him for the argument advanced for more humane punishment of criminals. He, like Jefferson, opposed any "unnatural" form of law that unnecessarily degraded the individual.

By early May, Jefferson obviously could no longer postpone his return to Philadelphia. His eargerness to share in making a new constitution for Virginia surpassed any interest in a declaration of independence or a confederation, which dealt more with the continent than with his "country," but no honorable way of prolonging his absence from Congress had appeared and so, reluctantly, he headed northward in early May.

Jefferson's impatience to get back to Virginia persisted for some time after the return to Philadelphia. But after two or three hints in letters to friends back home, he settled down to putting his ideas for a Virginia constitution on paper. Though Congress almost at once handed him a workload so heavy that only John Adams was serving on more committees, he found time to complete three full drafts between mid-May and Mid-June, when George Wythe carried the final version back to Virginia. (Jefferson may possibly have begun work on his constitution while back at Monticello, but one or two hints in the first draft—a mention, for example, that the King had dispatched Hessian troops to America, an event still only a rumor in mid-May—suggest that more likely he waited to begin until he returned to Philadelphia.)

We must linger a bit on this constitution. Understanding Jefferson's ideas on government as he revealed them here helps to illuminate what he was saying in the Declaration.

Jefferson knew that before he got down to specifics he must first justify the need for a constitution; men do not create new governments for casual reasons. He began with a brief preface, wherein he said that George III, "heretofore entrusted with the exercise of the kingly office in this government, hath endeavored to pervert the same into a detestable & insupportable tyranny." Now, George must be proved a tyrant. Prove this and you proved Americans were not rebelling but only resisting to protect their natural rights. The groundwork for this argument had been laid, so far as Jefferson was concerned, in *A Summary View*. From that he abstracted the grievances discussed there at length and condensed them into a list. The King had manifested the character of a tyrant

by putting his negative on laws the most wholesome & necessary for the public good

by denying to his governors permission to pass laws of im-

mediate & pressing importance, unless suspended in their operation for his assent &, when so suspended, neglecting to attend
to them for many years:

by refusing to pass certain other laws, unless the persons to
be benefited by them would relinquish the inestimable right of
representation in the legislature:

by dissolving legislative assemblies repeatedly & continually
for opposing with manly firmness his invasions on the rights of
the people:

when dissolved, by refusing to call others for a long space of
time, thereby leaving the political system without any legislative *head*.

by endeavoring to prevent the population of our country &
for that purpose obstructing the laws for the naturalization of
foreigners & raising the conditions of new appropriations of
lands:

by keeping among us in times of peace standing armies &
ships of war:

by affecting to render the military independant of & superior
to the civil power:

This seemed a satisfactory catalogue of the King's abuse of
his executive power. Jefferson turned now to a draft of the
Declaration of the Causes he had worked up in 1775, and there
collected several more charges that dealt with the King's
maledictions done in agreement with Parliament:

by combining with others to subject us to a foreign jurisdiction

giving his assent to their pretended acts of legislation

for quartering large bodies of armed troops among us:

for cutting off our trade with all parts of the world:

for imposing taxes on us without our consent:

for depriving us of the benefits of trial by jury:

for transporting us beyond seas to be tried for pretended offenses:

for suspending our own legislatures & declaring themselves invested with power to legislate for us in all cases whatsoever

The list still seemed deficient to Jefferson. No crimes of violence or cruelty had yet been included. Jefferson rounded up several of these, possibly depending to some extent on a list of twenty-one charges against the King that had appeared in the *Pennsylvania Evening Post* the day he had returned to Philadelphia:

by plundering our seas, ravaging our coasts, burning our towns, & destroying the lives of our people:

by inciting insurrections of our fellow subjects with the allurements of forfeiture & confiscation

by prompting our negroes to rise in arms among us; those very negroes whom by an inhuman use of his negative he hath refused us permission to exclude by law:

by endeavoring to bring on the inhabitants of our frontiers the merciless Indian savages whose known rule of warfare is an undistinguished destruction of all ages, sexes, & conditions of existence.

by transporting at this time a large army of foreign mercenaries to compleat the works of death, desolation, & tyranny already begun with circumstances of cruelty & perfidy so unworthy the head of a civilized nation

by answering our repeated petitions for redress with a repetition of injuries:

and finally by abandoning the helm of government & declaring us out of his allegiance & protection.

Jefferson had finished with his charges, at least for the moment; a frugal man when it came to getting wear out of his writings, he would find a way to serve up the list again, slightly altered but essentially the same. Jefferson had ended his preface with a long paragraph which stated that since George III had "put us out of his allegiance & protection" the colonies were no longer subject to him. Therefore, Jefferson concluded, the King "may now lawfully, rightfully, & by consent of both parties be divested of the kingly powers."

That done, Jefferson turned to the body of his constitution. His first draft obviously was written in haste. In the rush to get down his thoughts, words were abbreviated, interlined, and scratched out until the document was nearly unreadable. Jefferson labeled the paper "Constitution of Virginia, first ideas of...." He inaugurated no basic structural changes in the new government. Jefferson tossed away old titles—House of Burgesses, Governor, Council—as if once those went the taint of monarchy went with them. But the essence of the old pattern remained. He conceived a legislature composed of two houses—a House of Representatives elected annually by the voters and a Senate chosen by the lower house, and, in the original draft, chosen for life. The executive—Administrator, Jefferson called him—was "to possess the powers formerly held by the king save only..." and then followed a long list of exceptions, showing Jefferson's intent of avoiding the evils that strong royal governors had been able to commit. The Administrator could not, among other things, veto bills, dissolve the House, declare war or peace, raise an army, coin money, erect courts, or lay embargoes. All these powers resided in the legislature. The Administrator was to be no more than his title implied.

The orthodox form of Jefferson's government served to camouflage the innovations he slipped in. He introduced changes in the suffrage requirements. "Qualifications of electors," he wrote in this first draft, "shall be such as prove a fixed purpose of residence." Then, in brackets, he added that this should be determined on an as yet unestablished number of acres of land or on being an inhabitant who had paid his "scot and lot" tax, a town levy assessed proportionally on all members of a community.

As a further effort to widen the electorate, the constitution provided that "50 acres of land shall be appropriated without purchase money to every person not owning nor having ever owned that quantity...." In theory there was nothing shocking nor radical in this plan. Since the time of John Locke the land of a country was held to be the common stock of society to which all men had a right. But when Jefferson made provisions to apply the theory, he was attempting something many fellow Virginians would regard as shocking and radical, for a number of the colony's elite saw in the vast public domain a chance to build up a fortune through speculation. They were not anxious to do themselves out of a fortune.

Jefferson's first draft introduced two other innovations that would unsettle the minds of some of his countrymen. "Descents," he said, attacking both entail and primogeniture at once, "instead of being to the eldest son, brother, or other male cousin of the ancestor, . . . shall be to all the brothers & sisters of sd. heir. . . ." On the matter of religion Jefferson acknowledged not only religious freedom but freedom from religion. "All persons," he wrote, "shall have full & free liberty of religious opinion, nor shall any be compelled to frequent or maintain any religious service or institution...." But, he went on to add, they would be liable to punishment for "seditious behavior"—a vague phrase dropped from later drafts quite likely because of the many loopholes it left bigots.

Jefferson elaborated in drafts that followed many points touched on hastily in the first version. He made few basic changes but several additions. He decided against electing the Senate for life and instead limited the members' terms to nine years, and he made them ineligible for re-election. He modified his law of descents, insisting now only on equal division of the land among the heirs instead of all offspring but also making it clear "that females shall have equal rights with males." He had, curiously, overlooked in the first draft the slavery issue, which he rarely failed to condemn when the chance offered. He corrected that slip in the second draft by inserting the sentence: "No person hereafter coming into this country shall be held in slavery under any pretext whatever." In the first draft he had been of a mind to have justices of peace, hitherto appointed by the central government, elected. He now decided that the number of elective offices for all parts of the government should remain as they had been under the crown. He had left blank in the first version the number of acres of land a man needed to qualify as a voter. He settled at first on fifty acres for a rural resident and a half-acre for a town dweller, then on second thought lowered these requirements to twenty-five and to one-quarter acres respectively. He clearly sought to widen the electorate as far as feasible without raising the hackles of conservative members of the constitutional convention. And finally in the second draft he elaborated on the punishment of crimes, inserting a generous criminal code. Probably Beccaria's *On Crimes and Punishments* influenced him here. He abolished all capital punishment except for murder "& those offences in the military service for which they shall think punishment by death absolutely necessary."

In the process of revision Jefferson added a section dealing with western territories. "By act of the Legislature one or more territories shall be laid off Westward of the Alleganey mountains for new colonies, which colonies shall be established on the same fundamental laws contained in this instrument & shall be free & independent of this colony and of all the world." Jefferson here became the first to take a public stand on a question that would arise at the Constitutional Convention of 1787:

should the western territories enter the union as equals or as colonies, or should they remain independent? His views in 1776 were conditioned by a conviction, possibly obtained from Montesquieu, that republics could operate effectively only over small areas.

In the penultimate paragraph of the second and third drafts, Jefferson slipped in one final revision. He insisted that "none of these fundamental laws and principles of government shall be repealed or altered, but by the personal consent of the people on summons to meet in their respective counties...." He here underscored a belief that the phrase "consent of the governed" should be taken much more literally than John Adams and others in Congress were willing to take it. Soon after he had dispatched the final draft to Virginia, he urged a friend, then sitting in the constitutional convention there, to oppose any motion to draft a permanent constitution. Perhaps he wanted to delay the event until he could be on hand, but he advanced another reason. He said the people should elect deputies especially for the purpose of making a constitution. "He denied," Edmund Randolph later reported, "the power of the body elected (as he conceived them to be agents for the management of the war) to exceed some temporary regimen."

If the Virginia convention had accepted Jefferson's constitution in 1776, many of the battles of his later career would have been won at that date. This document contained, as one writer has noted, "most if not all of the leading principles to which Jefferson's entire career was dedicated." Jefferson had built on old traditions and at the same time moved ahead to new ground. He held to his old belief that the central government should remain weak and that what power it had should be dispersed among its three branches. Yet he also showed that government had positive things it could and should do. He believed, for example, that the power of the state must be used for the social good in order to eliminate extreme inequalities of

property, first by distributing public property to the deprived
and then by abolishing primogeniture and entail. He indicated
that the government should take the lead in humanitarian reform
by liberalizing the penal code and prohibiting the extension
of slavery.

His constitution blended the views of the aristocrat and the
democrat. Jefferson expected no one in the new government
to come from the poorer class, for he remarked that "no salaries
shall be given to the Administrator, members of the Legislative
houses, judges of the court of Appeals, judges of the County
courts, or other inferior jurisdictions, Privy counsellors, or
Delegates to the American Congress." He avoided any suggestion that the plain people would have much say in the government and cleared all doubt where he stood in a letter to a friend
soon after finishing the third draft: "I have ever observed that a
choice by the people themselves is not generally distinguished
for its wisdom," he wrote. "This first secretion from them is
usually crude and heterogeneous. But give to those so chosen
by the people a second choice themselves, and they generally
will chuse wise men. For this reason it was that I proposed the
representatives (and not the people) should chuse the Senate,
and thought I had notwithstanding that made the Senators
(when chosen) perfectly independent of their electors."

The constitutional convention rejected nearly all of Jefferson's
innovations. His alterations of voting requirements received
hardly passing attention. Though Jefferson still based the right
to vote on the possession of property, he had put the qualifications so low as to all but discard the old "stake in society"
concept. His friend Edmund Pendleton said, soon after reading the final draft of the constitution, that the right to vote
"should be confined to those of fixed Permanent property, who
cannot suddenly remove without injury to that property or Sub-
stituting another proprietor, and whom alone I consider as having
Political Attachment." Jefferson came back at once with a

full statement on the question: "I was for extending the right of suffrage (or in other words the rights of a citizen) to all who had a permanent intention of living in the country," he wrote. "Take what circumstances you please as evidence of this, either the having resided a certain time, or having a family, or having property, any or all of them. Whoever intends to live in a country must wish that country well, and has a natural right of assisting in the preservation of it. I think you cannot distinguish between such a person residing in the country and having no fixed property, and one residing in a township whom you say you would admit to a vote." Jefferson was carrying a natural right much too far for his friend.

The constitution Virginia eventually accepted solved the suffrage question by stating that "the right of Suffrage in the Election of Members for both Houses shall remain as exercised at present ..."—that is, a man must own at least fifty acres of cleared land. Years later Jefferson remarked that this refusal to extend voting rights in 1776 excluded first class citizenship to about "half of those on the roll of the militia, or of the tax-gatherers." It seems unbelievable that half the white males in a colony where almost anyone who owned land owned enough to vote were excluded from that right. Who were these disenfranchised? There were, of course, the worthless and the floaters, who regardless of the qualifications would never vote. A few of the non-voters were overseers, some were tenant farmers, others craftsmen and merchants and those who worked for them. Many were adult sons of small farmers who for a variety of reasons—they lacked the money perhaps, the inclination, or the energy—had failed to get established on their own. Jefferson believed this half of Virginia's male population had as much right to the vote as their more fortunate brethren. Fixed residence alone should be the determining suffrage requirement. He had not yet pushed this view to the point where he would grant universal male suffrage, but he had perhaps edged closer to that position in mid-1776 than any other man in the Continental Congress.

It is hard to fathom what started Jefferson along this line of thought. Obviously, the natural rights doctrine played a part. His willingness to include voting for adult white males among the natural rights seems less radical when it is recalled that he had previously attempted to include the Negro within the natural rights doctrine. And certainly Jefferson must have been influenced by the fact that many men serving in the armed forces lacked the vote, a point which had long been hammered home in the Philadelphia press by Tom Paine and his followers. A writer who called himself Elector had insisted in a newspaper article that appeared about the time of Jefferson's return that Pennsylvania's suffrage requirements—to qualify as a voter a man needed to own fifty acres of cleared land or fifty pounds worth of personal property—gave an advantage to "the *profligate* and *corrupt*." Elector went on to say that "every man who pays his shot and bears his lot"—words similar to those Jefferson used in his first draft—"is naturally and constitutionally an elector in a city. And, more especially, I will affirm, that every citizen who has armed and associated to defend the Commonwealth is and should be an elector." Possibly essays like Elector's—and there were several appearing in the press about this time—nudged Jefferson toward his position on suffrage.

Jefferson's views on property resist easy summary. He realized that unless the majority of people shared in the landed wealth of their country democratic government would fail. Others saw this equally clearly, but Jefferson differed from his friends in that he wanted, was eager in fact, to put theory into practice. He diverged still further from his friends by insisting that the amount of land a man owned had nothing to do with the right to first-class citizenship. "My observations," he said, "do not enable me to say I think integrity the characteristic of wealth." John Adams, for one, could have said that too, but

Adams would have meant that the political power of the wealthy must be checked, whereas Jefferson meant that the political rights of the poor must not be blocked by property qualifications for voting. Jefferson, in contrast to Adams, used the American past to foster liberalism where Adams, deeply involved through reading and inclination in European traditions, used the past to foster conservatism. Jefferson looked forward and worked to extend that liberal tradition he had been reared in. Adams looked backward to achieve his ideal.

Jefferson also diverged from Tom Paine—who he probably first met about the time he was writing the constitution for Virginia—in that he wished to build on the past to create the new and better world. Paine seemed convinced that Americans could disown the past, and whenever he contemplated new government for the states-to-be he talked of forms that had little in common with those the colonists were accustomed to. He suggested, for instance, a single house legislature when most of the colonies—Pennsylvania excepted—had a bicameral legislature. He argued for elected judges when Americans were accustomed to appointed judges, for a weak, multiple executive in place of the usual governor the colonists knew best. Paine talked with blithe enthusiasm about re-building from the ground up. Jefferson had been too long in politics to be cajoled into believing the old structure could be or should be completely razed. Nonetheless, Paine's democratical view held a nub of truth for Jefferson, and possibly from him and his followers he took the idea that whoever indicated a desire to settle in a "country" deserved to share in its government, regardless of his stake in society.

Laboring on the constitution had forced Jefferson to clarify and express ideas about government he had never before put on paper. He wrote when the "spirit of levelling," as John Adams called it, was afloat in Philadelphia. (And elsewhere, too, it should be noted. In February the Provincial Congress of New

Jersey had reduced the suffrage qualifications to males twenty-one years of age who had resided in the colony one year and possessed property worth £50 in "proclamation money," which, with inflation already underway, in effect gave the colony universal manhood suffrage.) It seems reasonable to suggest that Jefferson's presence in Philadelphia at a time when Paine and his friends there and elsewhere were agitating for the rights of the common man made him susceptible to views he might otherwise have been slower to adopt. In some ways Jefferson was still an impressionable young man, still open to new ideas and eager to incorporate them into his philosophy if it could be done without contradicting the old. His mind was still in the making. Monticello, that pastiche of architecture, constantly being torn down and rebuilt, exemplified his character. The older John Adams, on the other hand, long fixed in his ideas about man and government, would ride through the hullabaloo Paine was stirring up without being jarred an inch from his course.

As the middle of June neared, it was clear Jefferson would have no chance to present his ideas in person to the constitutional convention in Virginia. George Wythe and Richard Henry Lee were both returning home. Jefferson gave Wythe the third draft of the constitution. By this time—Wythe and Lee departed on June 13—an event had occurred which, while it did not dim Jefferson's eagerness to return to Virginia, eventually proved of greater importance in his life than the constitution he had been drafting.

Chapter 3

The Colossus of Independence

❋ ❋ ❋ ❋ ❋ ❋ ❋ ❋

I am a sincere inquirer after truth, but I find very few who
discover the *same* truth.

JOHN ADAMS

IT WAS Jefferson who, late in life, called John Adams "the
colossus of independence," but in 1783 he had this to say
when he heard his colleague had been made a member of the
peace commission to settle the war with England: "I am nearly
at a loss to judge how he will act in negotiation. He hates
Franklin, he hates Jay, he hates the French, he hates the English.
To whom will he adhere? His vanity is a lineament in his
character which had entirely escaped me. [But not Adams,
who admitted that vanity "is my cardinal vice and cardinal
folly."] His want of taste I had observed. Notwithstanding all
this he has a sound head on substantial points, and I think he
has integrity. I am glad therefore that he is of the commission
and expect he will be useful in it. His dislike of all parties, and
all men, by balancing his prejudices may give the same fair
play to his reason as would a general benevolence of temper.
At any rate honesty may be extracted even from poisonous
weeds."

Jefferson here only paraphrased Franklin's blunt remark that
Adams "is always an honest man, often a wise one, but sometimes and in some things absolutely out of his senses." But
in adapting the sentiment, Jefferson made it his own—something

at once fair ("I am glad therefore that he is of the commission"), tentative ("I think he has integrity"), vague ("his want of taste" —did Jefferson refer to Adams's bursts of temper, his tendency to gossip, his habit of chewing tobacco?), and cruel ("honesty may be extracted even from poisonous weeds").

Jefferson's ambivalence was not shared by John Adams, who to his diary and close friends censured his own failings relentlessly. "I am constantly forming, but never executing good resolutions," runs a typical entry. In another, he says: "Abroad, my appetites are solicited, my passions inflamed, and my understanding too much perverted, to judge wisely of men or things." He frankly admitted he lacked the ingredients for greatness. (This, however, meant little, for Adams had high standards. He knew no great men. He found abundant flaws in Franklin, in Washington, and eventually in Jefferson.) He could by turns be perverse, sulky, petty, and spiteful. He lacked wit. He often took himself too seriously and equally often could be unforgivably harsh toward those he admired. When his friend James Otis, then in the midst of a nervous breakdown, slighted Adams, the young lawyer saw only "a complication of malice, envy, and jealousy in this man" who had once been exceedingly kind to him.

Even if their physical differences were discounted, and a six-inch disparity in height was nothing easy to discount, especially for John Adams, no pair in Congress contrasted more sharply than Adams and Jefferson. While Jefferson, self-contained and restrained, sat by in silence, Adams more often than not was on his feet airing firm opinions. Jefferson had arrived in Philadelphia with an almost lavish equipage, while Adams on his first trip rode in on the back of his horse. The splendid way of life of Philadelphia's rich provoked no comment from the sophisticated southern aristocrat, but Adams, full of envy and awe, could report of little else for days in his diary. Jefferson bought what he desired in the well-stocked Philadelphia shops and showed little concern about prices; Adams, often pressed for cash and disturbed whether the income from his farm would suffice for his family, watched his expenses with care.

If style reveals the man, then the contrast between the two shows up clearest in their letters—Jefferson's articulate, graceful, and often dull; Adams's marked by that easy style Horace Walpole found so wanting in eighteenth century writers. ("Our writers of to-day have bodies of iron, not in their health, but in their style.") Adam's public writing could be ponderous, but his letters and diaries, usually dashed off in the midst of a full day, reveal vivid accounts of quarrels, characters, and events of the moment that have stirred his mind and feelings. In them Adams—by turns belligerent and compassionate, surly and sentimental, childish and wise—overwhelms by his vitality, his eagerness to seize hold of all sides of life. The days offered so much to see and do that at times the abundance tried Adams's patience: "My thoughts are roving from girls to friends, from friends to court, to Worcester, Newbury, and then to Greece and Rome, then to law; from poetry to oratory, and law. Oh! rambling imagination! Could I fix my attention and keep off every fluttering thought that attempts to intrude upon the present subject, I could read a book all day." The discipline Jefferson managed with seeming ease to impose on himself constantly eluded Adams. "I have smoked, chatted, trifled, loitered away this whole day almost," he could write in disgust, then go on to say that the morning had been spent reading ten pages of Justinian, translating four of those into English, then "in unloading a cart, in cutting oven wood, in making and recruiting my own fire, in eating victuals and apples, in drinking tea, cutting and smoking tobacco, and in chatting with Dr. Savil's wife at their house and this."

Though much that Adams judged as flaws in himself reveal only an attractively human side to his character, he nonetheless had real failings. Often in the uninhibited diary entries he resembles James Thurber's King Clode, who, when he heard that a huge pink comet had just missed the earth, said: "They aim these things at me! Everything is aimed at me." "I long to study sometimes, but have no opportunity," Adams remarked once in his God-how-I-pity-me mood. "But I have no books, no time, no friends. I must therefore be contented to live and die an ignorant, obscure fellow." And in 1775, after Congress had escorted Generals Washington, Lee, and Schuyler out of Philadelphia, he said: "Such is the pride and pomp of war. I, poor creature, worn out with scribbling for my bread and liberty, low in spirits and weak in health, must leave others to wear the laurels which I have sown; others to eat the bread which I have earned; a common case."

People fascinated Adams more than they did Jefferson, and vivid character sketches pervade much of his writing. Sometimes he required only a phrase to sum up a man, as when he dismissed one Andrew Oliver as "a very sagacious trifler." Adams admired Hogarth, and when he described an eighteenth century landlady as a "squaddy, masculine creature, with a swarthy face, a great, staring, rolling eye, a rare collection of disagreeable qualities," he attempted with words what the artist did with lines. A man named Lambert appears to Adams "like a little knurly, ill-natured horse, that kicks at every horse of his own size, and sheers off from everyone that is larger." It takes only a few, swift strokes to bring alive James Otis—"Otis is extremely quick and elastic; his apprehension is as quick as his temper. He springs and twitches his muscles about in his thinking."

Adams had an extraordinary sense of the dramatic, and long before Boswell supposedly invented the use of dialogue to recreate Johnson he had developed the same technique. Here, complete with stage directions, is a scene from his diary in 1772:

At the printing office this morning. Mr. Otis came in, with his eyes fishy and fiery, looking and acting as wildly as ever he did.

"You, Mr. Edes, you, John Gill, and you, Paul Revere, can you stand there three minutes?"

"Yes."

"Well, do. Brother Adams, go along with me."

Up chamber we went; he locks the door and takes out the key; sit down, *tête-à-tête*.

"You are going to Cambridge to-day?"

"Yes."

"Same I, if I please. I want to know, if I was to come into court and ask the court if they were at leisure a motion, and they should say, yes, and I should say . . .

And so the scene rolls on for two more pages. Jefferson rarely relaxed enough to record the sort of minor personal events that intrigued John Adams.

The contrast between Adams and Jefferson extends to their backgrounds. Adams came of a family that, as Montaigne said of his own, had "lived without tumult or lustre." No coat of arms lodged in the family tree, or if it did nothing urged Adams to hunt it out. Nothing he desired—neither fame nor wealth nor control over his temper—came easily to him. He rose slowly in the world, to his continual distress, and at thirty-three, when Jefferson knew continental fame, Adams by his own estimate lacked even local renown. Decisions that Jefferson drifted into with little difficulty—resistance against Great Britain, for instance —Adams reached only after prodigious effort. Both men searched steadily for truth, but the search always proved harder for John Adams, and the truth, when he found it, usually differed from that found by others.

For all that set the two men apart and sent them on divergent courses through life, they shared some things in common. Adams, much like Jefferson, spoke of his father as "a very capable and useful man," and obviously remembered him with deep affection. Almost nothing is known of either man's mother, for each said little about her. (Similarly, the illegitimate Alexander Hamilton, who might with reason have felt differently, spoke often and fondly of *his* father and rarely of his mother. Eighteenth century America in some ways seems a strange and foreign land.) The fathers of both insisted their sons should have a sound classical education. John Adams was hardly "out of petticoats," as he put it, when he was settled in Dame Belcher's classroom. A few years later he moved on to Latin school. He entered Harvard College in 1751, when he was fifteen. While the two boys went to college for different reasons—Adams, the eldest son and the family's tithe to God, was slated for the ministry; Jefferson was expected only to emerge with the outward graces of a gentleman—the effects of the experience were the same. Both were swept swiftly but gently into the intellectual life of the eighteenth century.

John Winthrop, Harvard's professor of natural philosophy, served as Adams's guide. Edward Wigglesworth, the professor of divinity, taught the boys Latin and Greek and took charge of their religious studies. Little completely new or unsettling emerged in his classes. Winthrop, on the other hand, opened a new world. His lectures on natural philosophy and his experiments, carried out in a laboratory stocked with mirrors, prisms, "a curious telescope," barometers, thermometers, and two dangling skeletons, exposed the boys to an experience their orthodox past had not prepared them for.

Winthrop himself was devout and showed no desire to disturb his students' religious beliefs. For him, as for William Small at a later date, Christianity and science nourished one another. Winthrop aimed to expand his students' knowledge of the universe and the world around them without shaking their religious beliefs. Possibly he failed, temporarily, with John Adams. It is hard to be certain, for Adams remained reticent throughout life about his four years at Harvard. It is only clear that by graduation time he had doubts that the church offered him a career he either wanted or was fit for.

A chance to postpone the decision of what to do with his life came with graduation. Adams had been chosen as one of the speakers for his class, and in the audience the day he spoke sat Reverend Thaddeus McCarty, who had come to the ceremonies to refresh old friendships and to search out a teacher for the grammar school in the backcountry town of Worcester. Adams's speech impressed him. He offered the young man the post and Adams accepted.

Worcester lay some sixty miles west of Boston. Adams decided after he had been there a few weeks that he had no complaints about the town, which he found "quite pleasant," nor about the inhabitants, whom he judged "sociable, generous, and hospitable people." But the school, he said, was "indeed a school of affliction." His students numbered about fifty—"a large number of little runtlings, just capable of lisping A B C, and troubling the master." Despite a friend's advice that "cultivating and pruning these tender plants" could be a rewarding occupation, Adams believed that "to keep this school any length of time, would make a base weed and ignoble shrub of me."

Adams, of course, had accepted the post only until he had thought through the problem of his future. If he had hoped Worcester would help strengthen his orthodoxy, the hope was misplaced. At the home of "one Green," where he first boarded, he came upon a copy of Thomas Morgan's *Moral Philosopher*, a deistic work Professor Wigglesworth would have reviled. Adams found out the book had been circulating around town and "that the principles of deism had made a considerable progress among several persons in that and other towns in the county." Soon he was reading *The Independent Whig* by Thomas Gordon and Francis Hutcheson's *A System of Moral Philosophy*, which used the principles and methods of science to create a social and political philosophy for men. But Adam's main source of wisdom at this time was Bolingbroke. He had carried to Worcester two of the political works, *The Study and Use of History* and *The Patriot King*. "Wrote out Bolingbroke's reflections on exile," goes an early Worcester entry in Adams's diary.

Later, on "a cloudy morn," he turned to Bolingbroke's *True Use of Retirement*. Such reading seemed appropriate for a young man who felt he had been banished to the hinterland.

Adams at twenty, like Jefferson at the same age, had begun to think Christianity was loaded with "whole cartloads of trumpery." Proddings from a new acquaintance named James Putnam, a Worcester lawyer who thrived on a good religious dispute, encouraged this view. Putnam called the apostles "a company of enthusiasts," certainly no compliment in an age that accepted Dr. Johnson's definition of enthusiasm as "a vain confidence of divine favor or communication." Adams decided Putnam verged close to viewing religion "as a cheat, a cunning invention of priest and politicians."

Adams refused to go that far, but his letters showed he now objected to "the frigid John Calvin." He worked hard to reconcile the orthodox Christianity he had been reared on with the Newtonian science he had met in Winthrop's laboratory. He decided after much thought that he still believed in miracles. "The great and Almighty author of nature," he wrote in his diary, "who at first established those rules which regulate the world, can easily suspend those laws whenever his providence sees sufficient reason for suspension." By late May of 1756 he had decided that "an intelligent and benevolent mind had the disposal and determination of these things." A few days later he appeared to have discarded the concept of original sin in favor of Locke's assumption that, as Adams phrased it in his diary, "when we come into the world, our minds are destitute of all sorts of ideas."

Other problems than those of religion plagued him during his months of exile. A deplorable lack of self-discipline tortured his conscience. He found himself constantly "forming, but never executing good resolutions." These losing bouts with sloth were despairing affairs. One day Adams "resolved to rise with the sun. May I blush whenever I suffer one hour to pass unimproved. I will rouse up my mind and fix my attention; I will stand collected within myself and think upon what I read and what I see. I will strive with all my soul to be something more than persons who have had less advantages than myself." After this fervent entry, Adams had to note the next day: "Rose not till seven o'clock. This is the usual fate of my resolutions." Once he decided public exposure of his failings might humiliate him into discipline. One evening he bet his landlord's wife "that she would not see me chew tobacco this month." (If he won, the victory was short-lived, for many years would pass before Adams finally abandoned chewing tobacco.)

For all his lack of discipline, Adams steadily faced up to the job of choosing a suitable career. One evening while reading Voltaire's *Age of Louis XIV*, he had paused to ask himself: "What is the proper business of mankind in this life?" The most acceptable answer was that "we should consider in what character we can do the most service to our fellow-men as well as to ourselves." The church, the most obvious choice, was out, partly because of "my opinion concerning some disputed points," partly because of the conformity demanded of a minister. He had been impressed when a bright young friend of his, a devout and well-meaning young man, had been called a heretic by the community he served, at the very time a dull-witted acquaintance of Adams, also in the ministry, was being touted as able and bright. "As far as I can observe," Adams said, "people are not disposed to inquire for piety, integrity, good sense, or learning, in a young preacher, but for stupidity (for so I must call the pretended sanctity of some absolute dunces), irresistible grace, and original sin.... Could you advise me, then, who you know have not the highest opinion of what is called orthodoxy, to engage in a profession like this?"

The church obviously was not for him. For a time Adams boarded with Dr. Nahum Willard in Worcester, and the association turned his thoughts to medicine. He read Dr. George Cheyne's *Works*, dipped in Thomas Sydenham and in Gerard

L. B. van Swieten's *Commentaries* on Boerhaave. For reasons kept to himself, Adams vetoed medicine as a career.

He decided instead, against the advice of friends and family, to enter the law. He signed a contract on August 21, 1756, with James Putnam to study under his guidance for two years. "Necessity drove me to this determination," Adams explained, "but my inclination, I think, was to preach." He then rapped out his complaints against the church. "The frightful engines of ecclesiastical councils of diabolical malice and Calvinistical good-nature never failed to terrify me exceedingly whenever I thought of preaching." More than negative reasons, however, prompted the decision. When he had first thought about law, he saw the profession as no more than "a fumbling and raking amidst the rubbish of writs, indightments, pleas...that have neither harmony nor meaning." But the law offered the one road open to wealth and political power for a man who had behind him distinctions neither of birth nor fortune.

Adams no doubt knew that the legal profession did not necessarily block off his chance to preach. He would remain a preacher of sorts all his life. The moral intensity that nearly drove him into the church would permeate his career in politics, much as it would Jefferson's. Both men tended to view public issues as a choice between good and evil rather than as a choice between the practical and impractical, the possible and the impossible. Issues that might have been presented to the people as questions of judgments they would discuss as questions of morality.

Adams, then, moved into the study of law loyal to much the same set of beliefs Jefferson held at the same age. He verged on deism in religion and found it no easier than Jefferson to admit his waywardness publicly. He respected the findings of natural philosophy and was inclined to extend those findings into the social and political world. He believed that natural law resembled the axioms of mathematics—"Self-evident principles, that every man must assent to as soon as proposed." He accepted as true that men are born with certain natural rights, among which were life, liberty, and property.

The few hints Adams dropped about his two-year apprenticeship with Putnam suggest he endured rather than enjoyed the stint. "I used to dread Putnam, because of his satirical and contemptuous smiles," he once remarked. He complained another time of Putnam's "insociability and neglect of me," but he said that in a sour, uneasy mood while working up his first court case. "Had he given me, now and then, a few hints concerning practice, I should be able to judge better at this hour than I can now."

As the end of the apprenticeship drew near, a delegation of leading figures in the town called and invited him to stay in Worcester to practice. Adams thanked them for the compliment and said ill-health had determined him to head back to the coast. Homesickness, too, entered into the decision. "I panted for want of the breezes from the sea, and the pure zephyrs from the rocky mountains of my native town," he explained.

He continued his studies back in Braintree and dismissed, or attempted as best he could to dismiss, thoughts of love and poetry. "I'd rather be lost in a whirlwind of activity, study, business, great and good designs of promoting the honor, grandeur, wealth, happiness of mankind," he wrote in his diary. He decided in October of 1758 the time had come to do something practical about realizing this goal, and in that month he traveled into Boston and stopped by the office of Jeremiah Gridley, one of the most eminent lawyers in the colony. With the assumed innocence of a country boy, he asked Gridley "what steps to take for an introduction to the practice of law in this county."

    Gridley: "Get sworn."
    Adams: "But in order to do that, sir, as I have no patron in this county..."
    Gridley: "I will recommend you to the court...."

Though Gridley had given Adams what he came for, the colloquy, as Adams reported it in his diary, had not ended. "I have a few pieces of advice to give you, Mr. Adams," the old gentleman went on. "One is, to pursue the study of law, rather than the gain of it; pursue the gain of it enough to keep out of the briers, but give your main attention to the study of it. The next is, not to marry early; for an early marriage will obstruct your improvement; and, in the next place, it will involve you in expense. Another thing is, not to keep much company, for the application of a man who aims to be a lawyer must be incessant; his attention to his books must be constant, which is inconsistent with keeping much company...."

Nothing remarkable turned up in this brief sermon. Experienced lawyers have handed it out to neophytes for centuries. The remarkable thing was that Adams listened and followed it.

Two weeks after he had been admitted to the bar, he bowed to his mother's "cruel reproaches" and took a case he saw no chance to win. He groused in his diary as he worked on it about Putnam's inadequate teaching and how it was his destiny "to dig treasures with my own fingers," as if real distinction could be won any other way. He lost the case and the client's "wrath waxed hot." That troubled him less than what friends were saying behind his back. "Let me see if Bob Paine don't pick up this story to laugh at," Adams wrote. "Lambert will laugh, no doubt, and will tell the story to every man he sees, and will squib me about it whenever he sees me."

Little business came Adams's way in the weeks that followed. Possibly, he thought, the fault lay with himself. "I have been very negligent and faulty in not treating Deacon S——, Nat B——, Deacon B——, &c., with more attention and sprightliness," he said. Adams began now to promote his career with the same assiduity if not the skill Jefferson would use. He cautioned himself that "popularity, next to virtue and wisdom, ought to be aimed at...." He warned himself that "reputation ought to be the perpetual subject of my thoughts, and aim of my behavior. How shall I gain a reputation! I feel vexed, fretted, chafed; the thought of no business mortifies me. But let me banish these fears; let me assume a fortitude, a greatness of mind."

Adams had his usual luck with resolutions. He seemed compelled to open his mouth when it was politic to keep it shut. One day he wrote: "Discharged my venom to Bill Veasey against the multitude, poverty, ill government, and ill effects of licensed houses; and the timorous temper, as well as criminal design of the selectmen, who grant them approbations."

It soon occurred to Adams that Braintree offered no living for a young lawyer, for the legal business of all but the most remote parts of Massachusetts centered in Boston. In 1759 he opened an office and took up bachelor quarters in the city. "Who can study in Boston streets?" Adams grumbled almost at once in his diary. "My eyes are so diverted with chimney-sweepers, sawyers of wood, merchants, ladies, priests, carts, horses, oxen, coaches, market-men and women, soldiers, sailors; and my ears with the rattle-gabble of them all, that I cannot think long enough in the street upon any one thing, to start and pursue a thought."

More than the city's distractions bothered him. Adams soon found material in Boston to depress his opinions of mankind. The colonies were then in the midst of the French and Indian War and, as a side-effect of the war, the city was enduring a wave of lawlessness. Newspaper and town talk revolved around the plethora of counterfeiting, burglaries, rapes, and murder. Citizens were warned to lock their houses tightly at night. Few any longer felt safe on the streets after dark and the ineffectual night watch could do little to improve the situation. When something dissatisfied the people, they collected in mobs and settled their grievances without recourse to law. The old habit of a strictly observed Sabbath went by the board as more and more shopkeepers stayed open for business on Sunday. Drinking increased.

Bawdy houses operated openly and "Strange Women" often solicited on the streets.

Boston pointed up unpleasant sides of life as Braintree and Worcester never had. Around Adams now spread disease and filth, slums, drunks, roistering sailors. Possibly "frigid John Calvin" had been rightly gloomy about the innate evil in man. Near the end of 1760, Adams admitted to his diary that "vice and folly are so interwoven in all human affairs, that they could not, possibly be wholly separated from them without tearing and rending the whole system of human nature and state; nothing would remain as it is." Adams had already started on the road back from deism to orthodoxy.

In 1761, when his father died, Adams moved back to Braintree to live with his mother, commuting into Boston when necessary. He now entered into the town's political life. Adams's interest in government, unlike Jefferson's, dated from youth. Politics in Virginia prior to 1765 had been tranquil and it had taken the Stamp Act and election to the House of Burgesses to rouse Jefferson's interest in government. Politics in Massachusetts, however, had never been tranquil, on either the provincial or the local level. Relations with England had been tense for over a century and that tension, fostered by personal rivalries, thrived in the town meetings throughout the province. It was thus not especially remarkable that in 1758, when Adams was twenty-three and had just decided to study law, he resolved to "aim at an exact knowledge of nature, end, and means of government; compare the different forms of it with each other, and each of them with their effects on public and private happiness."

Soon after he ventured into politics the town meeting elected him surveyor of the highways. He went at the job with his usual vigor, inquiring of neighboring towns their "methods of mending highways by a rate," and eventually setting up a system that lasted for over a half century. But the highway post occupied a small part of Adams's energy and time. His progress as a lawyer had been slow. He needed an issue that would satisfy his urge to make the world a better place and at the same time advance his career. He soon found it in the town's multitude of taverns. These taverns were, for Adams, the source of much evil, "the eternal haunt of loose, disorderly people...." "Here," he said, "the time, the money, the health, and modesty, of most that are young and of many old are wasted; here diseases, vicious habits, bastards, and legislators, are frequently begotten." Adams decided it was up to him to eliminate these nurseries of sin from Braintree.

Adams's project and his methods of carrying it out differed from Jefferson's on the Rivanna River. But then Adams's environment differed considerably from Jefferson's. A New England boy grew up accustomed to the church's and the town government's interfering in men's lives. Only a vague line existed between the two spheres of influence. The meetinghouse at times served as a forum where neighbors assailed the sins of one another, and it was accepted that the church do its best to order men's worldly affairs as well as supervise their religious life. What the church missed the local government, with its multitude of elected officials, picked up. Where Jefferson was reared to believe the least government the best, Adams assumed some strong formal institution was needed to control men's affairs. Since by the eighteenth century the power of the church had declined, he assumed further that this control came from government. His view of what was natural for government thus differed from Jefferson's. Moreover, the institution of government interested him more than the individual. He was willing to promote the strength of that government if it promoted efficient administration of society. He saw no reason, as Jefferson would have seen, to object to an interference in personal liberties if the interference aimed to promote "just" ends—such as the elimination of taverns.

Adams decided that the canker of taverns could be cut out if the number of these dens was limited by law and then supervised. He set out to see his views transformed into law. Life promptly turned difficult for him. "Last Monday had a passionate wrangle with Eben Thayer, before Major Crosby. He called me a *petty lawyer*. This I resented." In May of 1761 Adams's ideas were, despite strong opposition, accepted by the Braintree town meeting. Taverns permitted to serve alcohol were limited to three. Life now became more difficult for Adams. "I am creating enemies in every quarter of the town...," he observed. "I shall have the ill will of the whole town.... This will not do." Within a few months the ex-tavern keepers had found ways to evade the new law and Adams's attempt to regulate the personal habits of his neighbors had failed. His first venture to make the world a better place to live, in contrast with Jefferson's maiden effort, had ended in failure and did little to raise his opinion of mankind.

Gradually, it dawned on John Adams that society could not be overhauled in one swoop. People resisted improvement in the mass as vigorously as he himself, who, despite nightly resolves, still found the sun catching him abed. Adams put his time to less controversial matters. He worked at building up a law practice, cultivating popularity and making money. He fell in love and late in 1764 married a sprightly girl named Abigail Smith. The next year he reported in his diary that "1765 has been the most remarkable year of my life." Marriage delighted him, he had received praise for his work as surveyor, picked up several clients in a tour of the court circuit, and been charmed by the way the people had resisted the Stamp Act. "The people, even to the lowest ranks," he said, "have become more attentive to their liberties, more inquisitive about them, and more determined to defend them, than they were ever before known or had occasion to be...."

Also, in this year of the Stamp Act, Jeremiah Gridley had formed a "law club" or Sodality as it was called, and Adams had been asked to join. In one of the evening discussions, Adams read an essay entitled "A Dissertation on Canon and Feudal Law." A revised version of it, but with the scholarly title intact, appeared in a Boston newspaper. The point of the paper was to prove that the oppressions of feudalism had been left behind when America was settled. To make it, Adams was forced to recreate the seventeenth century pioneers as children of the eighteenth century—men inspired by natural law, who based their government on reason, who had an abiding faith in the virtue of knowledge, and who came to America not for religion alone but out of "a love of universal liberty." They came knowing "that government was a plain, simple, intelligible thing, founded in nature and reason, and quite comprehensible by common sense." New Englanders should know these facts, he said, for now "there seems to be a direct and formal design on foot, to enslave all America." At this point Adams slipped in a brief attack on the Stamp Act to make his essay topical. He called it "a design...formed to strip us in a great measure of the means of knowledge...and to introduce the inequalities and dependencies of the feudal system."

The essay revealed, among other things, how fully Adams had absorbed eighteenth century thought on the rights of man. "I say *Rights*, for such they [the people] have, undoubtedly, antecedent to all earthly government,—*Rights*, that cannot be repealed or restrained by human laws—*Rights*, derived from the great Legislator of the Universe," he said at one point. And then in his peroration he added: "Let it be known that British liberties are not grants of princes or parliaments, but original rights, conditions of original contracts, coequal with prerogative, and coeval with government; that many of our rights are inherent and essential, agreed on as maxims, and established as preliminaries, even before parliament existed. Let them search for the foundations of British laws and government in the frame of human nature, in the constitution of the intellectual world."

Adams talked in public about the Stamp Act's infringement of rights; in private he viewed the act bitterly for other reasons. It had required all court papers to be adorned with special stamps; refusal to use the stamps had closed the courts. "I have not drawn a writ, since the first of November," Adams remarked in his diary, continuing in a self-pitying mood. "I was but just getting into my gears, just getting under sail, and an embargo is laid upon the ship. . . . I have had poverty to struggle with, envy and jealousy and malice of enemies to encounter, no friends, or but few, to assist me; so that I have groped in dark obscurity, till of late, and had but just become and gained a small degree of reputation, when this execrable project was set on foot for my ruin as well as that of America in general, and of Great Britain."

The Stamp Act controversy pushed Adams into politics up to his ears. He drew up a set of instructions for Braintree's representative in the legislature to act on when the issue came up for discussion. In them he attacked the Stamp Act as "burthensome," unconstitutional, and an "alarming extension of the power of the courts of admiralty." His argument was so clear and persuasive that forty other Massachusetts towns adopted the Braintree instructions for their representatives. At the height of the dispute the town meeting of Boston asked him to act as its counsel to argue before the Governor and Council that the courts should be re-opened without the use of the stamps. The invitation pleased Adams, but he no doubt suspected, knowing of the rigged operations of the Boston meeting, he was being pulled into city affairs in the hope he would devote his legal skill to the side of the radicals. (John Adams had learned something about the way the Boston meeting worked in 1763. "This day," he reported in his diary, "learned that the Caucus Club meets, at certain times, in the garret of Tom Dawes, the Adjutant of the Boston Regiment. He has a large house, and he has a movable partition in his garret which he takes down and the whole club meets in one room. There they smoke tobacco, till you cannot see from one end of the garret to the other. There they drink flip, I suppose, and there they choose a moderator, who puts questions to the vote regularly; and selectmen, assessors, collectors, wardens, fire-wards, and representatives, are regularly chosen before they are chosen in the town. . . . They send committees to wait on the merchant's club, and to propose and join in the choice of men and measures.")

Eventually the Stamp Act was repealed, the courts were reopened, and Adams found himself traveling the circuit again. He began to wonder in the empty evenings away from home if the furor over liberty and rights had been wholly good. From what he had observed on the circuit, party spirit "seemed to have wrought an entire metamorphosis of the human character," he wrote in his diary. "It destroyed all sense and understanding; all equity and humanity; all memory and regard for truth; all virtue, honor, decorum, and veracity."

These postmortem doubts persisted. In the tranquil period after the Stamp Act's repeal, Adams resolved, as he later put it, "to avoid being concerned in counseling, or aiding, or abetting tumult or disorder; to avoid all exceptionable scribbling in the newspaper of every kind; to avoid all passion and personal altercation or reflections." He managed to keep this resolve better than most resolves. All his energy went into making money, and no doubt at least partly because of his reformed behavior his law business prospered. But a conscience as sensitive and an urge to do good as pronounced as his could not be easily satisfied with material things alone. "To what object are my views directed?" he asked himself early in 1766. "What is the end and purpose of my studies, journeys, labors of all kinds, of body and mind, of tongue and pen? Am I grasping at money, or scheming for power? Am I planning the illustration of my family or the welfare of my country?" He concluded he was "tossed so much from post to pillar" he lacked the leisure to think the questions through.

A few weeks later a chance event forced him to take something of a stand. His friend Jonathan Sewall, now Attorney-General for the province, stopped by the house one evening for a visit. He said he was empowered by the Governor to offer Adams the position of Advocate-General in the Court of Admiralty, one of

1. John Adams by
C. W. Peale, courtesy of
the Independence National
Historical Park Collection.

2. A northwest view of the State House in Philadelphia, taken in 1778 and printed in the Columbian Magazine, July, 1787, courtesy of the Rare Books Division, New York Public Library.

3. Monticello, the West Front. Photograph courtesy of the Thomas Jefferson Memorial Foundation.

4. The house where Thomas Jefferson wrote the Declaration of Independence. Drawing from John T. Scharf and Thompson Westcott's *History of Philadelphia*, 1884.

5. Thomas Jefferson
by C. W. Peale, courtesy of
the Independence National
Historical Park Collection.

6. Congress Voting Independence by Pine and Savage.

7. John Dickinson by
C. W. Peale, courtesy of
the Independence National
Historical Park Collection.

8. Richard Henry Lee
by C. W. Peale, courtesy of
the Independence National
Historical Park Collection.

9. "The Manner in which the American Colonies Declared Themselves Independent of the King of England, throughout the different Provinces on July 4, 1776," engraved for Barnard's *History of England*, courtesy of the Fort Ticonderoga Museum, Fort Ticonderoga, New York.

10. Fragment of the earliest draft written by Jefferson of the Declaration of Independence, discovered in 1947, reproduced from the Collections of the Library of Congress.

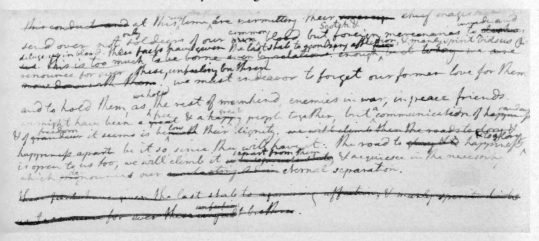

In CONGRESS, July 4, 1776.

A DECLARATION

By the REPRESENTATIVES of the

UNITED STATES OF AMERICA,

In GENERAL CONGRESS ASSEMBLED.

WHEN in the Course of human Events, it becomes necessary for one People to dissolve the Political Bands which have connected them with another, and to assume among the Powers of the Earth, the separate and equal Station to which the Laws of Nature and of Nature's God entitle them, a decent Respect to the Opinions of Mankind requires that they should declare the causes which impel them to the Separation.

We hold these Truths to be self-evident, that all Men are created equal, that they are endowed by their Creator with certain unalienable Rights, that among these are Life, Liberty, and the Pursuit of Happiness—That to secure these Rights, Governments are instituted among Men, deriving their just Powers from the Consent of the Governed, that whenever any Form of Government becomes destructive of these Ends, it is the Right of the People to alter or to abolish it, and to institute new Government, laying its Foundation on such Principles, and organizing its Powers in such Form, as to them shall seem most likely to effect their Safety and Happiness. Prudence, indeed, will dictate that Governments long established should not be changed for light and transient Causes; and accordingly all Experience hath shewn, that Mankind are more disposed to suffer, while Evils are sufferable, than to right themselves by abolishing the Forms to which they are accustomed. But when a long Train of Abuses and Usurpations, pursuing invariably the same Object, evinces a Design to reduce them under absolute Despotism, it is their Right, it is their Duty, to throw off such Government, and to provide new Guards for their future Security. Such has been the patient Sufferance of these Colonies; and such is now the Necessity which constrains them to alter their former Systems of Government. The History of the present King of Great-Britain is a History of repeated Injuries and Usurpations, all having in direct Object the Establishment of an absolute Tyranny over these States. To prove this, let Facts be submitted to a candid World.

He has refused his Assent to Laws, the most wholesome and necessary for the public Good.

He has forbidden his Governors to pass Laws of immediate and pressing Importance, unless suspended in their Operation till his Assent should be obtained; and when so suspended, he has utterly neglected to attend to them.

He has refused to pass other Laws for the Accommodation of large Districts of People, unless those People would relinquish the Right of Representation in the Legislature, a Right inestimable to them, and formidable to Tyrants only.

He has called together Legislative Bodies at Places unusual, uncomfortable, and distant from the Depository of their public Records, for the sole Purpose of fatiguing them into Compliance with his Measures.

He has dissolved Representative Houses repeatedly, for opposing with manly Firmness his Invasions on the Rights of the People.

He has refused for a long Time, after such Dissolutions, to cause others to be elected; whereby the Legislative Powers, incapable of Annihilation, have returned to the People at large for their exercise; the State remaining in the mean time exposed to all the Dangers of Invasion from without, and Convulsions within.

He has endeavoured to prevent the Population of these States; for that Purpose obstructing the Laws for Naturalization of Foreigners; refusing to pass others to encourage their Migrations hither, and raising the Conditions of new Appropriations of Lands.

He has obstructed the Administration of Justice, by refusing his Assent to Laws for establishing Judiciary Powers.

He has made Judges dependent on his Will alone, for the Tenure of their Offices, and the Amount and Payment of their Salaries.

He has erected a Multitude of new Offices, and sent hither Swarms of Officers to harrass our People, and eat out their Substance.

He has kept among us, in Times of Peace, Standing Armies, without the consent of our Legislatures.

He has affected to render the Military independent of and superior to the Civil Power.

He has combined with others to subject us to a Jurisdiction foreign to our Constitution, and unacknowledged by our Laws; giving his Assent to their Acts of pretended Legislation:

For quartering large Bodies of Armed Troops among us:

For protecting them, by a mock Trial, from Punishment for any Murders which they should commit on the Inhabitants of these States:

For cutting off our Trade with all Parts of the World:

For imposing Taxes on us without our Consent:

For depriving us, in many Cases, of the Benefits of Trial by Jury:

For transporting us beyond Seas to be tried for pretended Offences:

For abolishing the free System of English Laws in a neighbouring Province, establishing therein an arbitrary Government, and enlarging its Boundaries, so as to render it at once an Example and fit Instrument for introducing the same absolute Rule into these Colonies:

For taking away our Charters, abolishing our most valuable Laws, and altering fundamentally the Forms of our Governments:

For suspending our own Legislatures, and declaring themselves invested with Power to legislate for us in all Cases whatsoever.

He has abdicated Government here, by declaring us out of his Protection and waging War against us.

He has plundered our Seas, ravaged our Coasts, burnt our Towns, and destroyed the Lives of our People.

He is, at this Time, transporting large Armies of foreign Mercenaries to compleat the Works of Death, Desolation, and Tyranny, already begun with circumstances of Cruelty and Perfidy, scarcely paralleled in the most barbarous Ages, and totally unworthy the Head of a civilized Nation.

He has constrained our fellow Citizens taken Captive on the high Seas to bear Arms against their Country, to become the Executioners of their Friends and Brethren, or to fall themselves by their Hands.

He has excited domestic Insurrections amongst us, and has endeavoured to bring on the Inhabitants of our Frontiers, the merciless Indian Savages, whose known Rule of Warfare, is an undistinguished Destruction, of all Ages, Sexes and Conditions.

In every stage of these Oppressions we have Petitioned for Redress in the most humble Terms: Our repeated Petitions have been answered only by repeated Injury. A Prince, whose Character is thus marked by every act which may define a Tyrant, is unfit to be the Ruler of a free People.

Nor have we been wanting in Attentions to our British Brethren. We have warned them from Time to Time of Attempts by their Legislature to extend an unwarrantable Jurisdiction over us. We have reminded them of the Circumstances of our Emigration and Settlement here. We have appealed to their native Justice and Magnanimity, and we have conjured them by the Ties of our common Kindred to disavow these Usurpations, which, would inevitably interrupt our Connections and Correspondence. They too have been deaf to the Voice of Justice and of Consanguinity. We must, therefore, acquiesce in the Necessity, which denounces our Separation, and hold them, as we hold the rest of Mankind, Enemies in War, in Peace, Friends.

We, therefore, the Representatives of the UNITED STATES OF AMERICA, in GENERAL CONGRESS, Assembled, appealing to the Supreme Judge of the World for the Rectitude of our Intentions, do, in the Name, and by Authority of the good People of these Colonies, solemnly Publish and Declare, That these United Colonies are, and of Right ought to be, FREE AND INDEPENDENT STATES; that they are absolved from all Allegiance to the British Crown, and that all political Connection between them and the State of Great-Britain, is and ought to be totally dissolved; and that as FREE AND INDEPENDENT STATES, they have full Power to levy War, conclude Peace, contract Alliances, establish Commerce, and to do all other Acts and Things which INDEPENDENT STATES may of right do. And for the support of this Declaration, with a firm Reliance on the Protection of divine Providence, we mutually pledge to each other our Lives, our Fortunes, and our sacred Honor.

Signed by ORDER and in BEHALF of the CONGRESS,

JOHN HANCOCK, President.

ATTEST.
CHARLES THOMSON, Secretary.

11. The John Dunlap broadside of the Declaration of Independence, courtesy of the National Archives.

the choicest posts in the administration. Adams refused at once, saying he did not want to be under any restraints or obligations to the government "on account of the unsettled state of the country." He went on to say that "the government, including the King, his ministers, and Parliament, apparently supported by a great majority of the nation, were persevering in a system wholly inconsistent with all my ideas of right, justice, and policy...." Nothing Sewall said could budge Adams.

Adams not only refused to be associated with the government; he balked, too, at close ties with the radicals. In the late summer of 1769 he attended a picnic with three hundred and fifty Sons of Liberty, but he turned up more as a detached observer than as a man with intimate ties with the radical cause. "Otis and [Sam] Adams are politic in promoting these festivals," he said, "for they tinge the minds of the people; they impregnate them with the sentiments of liberty; they render the people fond of their leaders in the cause, and averse and bitter against all opposers." John Adams obviously approved of the purpose behind the picnics without feeling any urge to share in the cause. (At this particular gathering some forty-five toasts were drunk. "To the honor of the Sons, I did not see one person intoxicated, or near it," Adams remarked with a straight face.)

The tense mood in which Sam Adams managed by one device or another to keep the people of Boston erupted into the open one March evening in 1770 when a platoon of British soldiers fired on a mob that had gathered to taunt them. John Adams, by now respected as one of the most effective lawyers in Massachusetts, agreed to help defend the soldiers. Meanwhile, as if providence itself wished to help Adams maintain his balance between two camps, a vacancy had occurred in the legislature among the delegation representing Boston. In a special election no doubt engineered by his cousin Sam, John Adams was chosen to fill out the term of the vacant seat. This was his first venture into provincial politics, but it was not as a politician that Sam

Adams wanted John in the legislature. The radicals lacked an able lawyer and with Hutchinson, former chief justice of the colony, acting as governor they needed one badly.

During Adams's brief tenure in the legislature, an incident occurred that rankled all his life. The former governor, William Shirley, in reading of a dispute between the current governor and legislature in the newspapers, asked: "Who has revived these old words? They were expunged during my administration."

"The Boston seat," he was told.

"And who are the Boston seat?"

"Mr. Cushing, Mr. Hancock, Mr. Samuel Adams, and Mr. John Adams."

"Mr. Cushing I knew, and Mr. Hancock I knew," Shirley said, "but where the devil this brace of Adamses came from, I know not."

Shirley soon heard more of one half "this brace," for in October of 1770 came the trial of Captain John Preston and his soldiers involved in the Boston Massacre, as it had by now been dubbed. John Adams's eloquent and forceful argument got nearly all the accused acquitted and only minor sentences for those found guilty. The opprobrium heaped on Adams for defending the soldiers determined him definitely hereafter to steer clear of politics. He set about implementing that decision at once.

But nothing, of course, came easy for John Adams. He was a man of strong feeling, accustomed to taking sides in an issue. He could not tolerate the crown's position, yet the methods of the opposition equally disgusted him. It can be said of John Adams, as it has been said of Samuel Johnson, that "few men... have struggled more against the constant human temptation to say and believe, or pretend to believe, what is comfortable, conventional, lazy, or pleasant." From the day of his defense of the British soldiers until early 1773, John Adams wrestled constantly for honesty of mind. The battle drove him to a nervous breakdown. In the early spring of 1771, he abandoned his law office in Boston and moved back to Braintree. Law and politics, he said, "had exhausted my health, brought on a pain in my breast, and a complaint in my lungs, which seriously threaten my life, and compelled me to throw off a great part of the load of business, both public and private, and return to my farm in the country." He left for the country with thoughts tinged with bitterness. "I have stood by the people much longer than they would stand by themselves. But I have learned wisdom by experience; I shall certainly become more retired and cautious; I shall certainly mind my own farm and my own office."

Back in Braintree Adams found the days dragged by. His doctor advised a trip to mineral springs in Connecticut and Adams agreed to go, though he felt guilty about it. "I feel as if I ought not to saunter, and loiter, and trifle away this time; I feel as if I ought to be employed for the benefit of my fellow men in some way or other." But to work for his fellow men meant taking sides, and that Adams could not at the moment do. "I am, for what I can see, quite left alone in the world."

The lethargy lingered through the summer. A trip over the circuit proved "the most flat, insipid, spiritless, tasteless journey that ever I took.... I slumber and mope all day." Adams perked up once when, shortly after finishing a plea to the jury, someone told him that people were saying "That Mr. Adams has been making the finest speech I ever heard in my life. He's equal to the greatest orator that ever spoke in Greece or Rome." Adams's private comment on that was: "What an advantage it is to have the passions, prejudices, and interests of the whole audience in a man's favor."

John Adams knew he could win the audience over if he would only throw in with the patriots; he also knew he could have every honor possible if he would side with the government. His mind refused to let him join either side. The chance for wealth attracted him immensely, and during these months he referred off and on to the subject in his diary. Rich men, he wrote, "feel the strength and importance which their riches give them in the world; their courage and spirits are buoyed up, their imaginations are inflated by them."

The depth of his depression came in the fall of 1772, as his thirty-seventh birthday approached. He noted dismally that a house in Boston, his farm in Braintree, and three hundred pounds in pocket were "all that my most intense application to study and business has been able to accomplish. . . ."

About this time Adams determined to re-open an office in Boston and pick up the remains of his once thriving practice. The return proved rougher than expected. One October morning in 1772, Adams stood in a printing office talking with friends when James Otis entered, "his eyes fishy and fiery." After chatting of other things, this exchange took place:

> Otis: "You will never learn military exercises."
> Adams: "Ay, why not?"
> Otis: "That you have a head for it, needs no commentary, but not a heart."
> Adams: "Ay, how do you know? You never searched my heart."
> Otis: "Yes, I have;—tried with one year's service, dancing from Boston to Braintree, and from Braintree to Boston; moping about the streets of this town as hipped as Father Flynt at ninety, and seemingly regardless of everything but to get money enough to carry you smoothly through the world."

After reporting this dialogue, Adams added: "This is the rant of Mr. Otis concerning me, and I suppose of two thirds of the town."

Two months later, on December 29, Sam Adams stopped round with a friend to invite John Adams to give the Boston Massacre Day oration, which had by now become an annual event, pushed by Sam Adams to keep the people properly tensed up. John Adams refused. "...I should only expose myself to the lash of ignorant and malicious tongues on both sides of the question," he wrote in his diary. "Besides that, I was too old to make declamations."

However, the next night John spent the evening with Sam Adams. Previously, he had been disturbed by Sam's hot-headedness, his rantings against the government. This particular evening Sam seemed different. John found him "more cool, genteel, and agreeable than common; concealed and restrained his passions, &c." The next evening, December 31, uncovered something even more surprising to John Adams. "I found [this evening] that my constitutional or habitual infirmities have not entirely forsaken me." It had started out as an innocuous evening with old acquaintances, then in the midst of a quiet conversation "I found the old warmth, heat, violence, acrimony, bitterness, sharpness of my temper and expression, was not departed. I said there was no more justice left in Britain than there was in hell; that I wished for war, and that the whole Bourbon family was upon the back of Great Britain." All this filled Adams with remorse. "I cannot but reflect upon myself with severity for these rash, inexperienced, boyish, raw, and awkward expressions. A man who has not better government of his tongue, nor more command of his temper, is unfit for everything but children's play and the company of boys."

Having written that, John Adams went to bed. The next afternoon he wrote in his diary: "I have felt very well and been in very good spirits all day. I never was happier in my whole life than I have been since I returned to Boston. I feel easy and composed and contented." Adams went visiting again that evening and found out that his old friends among the patriots still held him in high regard. "Warren thought I was rather a cautious man," Adams reported, "but that he could not say I ever trimmed; when I spoke at all, I always spoke my sentiments. This was a little soothing to my proud heart, no doubt."

"It is hard to tell," La Rochefoucauld has said, "whether a

clean, candid and honest act springs from probity or shrewd judgment." Nor does it matter especially. Let it suffice to note that New Year's day, 1773, marked John Adams's re-entrance into politics on the side of the patriots. Though doubts, of course, arose off and on, he never abandoned the position he adopted that day.

Once John Adams had committed himself, he found it hard to censure any of the patriot's actions. In December of 1773 a group of masked men dumped three cargoes of tea in the Boston harbor. "This is the most magnificent movement of all," Adams wrote, forgetting for the moment his antipathy toward mob action or the willful destruction of property. "There is a dignity, a majesty, a sublimity, in this last effort of the patriots, that I greatly admire. The people should never rise without doing something to be remembered, something notable, and striking. This destruction of the tea is so bold, so daring, so firm, intrepid and inflexible, and it must have so important consequences, and so lasting, that I cannot but consider it as an epocha in history."

Enthusiasm for the patriot cause, however, did not dim Adams's awareness of what England's waywardness had done to his personal fortunes. "I don't receive a shilling a week," he told his wife in May of 1774. "We must contrive as many ways as we can to save expenses; for we may have calls to contribute very largely, in proportion to our circumstances, to prevent other very honest people from suffering for want, besides our own loss in point of business and profit."

Adams was now approaching forty and the fact disheartened him. "My life has been a continual scene of fatigue, vexation, labor and anxiety," he wrote to his wife in June, 1774, while on the circuit. "I have four children. I had a pretty estate from my father; I have been assisted by your father; I have done the greatest business in the province; I have had the very richest clients in the province. Yet I am poor, in comparison with others." The fault to some extent was, admittedly, his, the result of an expensive house in Boston and of spending "an estate in books." But must of the blame should fall on England. "These would have been indiscretions, if the impeachment of the Judges, the Boston Port Bill, etc., had never happened; but by these unfortunate interruptions of my business from these causes, these indiscretions became almost fatal to me. . . ."

Adams wrote this shortly after he had been told of his election as a delegate to represent Massachusetts in the impending first session of the Continental Congress. He wished, he told his wife, he were off the circuit and settled in his library at home, where "I might be furbishing up my old reading in Law and History, that I might appear with less indecency before a variety of gentlemen, whose educations, travels, experience, family, fortune, and everything will give them a vast superiority to me, and I fear even to some of my companions." Meekness was not a pose Adams could hold long, and as he continued his letter he quickly talked himself out of it. "I thank God I have a head, and heart, and hands, which, if once fully exerted altogether, will succeed in the world as well as those of the mean-spirited, low-minded, fawning, obsequious scoundrels who have long hoped that my integrity would be an obstacle in my way, and enable them to outstrip me in the race . . . I will not willingly see blockheads, whom I have the pleasure to despise, elevated above me and insolently triumphing over me."

Earlier commitments forced Adams to remain away from home and on the circuit the week before he set out for Philadelphia and, filled with loneliness and trepidation, he poured out his thoughts to his wife in a series of letters. The prevalence of sin dominated much of his thought. Vice overruns New England, he said, sounding much like a seventeenth century divine, and it all springs from "the political innovations of the last ten years." Not only England but the failings of New Englanders themselves were to blame. "There is not a sin which prevails more universally and has prevailed longer than prodigality in furniture, equipage, apparel, and diet. And I believe this vice, this sin, has as large a share in drawing down the judgments of Heaven as any. And perhaps the punishment that is inflicted may work medicinally and cure the disease."

The imminence of mob rule also troubled his thoughts. In early July of 1774, a mob had broken into the house of a Falmouth man and terrified his wife and family. Adams, in reporting the incident to his wife, said: "These private mobs I do and will detest. If popular commotions can be justified in opposition to attacks upon the Constitution, it can be only when fundamentals are invaded nor then unless for absolute necessity, and with great caution. But these tarrings and featherings, this breaking open houses by rude and insolent rabble in resentment for private wrongs, or in pursuance of private prejudices and passions must be discountenanced. It cannot be excused even upon any principle which can be entertained by a good citizen, a worthy member of society."

The Tories Adams encountered on the circuit talked of little else but the internal violence that would come to pass if the colonists rebelled. Adams admitted their picture "must be granted to be a likness," but he saw the choice as the lesser of two evils. "Shall we submit to Parliamentary taxation to avoid mobs? Will not Parliamentary taxation, if established, occasion vices, crimes, and follies infinitely more numerous, dangerous, and fatal to the community? ... Are insolence, abuse, and impudence more tolerable in a magistrate than in a subject? ..."

Mobs, he decided, were not the real trouble at all, but party spirit. "Parties may go on declaiming, but is it not easy to say which party has excited most riots, which has published most libels, which has propagated most slander and defamations? Verbal scandal has been propagated in great abundance by both parties; but there is a difference, that one party have enjoyed almost all public offices, and therefore their defamation has been spread among the people more secretly, more maliciously, and more effectually.

"We seldom ever hear any solid reasoning," he went on. "I wish always to discuss the question without all painting, pathos, rhetoric, or flourish of every kind. And the question seems to me to be, whether the American colonies are to be considered as a distinct community so far as to have a right to judge for themselves when the fundamentals of their government are destroyed or invaded, or whether they are to be considered as a part of the whole British empire, the whole English nation so far as to be bound in honor, conscience, or by the general sense of the whole nation. However, if this was the rule, I believe it is very far from the general sense of the whole nation, that America should be taxed by the British parliament.... It is very certain that the sense of parliament is not the sense of the empire, nor a sure indication of it.

"It is a fundamental, inherent, and unalienable right of the people, that they have some check, influence, or control in their supreme legislature. If the right of taxation is conceded to Parliament, the Americans have no check or influence at all left."

Adams saw more clearly than most of his day the way of the future. War between America and Great Britain could not be avoided, and Adams used all his spare time on this final tour of the circuit endeavoring to work out a rationale for revolt. In his travels he met a patriot who had arrived at his position casually, ignorant of "every rope in the ship." This angered Adams, who had reached his decision only after much thought and who, having sided at last with the patriots, even now went "mourning in my heart all the day long...."

Adams would act only when he had reasoned through the question, but once he had justified revolt in his mind, it did not follow that he held high hopes for the future. His sense of sin in man was too strong. "Great things are wanted to be done, and little things only I fear can be done," he wrote shortly before setting out for Philadelphia. "I dread the thought of the Congress's falling short of the expectations of the continent, but especially of the people of this province." For all his doubts about mankind, he remained a skeptic, not a cynic. His skepticism never reduced him to empty bitterness or the belief that all action was hopeless. He had hope things could be improved, slightly at least if approached slowly. He had, in short, the quality of a first-rate intelligence, the text for which, it has been said, "is the ability to hold two opposed ideas in the mind at the same time, and still retain the ability to function. One should, for example, be able to see that things are hopeless and yet be determined to make them otherwise."

Adams set out for Philadelphia with no great love for the plain people. He hated the elite, who had monopolized public offices. He hated the well-to-do, who, with less talents than he, lived more comfortably. He hated the English for the injuries done by them to his own fortunes as much as for their oppressions to liberty. Regardless of how he had reached his decision to fight for the patriot cause, it rested now on ground he would never abandon. "I cannot avoid exposing myself before these high folks," he told his wife, shortly before leaving for Philadelphia. "My feelings will at times overcome my modesty and reserve, my prudence, policy and discretion. I have a zeal at my heart for my country and her friends which I cannot smother or conceal; it will burn out at times and in companies where it ought to be latent in my breast.... Colonel Otis's phrase is: 'The zeal-pot boils over.'"

Soon after arriving in Philadelphia, Adams was enveloped in a work day arduous even for him. "We go to Congress at nine," he said, "and there we stay, most earnestly engaged in debates upon the most abstruse mysteries of state, until three in the afternoon; then we adjourn, and go to dine with some of the nobles of Pennsylvania at four o'clock, and feast upon ten thousand delicacies, and sit drinking Madeira, Claret, and Burgundy, till six or seven, and then go home fatigued to death with business, company, and care."

Adams never forgot that governments are run by men and not necessarily by laws, and in the early days of Congress he and his cousin Sam took "much time to get acquainted with the tempers, characters, and designs of persons, and to let them into circumstances of our province." As part of his homework, he took the time to sketch the characters of the delegates in his diary. There Edward Rutledge of South Carolina emerges as "a perfect Bob-o-Lincoln—a swallow, a sparrow, a peacock; excessively vain, excessively weak, and excessively variable and unsteady; jejune, inane, and puerile." Adams judged well; his sketch implied that in the face of strong opposition Rutledge would swing with the tide and the implication eventually proved correct. Philip Livingston of New York, "a great, rough rapid mortal," was something else again. "There is no holding any conversation with him," Adams said. "He blusters away; says, if England should turn us adrift, we should instantly go to civil wars among ourselves to determine which Colony should govern all the rest; seems to dread New England, the leveling spirit, &c." Livingston, as Adams sensed, would be a hard one to win over. The sketch of John Dickinson revealed the same perception of character: "He is a shadow; tall but slender as a reed; pale as ashes; one would think at first sight that he could not live a month; yet, upon a more attentive inspection, he looks as if the springs of life were strong enough to last many years."

Adams's close study of his colleagues was a necessary one, for the delegates of Massachusetts had no easy job. They must somehow cajole twelve other colonies to support Massachusetts's defiance of Great Britain. There were numberless prejudices to overcome. Among them, said Adams, was the fact that these "fifty gentlemen meeting together, all strangers, are not acquainted with each other's language, ideas, views, designs. They are, therefore, jealous of each other—fearful, timid, skittish."

The delegates from Massachusetts, led by the astute political sense of Sam Adams, moved through this confusion of minds cautiously. "We have been obliged," said John, "to keep ourselves out of sight, and to feel pulses, and to sound the depths; to insinuate our sentiments, designs, and desires by means of other persons, sometimes of one province, and sometimes of another."

The first victory came when they persuaded Congress to endorse the Suffolk Resolves. These resolves of a Massachusetts county declared that the Coercive Acts should be resisted "as the attempts of a wicked administration to enslave America." Congress then passed a series of boycott measures against the importation of British goods. Non-importation had worked before, and it was worth another try. Congress then created "The Association," a series of committees in every town and county throughout the colonies, to make sure the boycott measures were enforced.

Before Congress adjourned it obviously had to state exactly what the colonies considered their rights. John Adams, whose zeal some deplored but whose intelligence and abilities none could deny, was among those appointed to the committee to draw up the appropriate document. As Adams remembered it, the committee argued for some time whether it should "recur to the law of nature, as well as to the British constitution, and our American charters and grants." After hours of discussion, John Rutledge of South Carolina said: "Adams, we must agree on something; you appear to me to be as familiar with the subject as any one of us... Come, take the pen and see if you can produce something that will unite us." Adams took the pen and wrote:

That the inhabitants of the English colonies in North America, by the immutable laws of nature, the principles of the English Constitution, and the several charters or compacts, have the following Rights:
That they are entitled to life, liberty, and property. . . .

The words he wrote indicated Adams had learned a great deal, possibly from his cousin Sam, about the art of politics. He had eased out of the dilemma by combining all sides of the argument, and though no one was fully satisfied, "The Declaration and Resolves" went through Congress and on its way to England pretty much as he had written it.

Shortly after this declaration had been agreed to, Congress adjourned, a little less than two months after it had assembled. The session had already lasted several weeks beyond Adams's patience. "The business of Congress is tedious beyond expression," he had written midway in the session. "This assembly is like no other that ever existed. Every man in it is a great man, an orator, a critic, a statesman; and therefore every man upon every question must show his oratory, his criticism, and his political abilities. The consequence of this is that business is drawn and spun out to an immeasurable length. I believe if it was moved and seconded that we should come to a resolution that three and two make five, we should be entertained with logic and rhetoric, law, history, politics, and mathematics and then—we should pass the resolution unanimously in the affirmative."

For all Adams's grousing, the Congress had accomplished what it had set out to do. Massachusetts no longer stood alone in her defiance of Great Britain. Eleven other colonies—Georgia had not sent delegates—now stood with her. It had not created a new government, but it had not tried to. It had tried only to persuade England to back down, and on that the colonies stood united.

Adams did not rest while home. In late 1774 the *Boston Gazette* began to publish a series of his essays under the pseudonym "Novanglus." Among the pamphlets passed around among the delegates at Congress had been Jefferson's *A Summary View*. Jefferson's argument apparently left its mark on Adams, for in the Novanglus papers he appropriated the Virginian's theory of the British constitution. "I would ask," he wrote, "by what law the parliament has authority over America? By the law of

God...it has none; by the law of nature and nations, it has none; by the common law of England it has none...; by statute law it has none...." How then was America tied to Great Britain? "We owe allegiance to the person of His Majesty, King George III, whom God preserve." George was more than King of Great Britain and Ireland; he was also "King of Massachusetts, King of Rhode Island," Adams said, running through the colonies, "and I wish he would be graciously pleased to assume" these titles. Like Jefferson, Adams in the Novanglus papers based his argument on "the principle of nature and nations." But he went a step further by nothing that it was "not repugnant to the law of nature, for any one to repel injuries by force."

The first use of force occurred in April, 1775, as the last of Adams's essays was appearing. In the month following the clashes at Lexington and Concord, the second session of the Continental Congress convened. George Washington rode in from Virginia wearing the uniform of colonel of the Virginia militia, which prompted Adams to remark: "Oh that I were a soldier! I will be. I am reading military books. Everybody must, and will, and shall be a soldier." Obviously, the zeal-pot still boiled, and it continued to do so in mid-June when Adams reported good news: "I can now inform you that the Congress have made choice of the modest and virtuous, the amiable, generous, and brave George Washington, Esquire, to be General of the American Army, and that he is to repair, as soon as possible, to the camp before Boston." The outbreak of fighting had forced Congress to assume, in addition to its deliberative duties, those of administration. They had, in short, to create a national government for America. Congress effected the transition so swiftly that John Adams, clearly impressed, for a moment might have passed for an optimist.

The moment passed. Adams soon found Congress "not yet so much alarmed as it ought to be," and a majority still favoring "Negociations for Peace." Adams thought the colonies "ought immediately to dissolve all Ministerial Tyrannies, and Custom houses, set up Governments of our own, ... confederate together like an indissoluble Band, for mutual defence, and open our Ports to all Nations immediately." Congress, however, still wanted to negotiate. "This Negociation I dread like Death," Adams said. "But it must be proposed. We cant avoid it. Discord and total Disunion would be the certain Effect of a resolute Refusal to petition and negociate."

Adams wrote this in July of 1775, about the time at least one delegate was convinced he was splitting the colonies apart by his agitation for independence. "What is the reason, Mr. Adams," asked John Dickinson one afternoon, finding his opponent in the State House yard, "that you New Englandmen oppose our measures of reconciliation? Look ye! if you don't concur with us in our pacific system, I and a number of us will break off from you in New England and we will carry on the opposition by ourselves in our own way." Adams held his temper then, only to lose it later in a letter home. "A certain great Fortune and piddling Genius, whose Fame has been trumpeted so loudly, has given a silly Cast to our whole Doings," he wrote of Dickinson. The British picked up the letter and published it, and for several weeks Congress treated Adams coolly, omitting his name from all important committees and generally treating him as "an object of nearly universal detestation," as a friend phrased it.

Congress could not afford to prolong the punishment. There was too great a need for Adams's first-rate abilities, and within a few weeks he was again being voted a member of important committees. "...I am really engaged in constant business from seven to ten in the morning in committee, from ten to four in Congress, and from six to ten again in committee," he wrote home. When he could spare time from congressional duties, he worried about affairs in Massachusetts. "I want to know a Thousand Things..." became a recurring theme in his letters to friends back home. "I want to know what is become of the

Whalemen, Codfishers, and other Seamen belonging to our Province..." "...my Mind has been Constantly engaged with Plans and Schemes for the Fortification of the Islands and Channells in Boston Harbour..." He rarely relaxed to attend a ball, enjoy the theater, or waste an evening at cards, and his contempt for those who did, like Benjamin Harrison of Virginia, knew no bounds. But then Adams had rarely relaxed in life. "Business alone, with the intimate, unreserved conversation of a few friends, books, and familiar correspondence, have ever engaged all my time; and I have no pleasure, no ease, in another way," he told a friend.

By May of 1776 Adams was talking as though all the cares of Congress rode on his shoulders. Two days before Jefferson's return he wrote: "Cares come from Boston, from Canada, from twelve other Colonies, from innumerable Indian Tribes, from all Parts of Europe and the West Indies. Cares arise in this City, and in the most illustrious Assembly; and Cares spring from Colleagues—Cares enough! Don't you pity me? it would be some Comfort to be pitied; but I will scatter them all—Avaunt ye Demons!"

Among the Demons, one with priority was the job of persuading—or forcing—each of the thirteen colonies to establish its own government, free from all royal influence and control. "I have reasons to believe," he said, "that no colony, which shall assume a government under the people, will give it up. A whole government of our own choice, managed by persons whom we love, revere, and can confide in, has charms in it for which men will fight."

But what, Adams had begun to ask himself, were these new governments to be like? His concern in the spring and early summer of 1776 was, of course, one shared by Jefferson and others. A Philadelphian named William Shippen expressed a prevailing sentiment a few days after the Declaration of Independence had passed Congress when he wrote: "We now have in our Power what never happened to any People before in the World. I mean an opportunity of forming a plan of Government upon the most just rational & equal principles; not expressed as others have heretofore been to caprice or accident or the influence of some mad conqueror, or prevailing parties or fashions of Men—but full power to settle our Government from the very foundation *de Novo*—by deliberate council, directed solely to the publick Good with wisdom, impartiality, & disinterestedness, having before us the experience of past Ages, pointing out clearly the advantages & disadvantages of all form of Governments, to assist us in our choice of each particular & then we may look forward... to a more flourishing Country than ever we have had...."

Shippen's fuzzy enthusiasm for the future was the sort that could irritate Jefferson and enrage Adams. What, they might ask, did he mean by *de Novo?* Was this grandiloquent talk or a hint that a real revolution was in progress and the men involved in it planned to rip out the old and slip in an entirely new goverment? What assurance did Shippen have that with the chance to build a new wisdom would prevail? Sentiments like Shippen's sounded to Adams painfully akin to those of Tom Paine's. Paine saw man prone to good where Adams remained uncomfortably aware of his perversity.

Even in old age John Adams found it hard to accomodate himself to man's perversity. He never, for instance, could calmly accept the fact that the age he had tried so hard to shape came to be called the Age of Reason, after the book by that "disastrous meteor" Tom Paine. "I am willing you should call this the Age of Frivolity. . . ." he wrote at an unmellowed seventy-one, "and would not object if you had named it the Age of Folly, Vice, Frenzy, Fury, Brutality, Daemons, Buonaparte, Tom Paine, or the Age of the burning Brand from the bottomless Pitt: or any thing but the Age of Reason. I know not whether any Man in the World has had more influence on its inhabitants or affairs for the last thirty years than Tom Paine. There can be no severer Satyr on the Age. For such a mongrel between Pigg and Puppy, begotten by a wild Boar on a Bitch Wolf, never before in any Age of the World was suffered by the Poltoonery of mankind, to run through such a Career of Mischief. Call it then the Age of Paine."

Adams's contempt for Paine's ideas was not the result of hindsight or old age. It appeared full blown in January of 1776 when he first encountered Paine's thought in *Common Sense*. Paine had ignored the murky and confusing arguments over constitutionalism and had built his case on grounds that fit the test of experience. Adams had liked the common-sense arguments for independence—possibly because he had used so many of them himself in and out of Congress—but when Paine broached his thoughts on government Adams found here "some whims, some sophism, some artful addresses to superstitious notions, some keen attempts upon the passions...." Paine, an amateur devoid of practical experience, had stepped into a field where Adams judged himself an expert. As a young man embarking on the study of law, he had striven "at an exact knowledge of the nature, end, and means of government," and nothing since had deflected him from that target. Not even duties in Congress diminished his interest. In April of 1776, when other affairs might with reason have occupied his mind, he could write to a friend: "I know of no Researches in any of the sciences more ingenious than those which have been made after the best Forms of Government, nor can there be a more agreeable Employment to a benevolent Heart."

What Adams most resented in Paine were his "absurd democratical notions." Adams had studied himself and his fellow man too long to accept any political system based on the goodness in man. Occasionally, he could give a qualified endorsement of man ("Human nature, with all its infirmities and deprivation, is still capable of great things."), but generally he remained skeptical.

"...I have seen all along my Life such Selfishness and Littleness even in New England," he once remarked, "that I sometimes tremble to think that, altho We are engaged in the best Cause that ever employed the Human Heart yet the Prospect of success is doubtful not for Want of Power or of Wisdom but of Virtue." Virtue, so far as public life was concerned, meant to Adams "a positive Passion for the public good...and this public Passion must be Superiour to all private Passions." Men being what they were, Adams saw slim chance that public virtue would soon flower in America. He nonetheless persisted in a qualified hope for the future by assuming that well-constructed governments could obstruct man's bent for evil. Paine, however, had mapped out a conception of government that in Adams's view catered to man's weaknesses. "'Common sense,' by his crude ignorant Notion of a Government by one Assembly, will do more Mischief," said Adams not long after he had first looked at the pamphlet, "in dividing the Friends of Liberty, than all the Tory Writings together. He is a keen Writer but very ignorant of the Science of Government."

Paine and Adams agreed on one thing—that the end of government was "the happiness of society," as Adams put it. Thereafter they diverged. Paine wanted a government designed to be promptly responsive to the will of the people, one with a single, supreme legislature, unchecked by a cautious upper house, or by a strong executive or judiciary. Adams objected to a single assembly because, he said, it was liable to all the vice of an individual, it was apt to be avaricious and ambitious for more power, it was unfit to exercise executive power, and it would make arbitrary laws for its own interest. He preferred an assembly that would represent all the interests of the people and this would choose a council or senate and these two bodies would elect a governor. The judicial power would be distinct from both the legislative and executive and independent. "It is by balancing each of these powers against the other two, that the efforts in human nature toward tyranny can alone be checked and restrained, and any degree of freedom preserved in the constitution," Adams said.

Adams justified his affection for a government of balanced powers on intellectual and practical experience. In the first place, it was a pattern that he as well as most American politicians were accustomed to. When Great Britain after 1763 had striven to strengthen the executive in American government, especially in New England, the colonials had objected on the ground such change was unnatural, that it put the branches of government out of balance. They meant of course that it was an innovation that did not fit their political experience. Adams also favored a system of checks and balances because it impressed him as the best contrived to contain social strife. Contention between rich and poor, aristocrat and democrat, merchant and farmer had been something Adams had witnessed and participated in since youth. It was a government's job to both keep this contention within bounds and also see to it that none of these special interests dominated the government. A government devised on a system of checks and balances would perform this task best.

Adams's intellectual justification for his political ideas stemmed from Newtonian science. Newton had revealed that behind the orderliness and harmony of the universe lay a system of checks and balances. Upset this balance and chaos resulted. If, say, the moon deviated from its assigned path, the earth, deprived of its counterbalance, might smash into the sun. Thus the most natural and best form of government was that which reproduced the balanced harmony of the universe.

The man who swung Newtonianism swung a double-edged weapon. Tom Paine used the same Newtonian ideas to justify his ideas on government. Newton had supplied proof of a universal harmony, said Paine. Harmony implied a benevolent God who had created a universe pervaded with goodness. Since man was part of a divine plan he must be naturally good. He was corrupted, not originally by God, but by governments. Since human nature is not of itself vicious, according to Paine, and "the great mass of people are always just," it followed that governments will be as good as they directly, without checks, represented the will of the people.

These perverse views of Paine so disturbed Adams that soon after the appearance of *Common Sense* he wrote a lengthy letter to George Wythe setting forth his own ideas in some detail. Eventually the letter reached print as a pamphlet entitled *Thoughts on Government*. It was published anonymously, but informed men of the day knew its author. "Mr. Paine was so highly offended by it," Adams wrote long afterward, "that he came to visit me at my chambers at Mrs. Yard's to remonstrate and even scold me for it, which he did in very ungenteel terms."

In their argument, Paine and Adams found they agreed that all government originated in the consent of the people. But who were the people? Paine and his followers argued that all able-bodied men who paid taxes should share in the government, and they, like Jefferson, buttressed their arguments with natural law. They wished, they said, "only to establish the common rights of mankind on the firmest ground." Now, Adams willingly used natural law and argued for natural rights against Great Britain, but when that concept contradicted a basic idea of American society—which held that a man must have a certain "stake in society" to share in government—he balked. "It is certain, in theory, that the only moral foundation of government is, the consent of the people," he said. "But to what an extent shall we carry this principle?" Certainly not to the point of tampering with traditional voting qualifications, he went on. In the first place, "our people have never been very rigid in scrutinizing into the qualications of voters, and I presume they will not now begin to be so." More important, those "destitute of property, are also too little acquainted with public affairs to form a right judgment, and to dependent upon other men to have a will of their own." It followed logically, to Adams, that "if you give to every man who has no property, a vote, will you not make a fine encouraging provision for corruption by your fundamental law?" Men without property "talk and vote as they are directed by some man of property, who has attached their minds to his interest." The spirit of leveling and innovation Adams saw in Philadelphia and heard was now beginning to flourish in Massachusetts distressed him. "Depend upon it, Sir," he told a friend, "it is dangerous to open so fruitful a source of controversy and altercation as would be opened by attempting to alter the qualifications of voters; there will be no end of it. New claims will arise; women will demand a vote; lads from twelve to twenty-one will think their rights not enough attended to; and every man who has not a farthing, will demand an equal voice with any other, in all acts of state. It tends to confound and destroy all distinctions, and prostrate all ranks to one common level."

By the time Adams wrote these sentiments he had come to know and serve on several committees with Thomas Jefferson. If the two men ever took time to exchange views, Adams, otherwise impressed by the dissimilarities between his "country" and Jefferson's, must have been struck by how many ideas they shared in common. Both based their arguments against British usurpations on natural law. Both had little good to say about the world of merchants. "The Spirit of Commerce...," Adams said, "corrupts the morals of families...is incompatible with that purity of Heart and Greatness of soul which is necessary for an happy Republic." Both men stressed the importance of public virtue in government. "Public Virtue cannot exist in a Nation without private," said Adams, and Jefferson would have nodded in agreement, "and public Virtue is the only Foundation of Republics. There must be a positive Passion for the public good, the public Interest, Honor, Power, and Glory, established in the Minds of the People, or there can be no Republican Government, nor any real Liberty."

Behind this façade of agreement, of course, the two men diverged toward different paths. Possibly the circumspect Jefferson knew this and kept the conversation on topics they agreed about. Possibly the split, when it became apparent, surprised him as much as Adams, for both had been using the same words in different ways without realizing it until the pressure of events exposed the fact. Adams, for instance, always associated the Laws of Nature with the Laws of God, and he would boggle when they were tied to the Laws of Reason, as Jefferson and his friend Paine already verged on doing. Natural rights, a phrase both men mouthed frequently, would in time open up another area of disagreement.

Also in time would appear their divergent views on human nature. Adams, along with most in Congress, held that man, with his propensity for evil, needed to be restrained by such institutions as church and government. His view here led to a stand opposite from Jefferson's on political power. A strong government with sufficient force to carry out its decisions was not something Adams feared if it were properly constructed. "I have long been settled in my own opinion," he told Jefferson in 1787, when their friendship was about to end for a few years, "that neither Philosophy, nor Religion, nor Morality, nor Wisdom, nor Interest, will ever govern nations or Parties, against their Vanity, their Pride, their Resentment or Revenge, or their Avarice or Ambition. Nothing but Force and Power and Strength can restrain them."

Finally, both men differed on their views of the future. Jefferson held out high hopes for it. Adams despaired of any great reformation. He saw the future as hopeless and yet remained determined to make it otherwise. "We may please ourselves with the prospect of free and popular Governments," he wrote shortly before Jefferson returned to Congress in mid-May, "but there is great Danger that these Governments will not make us happy. God grant they may. But I fear, that in every Assembly, Members will obtain an Influence, by Noise not Sense, by Meanness not Greatness, by Ignorance not Learning, by Contracted Hearts not large Souls. I fear, too, that it will be impossible to convince and persuade People to establish wise Regulations."

The gulf between Adams and Jefferson remained buried in the haste and confusion of the summer of 1776. The urge to bring about independence as swiftly as possible united the two men and hid all differences. Jefferson's prudence as well as his literary skill would keep them hidden for several years longer.

Chapter 4

In the Very Midst of a Revolution

❀ ❀ ❀ ❀ ❀ ❀ ❀ ❀

What the absolute moralist calls "dirty politics" is its natural
condition. The politician is the scapegoat for what an absolute morality regards as the sin of compromise. But when
a necessity of nature becomes sinful, it is the morality that
is unnatural.

ABRAHAM KAPLAN

AMERICA arrived at independence simultaneously by two
roads—one, the actual route that involved considerable
political compromising along the way; the other, an illusory
route that Jefferson pictured in the Declaration, where the political situation is viewed as a drama between good and evil. The
noble sentiments, the illusion of innocence and purity that pervade
Jefferson's paper—and has shaped America's view of itself ever
since—is notably absent from the maneuverings and debates that
carried the colonies toward independence.

No one can fully understand the Declaration without knowing
something of the events that occurred along this second road.
Here shrewd practical men of politics will be found working
for and against independence with all the ingenuity at their
command. John Adams will dominate this part of the story.
Jefferson will remain only a silent figure absorbing what is said.
Yet all that goes on will be relevant in some way to the Declaration he must soon write. A wide split runs through Congress, and
feeling by the end of the debate is bitter. He knows that some-

how out of the raw material of the debate must be constructed a Declaration that will not only appeal to the world but must also unite the diverging groups within and without Congress.

The tactics John Adams used to urge Congress toward independence begin with his schemes to forge a pro-independent delegation for Pennsylvania. Pennsylvania was America's economic "keystone," or, to use Robert Morris's analogy, "what the heart is to the human body in circulating the blood." America could not move toward independence until the leaders of Pennsylvania accepted the idea, or were forced by the people to accept it. The people got their chance to bring about a change on May 1. The Pennsylvania Assembly had agreed to expand its size by seventeen seats, and these new seats were to be filled on that day. In a long warm campaign, the Moderates had made it clear they favored reconciliation and the Independents that they were for immediate separation from Great Britain. A landslide victory for the Independents would give them control of the Assembly and this, in turn, would let the Assembly remove its Moderate delegation from Congress and send a pro-Independent one in its place. A switch in Pennsylvania's stand would swing Congress into a favorable mood for independence. The Independents, however, lost the election, and the Assembly remained in control of the Moderates.

The election results momentarily blocked Adams's hopes for a quick decision on independence, but he refused to be thwarted. On May 10 he made a new move in Congress. He offered a resolution recommending that "where no government sufficient to the exigencies of their affairs have been hitherto established" the people should promptly set one up. Adams hoped that his resolve could be used to effect a change in Pennsylvania's government. John Dickinson, still firm for reconciliation and still powerful in Pennsylvania as well as congressional affairs, announced, doubtless to Adams's irritation, that he agreed entirely on the necessity for such a resolution. It did not apply, of course, to Pennsylvania, which already had a government "sufficient to the exigencies of their affairs," and one which the voters had just handed a mandate of approval. The liberties and rights the colonies now fought to preserve were amply protected in that colony. The Assembly functioned so smoothly that Pennsylvania's contribution to the war in men and materials exceeded that of any other colony. The emasculated resolution promptly passed.

John Adams refused to be out-maneuvered. All important resolutions of Congress were dignified with a high-sounding preamble before being released to the public. Adams used this device to plug the loopholes Dickinson had discovered. On the pleasantly warm spring morning of May 15, the day after Jefferson's return, the delegates assembled in the State House to debate his handiwork. The entire day was given over to the matter. The usual reading of the morning mail was dispensed with. Promptly after the chamber doors were shut, the preamble was read aloud. It stated, in essence, that "it appears absolutely irreconcilable to reason and good conscience, for the people of these colonies now to take the oaths and affirmations necessary for the support of any government under the crown of Great Britain, and it is necessary that the exercise of every kind of authority under the said crown should be totally suppressed. . . ."

The preamble was directed at Pennsylvania, where the Assembly still took oaths of loyalty to the crown, where the King's justice was still practiced in the courts, and where the official tone of the colony still acknowledged the King's authority, as every delegate in Congress knew the instant he stepped beneath the King's arms on his way into the State House. The formidable job of presenting Pennsylvania's view against the measure fell on thirty-three-year-old James Wilson. (John Dickinson was absent this day. He had left Congress for a short rest at his farm near Dover, Delaware, assuming that for a few days at least John

Adams had been silenced and the drive for independence stopped.) Without hedging, James Wilson put full responsibility for future events in Pennsylvania directly on Congress if it passed the measure under discussion. "In this Province," he said, "if that preamble passes, there will be an immediate dissolution of every kind of authority; the people will be instantly in a state of nature. Why then precipitate this measure? Before we are prepared to build a new house, why should we pull down the old one, and expose ourselves to all the inclemencies of the season?" (These words would soon have ironical significance for John Adams, now doing so much to pull down Pennsylvania's house. Within a few days he would hear of many disconcerting democratic "innovations" in Massachusetts. Such innovations had no part in his plan for independence. "Many of the projects that I have heard of," he wrote, "are not repairing, but pulling down the building, when it is on fire, instead of laboring to extinguish the flames.")

The plight of Pennsylvania alone would have been little reason to spend a full day debating the preamble. More compelling arguments existed. In the first place, Congress had no authority to interfere in any colony's internal affairs. The instructions every delegate carried from his colony made this clear. This had been the argument used twice against Pennsylvania when she had asked for aid in settling her boundary disputes with Connecticut and Virginia. James Duane of New York—a prosperous, plump lawyer, slightly squint-eyed and, in John Adams's judgment, "very sensible, I think, and very artful"—rose to make this point. "You have no right to pass the resolution, any more than Parliament has," he said.

Furthermore, the theoretical implications of the preamble trod new and dangerous ground. The focus on His Britannic Majesty was awkward. To deny the legality of Parliament's law, the colonies, in their constitutional debates with Great Britain, had been forced to deny Parliament's right to legislate for them. The effort to work out a scheme that permitted the colonies to exist within the framework of the British Empire without being responsible to Parliament had by now led to general acceptance of the ideas advanced in Jefferson's *A Summary View* and Adams's Novanglus papers—that is, to the theory that the colonies owed allegiance only to the King, that they were equals within the Empire and could make their own laws, levy their own taxes as Englishmen in Britain did. But to carry out this theory in practice meant in effect to declare independence. Such a declaration, though only implied, came at a lamentable time—to Duane's way of thinking, at least—for rumors persisted of the coming of peace commissioners. "Every account of foreign aid is accompanied with an account of commissioners," Duane said. "Why all this haste?" he asked. "Why this driving?"

Sam Adams, who seldom spoke in Congress, marked the importance of the debate by rising to answer Duane. His white hair and creased face, the congenital trembling of his hands and head, made him appear older than his fifty-seven years. Mr. Duane, he said, had asked Congress not to act until its petitions to the King had been answered. "Our petitions have not been heard, yet answered with fleets and armies, and are to be answered with myrmidons from abroad," Adams said. "We cannot go upon stronger reasons than that the King has thrown us out of his protection. Why should we support governments under his authority? I wonder that people have conducted so well as they have."

Other arguments were advanced to overcome Wilson's and Duane's objections. One was the ridiculous, humiliating aspect of pretended loyalty to a King who treated his subjects as rebels. "The Continuing to Swear Allegiance to the power that is Cutting our throats, and attesting jurors to keep the Secrets and Try Offenders against the peace of our Sovereign Lord the King &c is Certainly absurd," Caesar Rodney said.

The approaching summer campaign offered a forceful reason for ending royal influence in the colonies. The May 15 issue of

the *Pennsylvania Gazette* reported a late dispatch from London—
only three months old—that said a fleet of fifty-seven warships
and three armies totalling 35,000 men were enroute to the colonies. The summer would unquestionably be America's testing-
time. "The ensuing campaign is likely to require greater exertion
than our unorganized powers may at present affect," Jefferson
said shortly after the day's debate ended. Stable, effective governments were impossible, the argument went, so long as royal influence persisted. (Jefferson did not enter the debate, having
"been so long out of the political world that I am almost a new
man in it," he explained.)

John Adams's preamble forced the delegates to balance the
plight of Pennsylvania, the illegality of the measure, and its
theoretical implications of independence against the evident
necessity for strong, regular governments in all the colonies, a
necessity which even Pennsylvania admitted was valid. Pennsylvania insisted, however, that the body of the resolution cleared
the way for creating new governments in the colonies that lacked
them and that the preamble only threatened those colonies—
notably Pennsylvania—that already had effective governments.

The preamble came up for vote in the early afternoon. The
ballots were cast, as usual, by colonies. The result was close. Six
colonies (the four of New England, plus Virginia and South
Carolina) voted in favor of the measure, and four (North Carolina, New York, New Jersey, and Delaware) voted against it.
Georgia was absent, Pennsylvania and Maryland abstained.

Maryland did more than abstain. After the voting, her delegates gathered up their papers and walked from the chamber.
"[They] gave us to understand," Carter Braxton of Virginia said,
"they should not return nor deem our farther Resolutions obliga-
tory, untill they had transmitted an Acct. of their Proceedings
to their Convention and had their Instructions how to act or conduct themselves upon this alarming occasion. This Event is waited
for with Impatience and while it is in agitation the assembly of

this Province [Pennsylvania] will meet and it is not impossible but they may join in this extraordinary proceeding. What will be the consequence God only knows."

Until Maryland left the meeting room, many of the delegates who had favored the preamble apparently had failed to realize what they were voting for. The measure's proponents had emphasized in the day-long debate its utility—stable governments were needed to fight the "myrmidon's from abroad"—and implied that its opponents exaggerated the overtones of independence. (The skill and organization with which the proponents presented their side suggests the directing hand of Sam Adams. "He was constantly holding caucuses. . . ," Jefferson once said, "at which the generality of the measures pursued were previously determined on.") Once Maryland had left the hall, many of the delegates began to see that the measure held more than met the eye at first glance. "You will say [it] falls little short of Independence," Carter Braxton wrote a friend. "It was not so understood by Congress but I find those out of doors on both sides the question construe it in that manner." Caesar Rodney had been among those who at the time of voting had noted only the preamble's practical virtues. Two days later he wrote: "Most of those here who are *termed the Cool Considerate Men* think it amounts to a declaration of Independence. It Certainly savours of it," he added, still not positive of its implications, "but you will see and Judge for Your Self. . . ."

A few days before the preamble passed, John Adams had warned a friend at home not to let Massachusetts move too rapidly toward independence; her boldness might separate her from the other colonies. "The Union is our defence, and that must be most tenderly cherished," he said. He had now forced a crack in that union. If Maryland's defection spread to Pennsylvania and from her to the other Middle Colonies, that crack might widen into an irreparable split. More than ever now depended on the turn of events in Pennsylvania. "But, above all, let us see the conduct of the middle Colonies," James Duane cautioned a friend back in New York, "before we come to a decision: It cannot injure us to wait a few weeks: the advantage will be great for this trying question will clearly discover the true principles & the extent of the Union of the Colonies."

John Adams's preamble had given the Pennsylvania Independents the weapon they needed to recoup their recent defeat at the polls. Congress had recommended that *all* royal authority be "totally suppressed." The Assembly represented royal authority; thus Congress had ordained the Assembly's end. A paragraph of words backed up by the authority and dignity of Congress had discredited the Assembly, achieving in an instant what might have taken the Independents weeks, even months, to accomplish.

Chance now handed the Independents another opportunity. Two months earlier Congress had designated Friday, May 17, "a day of solemn fasting and humiliation to implore Almighty God the forgiveness of the many sins prevailing among all ranks, and to be the countenance and assistance of his providence in the prosecution of the present just and necessary war." On this Fast Day, after ministers throughout the city had invigorated flagging spirits, the Independents moved about gathering names on a petition which urged that "a general call be made of the inhabitants of the City and Liberties to meet next Monday at 9 o'clock forenoon at the State House in order to take the sense of the people respecting the resolve of Congress...." It so happened that Monday, May 20, was also the day the Assembly planned to convene.

The mass meeting came off as planned. "We have had an entertaining Maneuvre this Morning in the State House Yard," John Adams wrote. "The Weather was very rainy and the Meeting was in the open air like the Comitia of the Romans, a Stage was erected *extempore* for the Moderator and the few orators to ascend.... It was the very first Town Meeting I ever saw in Philadelphia and it was conducted with great order, Decency, and Propriety.

"The first step taken was this: the Moderator produced the Resolve of Congress of the 15th inst. and read it with a loud stentorian Voice that might be heard a Quarter of a Mile.... As soon as this was read, the Multitude, several Thousands, some say, tho so wett rended the Welkin with three Cheers, Hatts flying as usual, etc."

By the end of the meeting the multitude had resolved that the Assembly lacked the authority of the people and would be assuming arbitrary power if it sat again. It was agreed that the present government was not "competent to the exigencies of our affairs." And finally the crowd voted as one to call a provincial conference to draw up plans for a constitutional convention.

Caesar Rodney was impressed as he watched how neatly the intent of Congress had been twisted. A compelling argument for the preamble had been the necessity for regular governments. "By their mode," he said of the throng's action, "it will be impossible for them to have any Government for three months to Come, and during that time much Confusion—If the present assembly Should take order in the matter, the work would be done in one Quarter of the time."

Regardless of the paralyzing effect on Pennsylvania, the measure had served its purpose. America had advanced closer to independence. John Adams, for once, was exultant, and nothing could dim his buoyant mood: not even Maryland—"so eccentric a Colony—sometimes so hot, sometimes so cold; now so high, then so low"—nor the news that had arrived two days earlier— "the Dismals from Canada," he called it—informing Congress that the American forces had been completely routed and that the Canadian campaign had ended in disaster.

"Every Post and every Day rolls in Upon Us. Independence like a Torrent...." he wrote. "We can't be very remote from the most decisive Measures and the most critical events. What do you think must be my Sensations when I see Congress now daily passing Resolutions, which I most earnestly pressed for against

Wind and Tide Twelve Months ago? and which I have not omitted to labour for a Month together from that Time to this?"

Robert Penn Warren once tried to explain why the Revolution fails to appeal to the American imagination as does the Civil War. "The Revolution is too simple," he said. "That is, it comes to our imagination as white against black, good against bad. It is comfortable, of course, to think that way of the Revolution, even if somewhat unhistorical; but it is not very interesting. It lacks inner drama. We never think, for instance, of Washington or Jefferson caught in dark inner conflicts such as those Lincoln or Lee or Stonewall Jackson experienced."

Warren is right up to a point. "Dark inner conflicts" did exist; if John Adams had worked his way clear by 1776, John Dickinson, along with several others in Congress, had not, but historians have reduced these conflicts to the point where Dickinson, for instance, has gone down in the books as "timid." Tensions also existed ("We do not treat each other with that decency and respect that was observed heretofore," a delegate remarked in the spring of 1776 as talk of independence increased. "Jealousies, ill-natured observations and recriminations take the place of reason and argument. Our Tempers are soured."), but too often the tension was compounded with uninspiring back-biting and pettiness. All the dramatic elements of the Civil War, where an entire nation served as both actor and audience, were missing. No mobs stormed the State House; Philadelphia for the most part went placidly about its business while Congress debated the question of independence behind closed doors. And within the chamber, Congress sounded all too often like a debating society of lawyers rather than a mighty body leading thirteen resolute colonies into a revolution.

In spite of all this, the Revolution to some extent has failed to impress the American imagination because historians have refused to take it on its own terms. It is the absence of the very ingredients that normally excite the imagination that makes it re-markable. When before in western history was a great revolution accomplished in a debating chamber? When before have men been persuaded by reasonable argument, not by brute force, not by pressure from mobs pounding at the doors? (True, pressure was exerted at times—to swing Pennsylvania into line, for in-stance—but the tactics were always civilized, those of the poli-tician, not the militarist; no lives were lost or even threatened.) And when before in history have a nation's leaders, aware they were "in the very midst of a revolution," argued with a fair amount of good temper the philosophical question of the leaders' relationship to the people. Eloquence might be lacking in the debate Congress now approached; reasonableness would not be. It is this quality—a basic one in the American tradition—that makes the Revolution remarkable and, in its own way, dramatic.

Despite the events unleashed by John Adams's measure on May 15, no one in or out of Congress suspected that a declaration of independence was immediately at hand. Then, on May 27, news arrived from Virginia that the Convention sitting there, the one Jefferson wanted so much to attend, had resolved that its delegates in Congress should "propose to that respectable body to declare the United Colonies free and independent States, ab-solved from all allegiance to, or dependence upon, the Crown or Parliament of Great Britain; and that they give the assent of this Colony to such declaration, and to whatever measures may be thought proper and necessary by the Congress for forming for-eign alliances, and a Confederation of the Colonies, at such time and in the manner as to them shall seem best."

The resolution caught Congress by surprise—even John Adams. "It has ever appeared to me," he wrote to Patrick Henry a short while later, "that the natural course and order of things was this; for every colony to institute a government; for all the colonies to confederate, and define the limits of the continental

Constitution; then to declare the colonies a sovereign state, or a number of confederated sovereign states; and last of all, to form treaties with foreign powers. But I fear we cannot proceed systematically, and that we shall be obliged to declare ourselves independent States, before we confederate, and indeed before all the colonies have established their governments. It is now pretty clear that all these measures will follow one another in a rapid succession, and it may not perhaps be of much importance which is done first."

More than a week passed before Virginia's order to its delegates was placed before Congress officially. The delay did not result from apathy among the Independents in Congress. Richard Henry Lee told a friend back in Virginia the day after the resolution reached Philadelphia that "the sensible spirited resolve of my Countrymen on the 15th has gladdened the heart of every friend to human nature in this place, and it will have a wonderful good effect on the misguided Councils of these Propriety Colonies." By "Propriety Colonies" he meant the Middle Colonies in general and Pennsylvania in particular. Pennsylvania's political affairs were at the moment in a turmoil. The Assembly had managed to convene, but the Independents in that body, though still a minority, had acquired sufficient strength and political skill to all but bring legislative activity to a standstill. No doubt the Independents delayed introducing the Virginia resolution in Congress in order to assess its probable effect on Pennsylvania. Would it hasten or deter the cause in that colony?

No doubt, too, Sam Adams, in concert with his friend Richard Henry Lee as well as his cousin John, used, perhaps even created, the delay in order to map out a plan for the great debate he knew lay ahead. Lee, while he may have shared in planning the strategy for the debate, refused to let the question of independence prevent his long-planned trip home. As soon as his relief, Colonel Thomas Nelson, arrived, he said, "I shall sett out for Virginia, and after resting at home a day or two will attend the Convention at Williamsburg." Sam Adams, on the other hand, though also overdue for a rest, planned to remain in Philadelphia. On June 6 he tried to make clear to a friend in New England what detained him. "I have long wishd for the Determination of some momentous Questions," he wrote, putting his thoughts obliquely for fear that if the British intercepted the letter they might get wind of what was brewing in Congress. "If Delay shall prove mischeivous I shall have no Reason to reflect upon myself; Every one here knows what my Sentiments have been. However, tomorrow a Motion will be made, and a Question I hope decided, the most important that was ever agitated in America. I have no doubt but it will be decided to *your* satisfaction. This being done, Things will go on in the right Channel and our Country will be saved. The Bearer waits. Adieu."

June 7, the day Sam Adams expected to be so momentous, dawned bright and clear. Since in life the trivial invariably adulterates the momentous, the great day opened on a minor note. Hancock called the delegates to order, and they began the morning pondering a naval problem. The vessel of one Charles Walker had been commandeered by Esek Hopkins, commodore of the continental fleet. Congress agreed to the recommendation drawn by John Adams, chairman of the Marine Committee, that Walker should be paid for his vessel and cargo. Next, according to the Journal, Congress took note of a complaint about the quality of "powder manufactured at Mr. O. Eve's mill." Three delegates were chosen "to enquire into the defect, and take measures to have it remedied."

With these matters swept aside, Richard Henry Lee, as the senior delegate of his colony, now rose and, in line with the instructions of his government, introduced the following resolution:

That these United Colonies are, and of right ought to be, free and independent States, that they are absolved from all allegiance to the British Crown, and that all political connection between them and the State of Great Britain is, and ought to be, totally dissolved.

That it is expedient forthwith to take the most effectual measures for forming foreign Alliances.

That a plan of confederation be prepared and transmitted to the respective Colonies for their consideration and approbation.

(Congress knew it now trod on treasonable ground. Charles Thomson ignored Lee's remarks in the Journal and noted only "Certain resolutions being moved and discussed. . . .")

Lee's resolution—or resolutions, as the Journal noted, for three proposals were embodied in one—differed from that suggested by the Virginia Convention. The Convention, possibly confused by the subtleties of the constitutional question, had recommended independence from "the Crown or Parliament." The Lee resolution omitted mention of Parliament. The Virginia instructions had asked its delegation in Congress to go along with any measures dealing with foreign alliances or confederation. They did not order its delegation to introduce resolutions dealing with these matters. Lee, probably after conferring among the Independents, decided to embed those proposals in the resolution for independence.

Standard procedure required discussion of all important measures to be postponed a day after being introduced in Congress. This gave delegates a chance to ponder the matter and clarify their views. Standard procedure seems not to have been followed on June 7. At least one delegate—James Wilson of Pennsylvania —rose to speak at some length.

Two days earlier the Pennsylvania Assembly, faced with a militant group of Independents who had threatened to block all political activity until some change was made in the province's instructions to its delegation in Congress on the question of independence, had appointed a committee, headed by John Dickinson, to bring in a new set of instructions. The Assembly had still not agreed on these by the morning of June 7. With this background in mind and "after having stated the Progress of the Dispute between Great Britain and the Colonies," James Wilson went on to say, referring to himself in the third person, that it was "his opinion that the Colonies would stand justified before God and the World in declaring an absolute Separation from Great Britain forever, and that he believed a Majority of the People of Pennsylvania were in Favour of Independence." (Wilson's assumption that both God and the world were looking on at what was happening in America would turn up again in Jefferson's paper.) This was quite a concession for Wilson, who so recently had argued against the May 15 measure, and it indicated a clear break with his former mentor John Dickinson.

But, continued Wilson, "the Sence of the Assembly (the only representative Body then existing in the Province) as delivered to him by their Instructions, was against the Proposition." That being the case, he said, "he wished the question to be postponed, because he had Reason to believe the People of Pennsylvania would soon have an Opportunity of expressing their Sentiments upon this point and he thought the People ought to have an Opportunity given to them to Signify their opinion in a regular Way upon a Matter of such Importance." Pennsylvania's peculiar situation was not the sole reason for postponing a decision. "The Delegates of other Colonies were bound by Instructions to disagree to the Proposition and he thought it right that the Constituents of these Delegates should also have an Opportunity of Deliberation on Said Proposition, and communicating their Opinions thereon to their respective Representatives in Congress."

Others no doubt rose to oppose Wilson's suggestion, but further discussion of Lee's three proposals was soon cut short:

Resolved, That the consideration of them be referred till to morrow; and, that the members be enjoined to attend punctually at 10 o'clock, in order to take the same into consideration.

The next morning Congress assembled on time and at once resolved itself into a committee of the whole. John Hancock stepped down from the chair and Benjamin Harrison, who was always selected as chairman when Congress worked informally as a committee, replaced him. No full record of the debate that followed survives. Jefferson took detailed notes but failed to indicate who spoke what particular sentiments. He overlooked the identities of the speakers because, as usual, ideas interested him more than the men who advanced them. (Those who opposed independence were, said Jefferson, "Wilson, Robert R. Livingston, E. Rutledge, Dickinson and others," and "on the other side it was urged by J. Adams, Lee, Wythe and others.") It was unusual that he recorded the debate at all; he rarely bothered to take notes unless he expected to handle the matter under discussion in committee. Apparently he must have known he would have a major hand in the document that would declare America's independence. Perhaps Sam Adams had discussed this in caucus and had assured Jefferson a seat on the committee, for, since both Lee and Wythe would soon depart for home, he was the logical choice to represent Virginia on any such committee. This being true, Jefferson most likely expected his notes of the debate to guide him in whatever committee assignment he drew.

The essence of the issue—of all great political issues in a democracy, for that matter—appeared near the start of the discussion. Those who resisted independence said America should defer " to take any capital step till the voice of the people drove us into it." The people, these men said, "were our power, & without them our declarations could not be carried into effect." Those for independence answered: "the people wait for us to lead the way." Furthermore, "*they* are in favor of the measure, tho' the instructions given by some of their *representatives* are not," Jefferson recorded with the appropriate underlining.

Much of the debate centered on the stand of the Middle Colonies. One of those resisting independence, most likely Dickinson or Wilson, said: "the people of the middle colonies...were not yet ripe for biding adieu to British connection but that they were fast ripening & in a short time would join in the general voice of America." Another delegate answered that this was wishful thinking, that probably Pennsylvania and Maryland would never be ready. The people's will in those colonies, he said, was still subject to the Penn and Calvert families and to the host of lackeys who tended to the proprietors' affairs. Also, neither of these colonies had been attacked by British soldiers and "these causes were not likely to be soon removed, as there seemed no probability that the enemy would make either of these the seat of this summer's war."

One argument that must have struck the lawyers in Congress as effective dealt with the fact that several delegations lacked the power to vote for independence. "The assembly of Pennsylvania was now sitting above stairs," a delegate eager for delay said, "their convention would sit within a few days, the convention of New York was now sitting, & those of the Jersies & Delaware counties would meet on the Monday following & it was probable these bodies would take up the question of Independence & would declare to their delegates the voice of their state." Those for immediate independence rebuffed this plea for delay with weak rejoinders. They said the crown had declared the colonies in a state of rebellion and thus no longer under its protection. "No delegates then can be denied, or ever want, a power of declaring an existent truth," one man said. It was argued that only two colonies—Maryland and Pennsylvania—were absolutely tied up by forbidding instructions. This strained the truth. The New Hampshire delegation, for one, admitted uncertainty over whether or not it had the right to vote for independence.

When one of the delegates raised the probability of secession if a declaration of independence were forced through now, the debate touched on a subject that had haunted Congress from the start. John Dickinson's warning of a year ago—"Look ye! If you don't concur with us in our pacific system, I and a number of us will break off from you in New England..."—had been stamped on John Adams's mind. Perhaps it was Dickinson again who now said that "if such a declaration should now be agreed to, these delegates must retire & possibly their colonies might secede from the Union....Such a secession would weaken us more than could be compensated by any foreign alliance." Those for a prompt declaration drew on the past for their answer. "The history of the Dutch revolution, of whom three states only confederated at first, proved that a secession of some colonies would not be so dangerous as some apprehended," said a well-read delegate who might have been John Adams. This argument came close to whistling in the dark. Certainly none of the delegates believed a divided America could long hold off the British.

While Congress debated in the first-floor chamber of the State House, the Pennsylvania Assembly had been enduring an equally warm controversy of its own on the second floor. That discussion came to an end in the afternoon when the Assembly agreed to new instructions for its delegates in Congress by a vote of thirty-one to twelve. These revised instructions side-stepped mention of independence. Pennsylvania Independents called them "an artful and selfish compromise." Artful they were meant to be. Dickinson devised the delaying tactic in the hope that within the coming weeks, before a final step had been taken, the King's peace commissioners would arrive offering a reasonable settlement.

The new instructions were hurried into Congress. James Wilson obtained the floor and, probably after reading the instructions aloud, announced that since he was no longer restrained he would vote for independence if the question were put to Congress. But, he went on, repeating sentiments uttered the previous day, "he still wished a determination on it to be postponed a short time" to let the people of Pennsylvania express their thoughts on the issue and also "for the Purpose of giving the Constituents of several Colonies an opportunity of removing their respective instructions whereby unanimity would probably be obtained."

As the hours slipped past, the nub of the debate revolved around the unity of the colonies. Opponents of an immediate declaration fell back repeatedly on this point. Division among the colonies would not only destroy hope of victory; it would weaken any chance for a foreign alliance, one delegate remarked. Let us wait, said another, for we may in a few days "receive certain information of the disposition of the French court, from the agent whom we had sent to Paris for that purpose.... If this disposition should be favorable, by waiting the event of the present campaign, which we all hoped would be successful, we should have reason to expect an alliance on better terms."

The Independents had a ready answer to "waiting the event of the present campaign." That would only work delay, the reply reads in Jefferson's notes, "because during this summer France may assist us effectually by cutting off those supplies or provisions from England & Ireland on which the enemy's armies here are to depend; or by setting in motion the great power they have collected in the West Indies, & calling our enemy to the defence of the possessions they have there."

Only one speaker appears to have held that with or without a declaration America's chance for a foreign alliance of any sort was slim. "France & Spain," he said, "had reason to be jealous of that rising power which would one day certainly strip them of all their American possessions," and so naturally they would never help the colonies win their freedom. (The argument, of course, eventually proved false, but this early anonymous advocate of "manifest destiny" showed extraordinary prescience in sensing that America would one day stretch to the Pacific.) "Tho' France & Spain may be jealous of our rising power," came the rebuttal, "they must think it will be much more formidable with the addition of Great Britain; and will therefore see it their interest to prevent a coalition; but should they refuse, we shall be but where we are; whereas without trying we shall never know whether they will aid us or not."

Three weeks earlier John Adams and others for independence had favored foreign alliances as a necessary step leading toward separation. Now they advanced a host of arguments for the reverse position. "A declaration of Independence alone could render it consistent with European delicacy for European powers to treat with us, or even to receive an Ambassador from us," said one. Moreover, "it is necessary to lose no time in opening a trade for our people, who will want clothes, and will want money too for the paiment of taxes." (This last point may well have been put forth by Richard Henry Lee, who a few days earlier had written: *"It is not choice but necessity that calls for Independence, as the only means by which foreign Alliance can be obtained."*)

The usual three o'clock adjournment time came and went. Possibly some of the delegates stepped across Chestnut Street to the tavern for refreshment and others stretched their legs in the State House yard, but the debate rolled on without interruption. Afternoon merged into early evening and still it continued. It became obvious as the discussion meandered on that the opponents to independence were not essentially arguing against independence itself—regardless of their personal views on the matter, most saw the event as inevitable—but only to delay a declaration of it. Some wished for a foreign alliance first, others believed the colonies must confederate before they separated, and still others hoped that future events might obviate the necessity for independence, if the act could only be postponed for a few weeks. The question of natural rights turned up in none of their arguments. These were practical politicians arguing the facts of a specific issue. They resorted to no moralizing, no theorizing to buttress their positions.

It became apparent as the evening wore on that no decision would be reached this day. Congress resolved itself out of the committee of the whole, and John Hancock resumed the chair. "Mr. Harrison reported," the Journal entry reads, "that the committee have taken into consideration the matter to them referred, but not having come to any resolution thereon, desired leave to sit again on Monday next." During the intervening Sunday, the delegates out of doors might be able to approach some agreement among themselves.

That night Edward Rutledge, soon after leaving the State House, gave out a disgruntled and biased report ("No reason could be assigned for pressing into this Measure," he said, "but the reason of every Madman, a shew of our spirit.") of the day's proceedings to his friend John Jay, who was attempting to retard the rising feeling for independence back in New York. He told Jay he had a plan, that on Monday he meant to move that the question of independence "should be postponed for 3 Weeks or Months." He added, with little enthusiasm: "In the meantime the plan of Confederation and the Scheme of Treaty may go on. I don't know whether I shall succeed in this Motion; I think not, it is at least Doubtful. However I must do what is right in my own Eyes, and Consequences must take Care of themselves. I wish you had been here."

The now ebullient John Adams counter-balanced Rutledge's dark mood perfectly. Adams believed his year-long battle for independence was at last nearing the end. "Objects of the most stupendous magnitude, and measures in which the lives and liberties of millions yet unborn are intimately interested, are now before us," he said in a letter written home Sunday. "We are in the very midst of a revolution, the most complete, unexpected, and remarkable, of any in the history of nations. A few important subjects must be dispatched before I can return to my family. Every colony must be induced to institute a perfect government. All the colonies must confederate together in some solemn band of union. The Congress must declare the colonies free and independent States, and ambassadors must be sent abroad to foreign courts, to solicit their acknowledgment of us, as sovereign States, and to form with them, at least with some of them, commercial treaties of friendship and alliance. When these things are once completed, I shall think that I have answered the end of my creation, and sing my *nunc dimittis*, return to my farm, family, ride circuits, plead law, or judge causes, just which you please."

Congress came to order at the usual ten o'clock on Monday morning. An awaiting pile of letters that could no longer be ignored was read—two from General Washington, together with copies of twenty letters and papers from General Schuyler and others detailing the dismal trend of events in Canada and creating a far from cheerful backdrop for a debate on independence. After further minor business, Congress again resolved itself into a committee of the whole and the debate of the previous Saturday went on. One of the key arguments on Saturday had been that the plain people were not yet ready for independence. It is possible that several of the delegates firm for immediate independence had spent their Sunday gathering information to prove the opposite and that when Congress began to debate the issue again on Monday considerable time was given over to reading documents and letters from the various colonies to show that the sense of the people favored independence. Even the generally silent Jefferson may have risen at some point to announce the results of his informal survey of the Virginia back-country. This is only supposition; no evidence exists to substantiate the point. It is a fact, however, that on Monday, while the debate continued in the State House, the Independents of Philadelphia, as if to create the proper setting for that debate, had the city troops polled on their views. The troops almost unanimously condemned any temporizing attitude toward independence. The poll was rigged ("Any man who dared oppose their opinion was insulted and hushed...," one observer said), but to the unknowing the results were impressive. Quite likely moments after the poll had been completed someone rushed the results to the State House.

Two days discussion surely must have convinced at least one or two delegates who had been wavering toward an immediate declaration before the debate began. John Adams long afterward told of an incident about Joseph Hewes of North Carolina which, though Adams never precisely fixed it in time, may well have occurred toward the end of the second day's debate. The incident, regardless of when it took place, at least suggests something of the atmosphere in the State House chamber at this time. Hewes, whom Jefferson recalled as "sometimes firm, sometimes feeble, according as the day was clear or cloudy," had resisted independence up to this point. "For many days the Majority depended on Mr. Hewes, of North Carolina," according to Adams's recollection. "While a Member, one day, was speaking and reading documents from all the Colonies to prove that the Public Opinion, the general Sense of all, was in favour of the Measure, when he came to North Carolina and produced letters and public proceedings which demonstrated that the Majority of that Colony were in favour of it, Mr. Hew[e]s, who had hitherto constantly voted against it, started suddenly upright, and lifting up both his Hands to Heaven as if he had been in a trance, cry'd out 'It is done! and I will abide by it.' I would give more for a perfect painting of the terror and horror upon the Faces of the Old Majority at that critical moment than for the best Piece of Raphaelle."

Whenever Mr. Hewes threw up his hands to heaven, it is clear that the two-man North Carolina delegation came out for independence when an off-the-record test vote was taken near the end of June 9. The results showed seven states—New Hampshire, Massachusetts, Rhode Island, Connecticut, Virginia, North Carolina, and Georgia—for immediate separation and five—Pennsylvania, New York, Delaware, New Jersey, and South Carolina—against it. Maryland abstained.

Defeat rode with the Independents' victory. Two days of debate and a day of discussion out of doors had failed to win even a strong majority for them, and without something close to unanimity a declaration of independence was out of the question. The thirteen clocks must strike as one if the world was to be impressed. Adams may have been somewhat cheered by a remark of his made a year earlier: "But America is a great, unwieldy body. Its progress must be slow.... Like a coach and six, the swiftest horses must be slackened, and the slowest quickened, that all may keep an even pace."

Compromise of some sort was inevitable, and after the test vote discussion resumed. Once again it continued past the usual adjourning hour and into the early evening. "After some time spent thereon," the Journal finally notes, "the president resumed the chair, and Mr. Harrison reported, that the committee have had under consideration the resolutions to them referred, and have come to a resolution, which he read."

The road to agreement had been arduous to the end. The new resolution was written on the reverse side of the slip of paper on which Richard Henry Lee had drawn up his resolution of June 7. It began, in Benjamin Harrison's handwriting:

> Resolved that it is the opinion of this Committee tha[t] the first Resolution...

At this point Secretary Thomson picked up the pen and wrote:

> ...be postponed to this day three weeks and that in the mean time a committee be appointed to prepare a Declaration to the effect of the said first resolution....

This still failed to please a majority of the delegates. After the words "in the mean time" Robert R. Livingston inserted:

least any time should be lost in case the Congress agree to this resolution

The completed resolution, written in these three hands, now read:

Resolved that it is the opinion of this Committee tha[t] the first Resolution be postponed to this day three weeks and that in the mean time least any time should be lost in case the Congress agree to this resolution a committee be appointed to prepare a Declaration to the effect of the said first resolution.

The Independents had allowed Rutledge and Wilson the delay they wanted in return for the right to begin at once preparing a declaration of independence. The victory for the moderates meant little unless within the three weeks the King's peace commissioners brought a conciliatory offer. If no such offer was forthcoming—Adams was certain none would be—independence was all but declared. On June 11 Oliver Wolcott of Connecticut, sober, dignified, and seldom given to exaggeration, expressed in a letter to his wife what all in Congress knew to be true: "We seem at present to be in the Midst of a great Revolution, which I hope God will carry us safe thro with."

Chapter 5

The Skiff Constructed

❀ ❀ ❀ ❀ ❀ ❀ ❀ ❀

The spirit of the place, this American place ... is the spirit of men who are after strange gods. To be after them is the artist's calling: to find and serve them is his proper function. His individual talent, if he has one, will displace an old god with a new one—but the new one will bear an astonishing resemblance to the one it displaced. Tradition, insofar as it is living, lives on in him, and he is powerless to thwart it; but what is dead in tradition, the heavy hand of it, he destroys.

WRIGHT MORRIS

CONGRESS resolved on June 11 "That the Committee to prepare a declaration consist of five members: The members chosen, Mr. Jefferson, Mr. J. Adams, Mr. Franklin, Mr. Sherman, and Mr. Livingston." No question existed in the mind of Congress who among the five members would head the committee and write the Declaration. It was an accepted rule of Congress that the first chosen for any committee automatically became its chairman and responsible for any written reports. And yet long afterward, John Adams suggested that he had turned down the chance to write the Declaration. He recalled a conversation in which Jefferson proposed that Adams prepare it:

"I will not," Adams remembers answering.

"You should do it," replied Jefferson.

"Oh! no."

"Why will you not?" asked Jefferson. "You ought to do it."

"I will not," said Adams.

"Why?"

"Reasons enough."

"What can be your reasons?" Jefferson insisted.

"Reason first—You are a Virginian, and a Virginian ought to appear at the head of this business. Reason second—I am obnoxious, suspected, and unpopular. You are very much otherwise. Reason third—You can write ten times better than I can."

"Well," said Jefferson, capitulating perhaps too rapidly for Adams's taste, "if you are decided, I will do as well as I can."

"Very well," said Adams. "When you have drawn it up, we will have a meeting."

Jefferson, once questioned about this conversation, doubted it ever occurred, and historians have been inclined to agree with him. But the fact that Congress expected Jefferson to prepare the Declaration is no reason to doubt that as a courteous young southerner of thirty-three he made, and promptly forgot, a perfunctory offer—much the same offer he had made a year earlier to William Livingston—to a man eight years his senior and distinguished above all other delegates for his tenacious, year-long battle to force such a declaration through Congress. Given a free hand, Congress might well have chosen Adams to head the committee. Despite an almost perverted pride in being considered obnoxious and unpopular, Adams was in fact respected, even liked, by his fellow delegates. Nor was he the inept writer he pretended to be. Politics alone eliminated his chance to head the committee. The resolution for independence had been forced on Congress by Virginia, and a Virginian, of course, had to be selected to prepare the document. Since both Lee, the obvious choice, and Wythe had refused to defer their trips home, the task fell almost automatically to Jefferson.

The committee of five apparently convened within a day or two of its appointment, but it met as a committee of four. Benjamin Franklin was absent and remained so through all the meetings. He had returned only recently from an arduous trip to Canada for Congress. Weariness alone might not have kept Franklin from Congress, but an accompanying and painful attack of gout convinced him that as a man of seventy years he had a right to a brief vacation. He spent most of June on a friend's farm outside the city.

Franklin's presence on the committee, if only in name, indicated the voting strength in Congress of those for immediate independence. All three regions—New England, the Middle Colonies, and the South—were represented, but with the exception of Robert R. Livingston of New York none among those urging delay had won a seat. Livingston was thirty years old, a wealthy landowner, a lawyer, and like most lawyers reluctant to break with tradition. His presence on the committee—a maneuver manipulated perhaps by Sam Adams—sought to assure those for postponement that, while separation from Great Britain might be inevitable, the document that would declare that separation to the world would contain nothing to offend the more conservative delegates.

Roger Sherman gave New England its second seat on the committee. Sherman struck many in Congress as a relic of the past. Puritanism survived in him undiluted by what to him was the looseness of eighteenth century morality. Delegates strained in their letters home to transmit a word picture of this antediluvian from Connecticut. When he rose in Congress he talked, said one in a "very odd and countrified cadence." John Adams, who liked Sherman, remarked that "he has a clear head and sound judgment," but the man's appearance fascinated him—"when he moves a hand in anything like action, Hogarth's genius could not have invented a motion more opposite of grace;—it is stiffness and awkwardness itself, rigid as starched linen. . . ." All the while delegates joked about Sherman, however, they also acknowledged his political skill—"it is remarked he seldom fails"—and admitted that "in his train of thinking there is something regular, deep, and comprehensive." Sherman had backed the brace of Adamses on independence from the beginning and had not budged from that stand since.

At the first of what appears to have been several meetings, Sherman, Adams, Livingston, and Jefferson no doubt discussed the form and content of the proposed Declaration. Though no record survives of these conversations, it certainly became apparent, if it had not been so before, that Jefferson's task was to find arguments that not only would justify to the world the step America was about to take but also would prevent the loose union of thirteen colonies from splintering apart. The assignment involved something more, too. The delegates in their June debate had considered independence as a question of practical politics. Those in favor had argued that necessity demanded it, that independence would improve the chances for treaties of commerce and for foreign loans, that it would animate the people, that the coming summer campaign required it. These were the immediate reasons for separating, and Jefferson had to avoid them without denying them. He had to argue from a loftier plane than that of self-interest. Previous Declarations issued by Congress—the Declaration and Resolves of the First Continental Congress in 1774 and the Declaration of Causes and Necessity for Taking Up Arms in 1775—gave a lead here but at the same time added to Jefferson's problems. Those papers tended to be long, dull, and somewhat legalistic. Moreover, they argued only for American rights within the British Empire. Jefferson must cover much the same ground without sounding repetitious and in a more stirring manner if he hoped to reach the minds and hearts of all men.

It was apparent, too, that Jefferson must broaden the ground if America, which was about to be born into a world of aggressive empires, was to win wide support for her war. He had, then, to draw on universally accepted principles—or what seemed to be universally accepted—and then produce facts to prove these principles had been violated by Great Britain. These facts needed not necessarily be true, but they must seem true enough to give others an excuse for aiding the infant nation. Late in life Jefferson remarked that "an appeall to the tribunal of the world ... for our jutification ... was the object of the Declaration."

That object, for all its importance, ranked as trivial alongside the final part of Jefferson's assignment. He must animate Americans to disobey, to revolt against established authority and at the same time keep alive a spirit of respect for authority. The Americans were "not against authority as such, but against the abuse of authority," Walter Lippman has remarked. "Far from wishing to overthrow the authority of government, or to deny and subvert, as Diderot did, the moral foundations of authority, they went into rebellion first in order to gain admittance into, and then to take possession of, the organs of government." The question was, could Jefferson make this clear to Americans as well as to Europe?

All this Jefferson had to do. He was not required but he had the chance also to shape an ideology for the new nation about to be born. Among the forces that up to now had held the diverse colonies together were a common heritage from England and the binding power of imperial control. Opposed to these were divisive forces within each colony and among the three regions of the country, forces that impelled men like Adams and Jefferson to call their colonies "my country." Once imperial control vanished many wondered if the English heritage would suffice to cement the new states into a single nation. If from that heritage an ideology that fitted the American experience could be fashioned, one nation might emerge. Much could depend on Jefferson's handiwork.

Sometime not long after the first committee meeting, Jefferson began his first draft of the Declaration of Independence. Precisely how long it took to complete this original draft must be left to speculation. He may have spent no more than an hour or two on it. Jefferson always wrote swiftly, and a surviving fragment of the original draft shows that his pen hurried as usual to keep pace with his thoughts. If anything, he worked with more than customary speed, for the Declaration required nothing in the way of facts or thoughts he had not already worked out in earlier writings. Moreover, he could compose rapidly because his thoughts had been ordered before he put pen to paper. Though he may have paused occasionally to grope for the right word, the exact phrase, he knew clearly where he was going and what he planned to do from the moment he began to write. Little in the Declaration came about by accident. The surviving drafts reveal Jefferson nearly always was in complete control of his material and knew at every step along the way exactly what he was up to.

Jefferson wrote the Declaration in the second-floor apartment he had taken in a house on the outskirts of Philadelphia, as the corner of Seventh and Market Streets was then considered. He had moved there to escape "the excessive heats of the city" and to "have the benefit of a freely circulating air." He worked at a portable desk light enough to rest comfortably on his knees. One mid-June morning—since Jefferson worked best in the morning it is likely he began the Declaration then—he lifted the hinged, felt-covered top of the desk and pulled out a sheet of paper, folded it in half to make four leaves, and then wrote across the top of the first leaf:

A Declaration of

It looks as though Jefferson began to write "A Declaration of Independence" then changed his mind. Did he hesitate, as Julian Boyd suggests, "because he thought, perhaps, that the basic philosophy of government and of rights in this document was more inclusive than a mere declaration of the severance of dependency on Great Britain?" Whatever the reason, "of" was changed to "by" and the paper's heading now read:

A Declaration by the Representatives of the UNITED STATES OF AMERICA, in General Congress assembled.

The opening sentence of the Declaration, as it reads in the second or "rough" draft, this part of the original having been lost, went this way:

> When in the course of human events it becomes necessary for a people to advance from that subordination in which they have hitherto remained, & to assume among the powers of the earth the equal & independant station to which the laws of nature & of nature's god entitled them, a decent respect to the opinions of mankind requires that they should declare the causes which impel them to the change.

This statement of purpose was more than a rhetorical flourish, and it points up at the start the divergence between Jefferson and others in Congress. "The people," says Bernard Wishy, were to the leaders of the day "the wealthy, the talented, the leisured—in short, men whose experience and sobriety qualified them to speak, in the long run, for the rights of man." This may hold true for others in Congress; certainly it does for John Adams. It does not hold true for Jefferson. His constitution for Virginia indicated a broad conception of who "the people" were, and his demand that any constitution be ratified by "the people" showed he did not take the phrase "consent of the governed" solely as a handy abstraction.

Nor was the phrase "opinions of mankind" another flourish. "Opinion is power," Jefferson once said. He knew his job was to win that opinion not only at home but also abroad. With it on America's side would come foreign alliances, money possibly even troops. Without it, American chances for victory dimmed considerably.

Jefferson's haste to state his purpose may explain how the word "subordination" slipped past. It lent an awkward, even an illogical, cast to the context he gave it. To imply that the colonies had once been subordinate to England undermined the currently accepted argument that the colonies had been and remained equal to the mother country. That the word crept into the sentence suggests that all the subtleties of the colonial argument had not been fully absorbed even by Jefferson's eclectic mind. If the inconsistency caught his attention, it failed to slow his pen.

For the lead of the second paragraph Jefferson wrote:

> We hold these truths to be sacred & undeniable;

hoping thus to disarm those who did not accept or know of the natural rights philosophy. Others—the English, perhaps even the French—might regard these truths differently, but *we* hold them sacred and undeniable. Jefferson now proceeded to list "these truths":

> that all men are created equal & independant, that...

and here, consciously or not, he leaned on a friend named George Mason. Back in Virginia, Mason had in recent weeks headed a committee assigned to draft a Declaration of Rights for Virginia. These rights were eventually to be incorporated into the colony's new constitution, which was also being drafted at this time, as Jefferson knew only too well. Mason had completed a draft of *his* Declaration late in May; soon afterward it had reached the hands of Richard Henry Lee in Philadelphia. Lee, possibly out of provincial pride, turned the document over to the editor of the *Pennsylvania Evening Post*, and it appeared there in full on June 6, a fitting backdrop for the great debate that was to begin in Congress the following day.

The first of eighteen rights delineated in this draft of Mason's Declaration was:

> That all men are born equally free and independant and have certain inherent natural rights, of which they can not, by any compact, deprive or divest their posterity; among which are the enjoyment of life and liberty, with the means of acquiring and possessing property, and preserving and obtaining happiness and safety.

Six days later a slightly revised version of Mason's paper, the one finally accepted by the Virginia Convention, appeared in the *Pennsylvania Gazette*. The first of what were now sixteen rights read essentially as before. Among the minor changes was the substitution of "pursuing... happiness" for Mason's earlier phrase "preserving... happiness."

All the sentiments and most of the words of Mason's sentence came straight from John Locke's "Essay Concerning the... End of Civil Government" in the second of *Two Treatises of Civil Government*. Though Jefferson knew Locke's work as well as his friend, he must have been struck by Mason's succinct summary of the natural rights philosophy, for after noting that "We hold these truths to be sacred & undeniable," he continued:

> that all men are created equal & independant, that from that equal creation they derive rights inherent & inalienable, among which are the preservation of life, & liberty & the pursuit of happiness;

At first glance it appears Jefferson did little more than edit Mason's sentence sufficiently to call it his own, that he did this largely by cutting eight lines to five. He did much more. In the first place, when he altered Mason's

> all men are born equally free and independant and have certain inherent natural rights

to

> all men are created equal & independant; that from that equal creation they derive rights inherent & inalienable

he underscored equality as *the* basis of natural rights, just as he had done a few years earlier when pleading for the freedom of a mulatto slave. Jefferson says nothing here that any member of Congress who had read his Locke or was a devout Christian—for Jefferson was only giving a secularized version of a fundamental Christian belief—could have disagreed with. The difference is he emphasized as a fact and a moral absolute what others would have been pleased to pass over. They would have been glad to trace back their grievances to natural law and stop there, as had been done in other Declarations of Congress.

Jefferson edited Mason's thought further when he eliminated the word "property." The omission is a curious one, for Jefferson does not avoid allusions to property elsewhere in the Declaration. An argument can be made that he omitted it for stylistic reasons, that its inclusion here would have destroyed the balance of his sentence. Yet in succeeding drafts Jefferson continued to work over this sentence without once attempting to force "property" from it. Moreover, he was too facile to have been thwarted from using a word he really wanted in a sentence. Jefferson used words precisely, or failed to use them for precise reasons. (An event that occurred years later dispels any doubt that the omission was purposeful. During the time when Jefferson was ambassador to France, his friend Lafayette brought around an early draft of the Declaration of Rights of Man for him to look over. Among the inalienable rights listed there was man's right to property. Jefferson suggested that the word be dropped out.)

Omitting the word in his Declaration did not in Jefferson's eyes deny the right to acquire property as one of man's natural rights. He makes clear with the phrase "among which are" that he is listing only some of the natural rights. As he indicated in his recent constitution for Virginia, the emphasis on property in America was being used to deny men other natural rights— mainly the right to share in government, to become first-class citizens. Jefferson wanted to de-emphasize the right to property here as he had done in his constitution. In his oblique way, he was arguing from the same side of the line as Tom Paine. Neither Paine nor his followers rejected the right to own or acquire property as a basic natural right. Nor did they deny that the essential purpose of government was to protect men's property. They insisted only that the amount of property a man held should not deny him or qualify him for a chance to share in his government.

Regardless of what prompted Jefferson, "property" slipped from sight with the same calculation that brought forth "pursuit of happiness." Mason had said that among man's rights was that of "pursuing and obtaining happiness." Jefferson revealed realism as well as precision of thought in his revision of Mason's phrase. Man does not necessarily have a right to obtain happiness. He does, said Jefferson, have a right to pursue it. Jefferson was wise, too, in shunning a definition of happiness, though it would permit his phrase to be wildly misused.

Jefferson now put Mason's Declaration out of mind as he continued a summation of the natural rights philosophy.

> that to secure these ends, governments are instituted among men, deriving their just powers from the consent of the governed; that whenever any form of government shall become destructive of these ends, it is the right of the people to alter or **to abolish it, & to institute new** government, laying it's foundation on such principles & organizing it's power in such form, as to them shall seem most likely to effect their safety & happiness.

The phrase "consent of the governed" that Jefferson used here would please few leaders of the day—neither those monarchs of Europe who still insisted they held their crowns by divine right, nor those Americans who believed it had a chance of being applied literally. Jefferson side-stepped controversy by presenting the phrase as an abstract concept and omitting any hint of his own generous interpretation. He had written nothing that the most conservative member of Congress could object to either here or in the sentence that followed:

> prudence indeed will dictate that governments long established should not be changed for light & transient causes: and accordingly all experience hath shewn that mankind are more disposed to suffer while evils are sufferable, than to right themselves by

abolishing the forms to which they are accustomed. but when
a long train of abuses & usurpations, begun at a distinguished
period, & pursuing invariably the same object, evinces a design
to subject them to arbitrary power, it is their right, it is their
duty, to throw off such government & to provide new guards
for their future security.

Jefferson's borrowings from others and from himself here rise
to the surface again. Late in life, when political enemies accused
him of plagiarizing much of the Declaration, Jefferson insisted
he had written the document without referring to any book or
paper. It seems reasonable to assume that, except for the list of
crimes against the King, he spoke the truth. Nonetheless, his
retentive mind gave his enemies reason for their charges. The
phrase "begun at a distinguished period" is lifted directly from
A Summary View. Even a charitable critic finds it hard to
believe Jefferson wrote the long sentence above without referring to chapter nineteen of Locke's *An Essay Concerning...
Government*. He not only borrowed phrases—Locke's "a long
train of abuses, prevarications and artifices" becomes in the
Declaration "a long train of abuses & usurpations" and "make
the design visible" turns into "evinces a design"—but there is a
strikingly parallel development of thought. In this passage
Thomas Jefferson's ideas move step by identical step with John
Locke's.

The parallel is understandable, for both men wrote with the
same end in view. Jefferson in 1776, like Locke in 1688, sought
to justify rebellion against the "usurpations" of a specific King,
not against monarchy nor authority in general. The monarchs
of Europe, especially Louis XVI, must grasp this point or Jefferson's paper would fail in one of its major purposes. Once they
sensed that the revolution going on in America was a conservative affair safely in the hands of gentlemen who respected authority, then they might be able to forget some of the earlier

phrases in the Declaration, like "consent of the governed," and such words as "liberty" and "equality."

Having laid a reasonable basis for revolt, one that would be acceptable, it was hoped, at home and abroad, Jefferson went on to say:

> & such is now the necessity which constrains them to expunge their former systems of government. the history of his present majesty, is a history of unremitting injuries and usurpations, among which no one fact stands single or solitary to contradict the uniform tenor of the rest, all of which have in direct object the establishment of an absolute tyranny over these states. to prove this, let facts be submitted to a candid world, for the truth of which we pledge a faith yet unsullied by falsehood.

Jefferson did not pause after that build-up of American innocence to give the world the "facts" that proved George III a tyrant. He moved directly from these introductory remarks into his summation.

> a prince whose character is thus marked by every act which may define a tyrant, is unfit to be the ruler of a people who mean to be free. future ages will scarce believe that the hardiness of one man, adventured within the short compass of 12 years only, on so many acts of tyranny without a mask, over a people fostered & fixed in principles of liberty.

George III alone must not bear the blame for what was happening.

> Nor have we been wanting in attentions to our British brethren. we have warned them from time to time of attempts by their legislature to extend a jurisdiction over these our states. we have reminded them of the circumstances of our emigration & settlement here, no one of which could warrant so strange a pretension: that these were effected at the expence of our own

blood & treasure, unassisted by the wealth or the strength of Great Britain:

Jefferson here handled the question of emigration, about which there had been considerable argument in and out of Congress, in a gingerly manner. During his "vacation" in early 1776, he had worked up an essay entitled "Refutation of the Argument that the Colonies were Established at the Expense of the British Nation." The essence of that essay now turned up in the "rough" draft, but it so palpably warped historical truth that Congress eventually amended the sentence to read simply: "We have reminded them of the circumstances of our emigration and settlement here."

More remained to be said about "our British brethren," but first Jefferson had to advance the currently accepted theory of empire.

that in constituting indeed our several forms of government, we had adopted one common king, thereby laying a foundation for perpetual league & amity with them: but that submission to their parliament was no part of our constitution, nor ever in idea, if history may be credited:

Jefferson obviously had forgotten the word "subordination" used earlier and had thus, whether he knew it or not, put himself in a position that exposed his entire argument to challenge. Would he catch the awkward error himself or would he be forced to endure the embarrassment of having a colleague on the comittee or, worse yet, someone in Congress pick him up on it?

More still remained to be said about the conduct of the British people in all this.

and we appealed to their native justice & magnanimity, as well as to the ties of our common kindred to disavow these usurpations which were likely to interrupt our correspondence &

connection. they too have been deaf to the voice of justice &
consanguinity, & when occasions have been given them, by the
regular course of their laws, of removing from their councils
the disturbers of our harmony, they have by their free election
re-established them in power.

Though still not finished with the British people, Jefferson
was ready for his peroration. Because the original draft of this
part of the Declaration has survived, the course of his composition can be followed exactly. After putting a period to the word
"power" in the previous sentence, he wrote "this conduct and,"
crossed that out and began again:

> very   too, they
> at this ∧ time ∧ are permitting their ~~sovereign~~ chief mag-
>   only   common
> istrate to send over not ∧ soldiers of our ∧ ~~own~~ blood
> Scotch &
> but ∧ foreign mercenaries to destroy us.

From this point to the end the composition flowed smoothly.

> this is too much to be borne even by relations. enough then
> be it to say, we are now done with them. we must endeavor
> to forget our former love for them and to hold them, as
> we hold
> ∧ the rest of mankind, enemies in war, in peace friends.
>   free   great
> we might have been a ~~great~~ & a ~~happy~~ people together, but
> a   [g]randeur   freedom
> ∧ communicated~~ion~~ of ~~happiness~~ & of ~~grandeur~~ it seems is
> low
> ~~beneath~~ their dignity. ~~we will climb then the road to glory~~
> ~~& happiness apart~~ be it so, since they will have it: the road
> to glory & to happiness is open to us too. we will climb it
> in a separate state and acquiesce in the necessity which pro-
> nounces our everlasting Adieu

On the word "Adieu" Jefferson ended his first draft of the Declaration of Independence. The lack of a period suggests he was still not fully satisfied with the conclusion and would return to add to it later.

It may be that Jefferson carried his original draft down to the State House to work on while attending Congress, for in making a clean copy—that which has come down as the "rough draft" —he committed several mistakes, the sort made when a person does a piece of work in a room full of distractions, where the touch of a friend's hand on the shoulder or a discussion nearby momentarily takes the mind off the job in hand.

Regardless of where Jefferson copied off the first draft, he performed no rote piece of work. He made at least fifteen changes in the text that can be traced directly on the rough draft; undoubtedly many more could be spotted if all the first draft had survived. Most of these were minor changes and did not affect the sense of the paper. One worth mentioning occurred near the start of the document. He altered "We hold these truths to be sacred & undeniable;" to "We hold these truths to be self-evident." The change did more than reduce three words to one. A person received a sacred truth on faith. It was of divine origin, not perceived by reason. The original phrasing implied that the Law of Nature was the Law of God. By shifting to "self-evident," Jefferson adapted a word from natural philosophy to politics and made the Law of Nature akin to the Law of Reason. More than that, however, was involved. These truths, as Louis Hartz has pointed out, were singularly self-evident to Americans as they were not to Europeans. The middle class, even in the eighteenth century, predominated in America. There were few extremes of wealth or poverty, a condition which gave the people, spread though they were along some thousand miles of coastline, a peculiar sense of community, and, in turn, led to a single code of morals in America as opposed to the several codes prevailing in Europe among the variety of classes. "This then," says Hartz, "is the mood of America's absolutism: the sober faith that its norms are self-evident. It is one of the most powerful absolutisms in the world."

Once Jefferson had recopied the introductory part, he searched through his papers for the first draft of his constitution. The list of charges in the preamble had served to justify a new government for Virginia. With the same purpose in mind, only now applied to the continental scene, he slipped the charges intact into the Declaration. His constant need to rewrite, to polish, and possibly to disguise old material in new dress forced several changes on the list. First, he altered the style. The charge in the constitution.

> by putting his negative on laws the most wholesome & necessary for the public good

now became

> he has refused his assent to laws the most wholesome and necessary for the public good.

Next, he lengthened the list. He had conjured up—either on his own or with the help of those on the committee—four more by the time he began to work on the Declaration. On the manuscript of the constitution's preamble he jotted down the headings of three of them after the sixth charge:

> refused judiciary establmts to some without unjust & partial judges dependant
> · erected swarms of offices

These notations, all of them further reminders of the King's abuse of his executive power, were expanded in the "rough" draft to:

> he has suffered the administration of justice totally to cease in some of these colonies, refusing his assent to laws for establishing judiciary powers:
> he has made our judges dependant on his will alone, for the tenure of their offices, and amount of their salaries:
> he has erected a multitude of new offices by a selfassumed power, & sent hither swarms of officers to harrass our people & eat out their substance:

The constitution's list had ended accusing the King of abandoning the helm of government and declaring "us out of his allegiance & protection." That charge was now moved into the body of the list and a new one was introduced for the conclusion. It was a lengthy diatribe against slavery, that crime which he had charged against the King in *A Summary View* but had failed to mention in his list in the constitution. Here was a fine chance to proclaim to the world that America acknowledged the blight, wanted to be rid of it, and, above all, that the King, not Americans, must shoulder full blame for it.

> he has waged cruel war against human nature itself, violating it's most sacred rights of life & liberty in the persons of distant people who never offended him, captivating & carrying them into slavery in another hemisphere, or to incur miserable death in their transportation thither. this piratical warfare, the opprobrium of *infidel* powers, is the warfare of the CHRISTIAN king of Great Britain. determined to keep open a market where MEN should be bought & sold, he has prostituted his negative for suppressing every legislative attempt to prohibit or to restrain this execrable commerce: and that this assemblage of horrors might want no fact of distinguished die, he is now exciting these very people to rise in arms among us, and to purchase that liberty of which *he* has deprived them, by murder-

ing the people upon whom *he* also obtruded them; thus paying off former crimes committed against the *liberties* of one people, with crimes which he urges them to commit against the *lives* of another.

Here, for the first time, Jefferson loses control of his material. The heart and not the head guides his pen. The paragraph reads like a first draft. The writing is verbose, and it depends on adjectives and on such stylistic tricks as italics and capitalization to make its point. The tight, restrained writing of the other charges, where the weight of spare sentences is carried by verbs, is gone. The paragraph rings false, as though Jefferson were trying to convince himself of something he did not really believe to be true.

The comments on slavery ended, for the time being at least, Jefferson's charges against the King. He turned now to the concluding portions of his paper. The surviving fragment of the original draft indicates the amount of rewriting he did on the fresh copy. The work on this part of the document went along with few changes at first.

at this very time too, they are permitting their chief magistrate to send over not only soldiers of our common blood but Scotch & foreign mercenaries to destroy us.

Jefferson paused here. The words "destroy us" seemed mild for the point he wanted to make. He scratched them out and substituted the gaudier phrase "invade and deluge us in blood." Having paused, he found that the next sentence now displeased him. On a blank space below the concluding words of the first draft he tested out a new sentence and after making a change or two in the trial run inserted it in the text above, which now read:

invade and deluge us in blood.
...& foreign mercenaries to ~~destroy us.~~

these facts have given the last stab to agonizing
~~this is too much to be borne even by relations.~~

affection, & manly spirit bids us to renounce forever these
~~enough then be it to say, we are now done~~

unfeeling brethren
~~with them!~~

Jefferson skimmed through the next two sentences without pausing for changes, but the final one gave trouble. He tinkered until it flowed as he wished:

be it so, since they will have it; the

& to glory
road to ~~glory & to~~ happiness is open to us too,

apart from them
~~separately~~
we will climb it ~~in a separate state~~ and

de
acquiesce in the necessity which ~~pre~~nounces

eternal separation
our ~~everlasting Adieu!~~

It was now time to draft the conclusion, a formal statement of the intentions of Congress. Jefferson added a final paragraph stating that "We therefore the representatives of the United States of America in General Congress do...." He ended this formal renouncement of all ties to Great Britain with a sentence Carl Becker has called "perfection in itself"

And for the support of this declaration we mutually pledge to each other our lives, our fortunes, & our sacred honour.

After completing this second or "rough" draft of the Declaration, Jefferson handed it over to John Adams for an opinion. Adams apparently thought his colleague had turned in a first-rate job, for he took time to copy the entire document. He felt the need to make only one change in the process. Among the charges against the King was one that read:

> he has refused for a long space of time to cause others to be elected....

Adams altered that to read

> he has refused for a long space of time after such dissolutions to cause others to be elected,...

Adams inserted the change in both his and Jefferson's copy. When he returned the document and pointed out what he had done, Jefferson agreed to the refinement and, with his attention now drawn to the charge, saw where he could improve the sentence still further. He altered it to read:

> he has refused for a long time after such dissolutions to cause others to be elected,...

A haze now begins to envelop the evolution of the Declaration's text. From the time John Adams returned the rough draft to Jefferson until it was laid before Congress, some thirty-one changes were made either by Jefferson, by the committee, which he certainly called into session soon after Adams had finished reading the Declaration, or, more likely, by both the committee and Jefferson.

The first change dealt with the introduction and seemed aimed principally at eliminating the word "subordination." There is no record of who called attention to this flaw in Jefferson's argument.

When in the course of human events it

dissolve

becomes necessary for a people to ~~advance~~

the political bands which have connected them

~~from that subordination in which they have~~

with another, and to

~~hitherto remained, & to~~ assume among the

separate and equal

powers of the earth the ~~equal & independant~~

station to which the laws of nature & of

nature's god entitle them, ...

Changes in the second sentence seem for the most part of the sort an author anxious to improve his phrasing would make, and quite possibly Jefferson carried them out before showing his document to the committee:

We hold these truths to be self-evident; that

all men are created equal ~~& independant~~; that

they are endowed by their creator with ~~equal rights, some~~

~~from that equal creation they derive rights~~

~~of which are~~   rights; that   these

inherent & inalienable   ∧   among ~~which~~ are ~~the~~

~~preservation of~~ life, ~~& ~~liberty, & the pursuit

rights

of happiness; that to secure these ~~ends,~~

governments are instituted among men, ...

One of these changes—the excision of "& independant"—exceeded a concern for style. Either Jefferson or someone on the committee saw that while all men may be created equal so far as God is concerned, all men obviously are not created independent. Logic demanded the word be eliminated.

Except for three new charges against the King which were doubtless suggested by the committee members—certainly by now Jefferson had exhausted his ingenuity—other changes in the rough draft were relatively minor and mainly stylistic. The first of the three additions Jefferson wrote out on a separate slip and pasted onto his manuscript in a way to indicate it would appear after charge number three ("he has refused to pass other laws for the accomodation of large districts...").

> he has called together legislative bodies at places unusual, uncomfortable, & distant from the depository of their public records, for the sole purpose of fatiguing them into compliance with his measures.

The second was slipped in among the crimes levelled at both the King and Parliament. It read:

> for abolishing the free system of English laws in a neighboring province, establishing therein an arbitrary government and enlarging it's boundaries so as to render it at once an example & fit instrument for introducing the same absolute rule into these colonies.

The final addition was eased in just ahead of the philippic on slavery.

> he has constrained others ~~falling into~~
> ~~his hands~~ taken captives on the high
> seas to bear arms against their country
> ~~& to destroy & be destroyed by the brethern~~
> ~~whom they love~~ to become the executioners of
> their friends & brethren or to fall themselves by
> their hands.

The Declaration had now cleared the committee and was ready for Congress. Benjamin Franklin, however, had still not seen it, and Jefferson especially wanted his approval as well as his suggestions for improvement. A close though not intimate relationship existed between the two. The old gentlemen had high respect for Jefferson, and some six months earlier had gone out of his way to lend him a copy of his ideas on a confederation for the colonies. On Friday, June 21, Jefferson wrote the following note:

TH: J. TO DOCTR. FRANKLYN   Friday morn.

The inclosed paper has been read and with some small alterations approved of by the committee. Will Doctr. Franklyn be so good as to peruse it and suggest such alterations as his more enlarged view of the subject will dictate? The paper having been returned to me to change a particular sentiment or two, I propose laying it again before the committee tomorrow morning, if Doctr. Franklyn can think of it before that time.

Doctr. Franklyn read it and appears to have made about five changes, all of them minor and only two of any interest. One dealt with style. In the first draft of his peroration, Jefferson had complained that Great Britain was sending over

Scotch & foreign mercenaries to invade & ~~destroy us~~ deluge us with blood.

Franklin, unaware of the original wording, crossed out the florid substitution and replaced it, curiously, with the identical phrase Jefferson had rejected. The second change worth mentioning occurred at the beginning of the Declaration and seemed equally insignificant.

When in the course of human events

one
it becomes necessary for ~~a~~ people to . . .

Franklin's intent seems clear. The Declaration must appear as the voice of a united people, and this slight change tended to increase that illusion. Unfortunately, Franklin lacked the energy to trace down the nine other uses of the word "people" in the paper and make certain each gave the impression of a single and united populace. As a result, debate would rage for three-quarters of a century whether the Declaration spoke for a single people or for thirteen separate and independent peoples. Only a long and bloody war would eventually silence discussion on the point.

Once the Declaration had been retrieved from Franklin, Jefferson apparently called a final committee meeting. With his colleagues' approval at last, Jefferson took back his scarred paper and made a fresh copy. This fair copy, which has since been lost, was placed on Charles Thomson's desk on Monday, June 28. It read this way:

> A Declaration by the Representatives of the UNITED STATES OF AMERICA, in General Congress assembled.
>
> When in the course of human events it becomes necessary for one people to dissolve the political bands which have connected them with another, and to assume among the powers of the earth the separate and equal station to which the laws of nature & of nature's god entitle them, a decent respect to the opinions of mankind requires that they should declare the causes which impel them to the separation.
>
> We hold these truths to be self-evident; that all men are created equal; that they are endowed by their creator with inherent & inalienable rights; that among these are life, liberty, & the pursuit of happiness; that to secure these rights, governments are instituted among men, deriving their just powers from the consent of the governed; that whenever any form of government becomes destructive of these ends, it is the right of the people to alter or to abolish it, & to institute new government, laying it's foundation on such principles & organising it's power in such form, as to them shall seem most likely to

effect their safety & happiness. prudence indeed will dictate
that governments long established should not be changed for
light & transient causes: and accordingly all experience hath
shewn that mankind are more disposed to suffer while evils are
sufferable, than to right themselves by abolishing the forms to
which they are accustomed, but when a long train of abuses &
usurpations, begun at a distinguished period, & pursuing invariably the same object, evinces a design to reduce them under
absolute Despotism, it is their right, it is their duty, to throw
off such government & to provide new guards for their future
security. such has been the patient sufferance of these colonies;
& such is now the necessity which constrains them to expunge
their former systems of government. the history of the present
King of Great Britain, is a history of unremitting injuries and
usurpations, among which appears no solitary fact to contradict
the uniform tenor of the rest, all of which have in direct object
the establishment of an absolute tyranny over these states. to
prove this, let facts be submitted to a candid world, for the
truth of which we pledge a faith yet unsullied by falsehood.

he has refused his assent to laws the most wholesome and   necessary for the public good:
he has forbidden his governors to pass laws of immediate &
  pressing importance, unless suspended in their operation till
  his assent should be obtained; and when so suspended, he has
  neglected utterly to attend to them.
he has refused to pass other laws for the accomodation of large
  districts of people unless those people would relinquish the
  right of representation in the legislature; a right inestimable
  to them, & formidable to tyrants only:
he has called together legislative bodies at places unusual, uncomfortable, & distant from the depository of their public
  records, for the sole purpose of fatiguing them into compliance with his measures.
he has dissolved Representative houses repeatedly & continually,
  for opposing with manly firmness his invasions on the rights
  of the people:

he has refused for a long time after such dissolutions to cause others to be elected, whereby the legislative powers, incapable of annihilation, have returned to the people at large for their exercise, the state remaining in the mean time exposed to all the dangers of invasion from without, & convulsions within:

he has endeavored to prevent the population of these states; for that purpose obstructing the laws for naturalization of foreigners; migrations hither; & raising the conditions of new appropriations of lands:

he has suffered the administration of justice totally to cease in some of these states, refusing his assent to laws for establishing judiciary powers:

he has made our judges dependant on his will alone, for the tenure of their offices, and the amount & payment of their salaries:

he has erected a multitude of new offices by a self-assumed power, & sent hither swarms of officers to harass our people & eat out their substance:

he has kept among us in times of peace standing armies & ships of war without the consent of our legislatures:

he has affected to render the military, independant of & superior to the civil power:

he has combined with others to subject us to a jurisdiction foreign to our constitutions and unacknologed by our laws; giving his assent to their acts of pretended legislation, for quartering large bodies of armed troops among us;

for protecting them by mock-trial from punishment for any murders which they should commit on the inhabitants of these states;

for cutting off our trade with all parts of the world;

for imposing taxes on us without our consent;

for depriving us of the benefits of trial by jury;

for transporting us beyond the seas to be tried for pretended offences:

for abolishing the free system of English laws in a neighboring province, establishing therein an arbitrary government and enlarging it's boundaries so as to render it at once an example & fit instrument for introducing the same absolute rule into these states;

for taking away our charters, abolishing our most valuable laws & altering fundamentally the forms of our governments;

for suspending our own legislatures & declaring themselves invested with power to legislate for us in all cases whatsoever:

he has abdicated government here, withdrawing his governors, & declaring us out of his allegiance & protection:

he has plundered our seas, ravaged our coasts, burnt our towns & destroyed the lives of our people:

he is at this time transporting large armies of foreign mercenaries to compleat the works of death, desolation & tyranny, already begun with circumstances of cruelty & perfidy unworthy the head of a civilized nation:

he has endeavored to bring on the inhabitants of our frontiers the merciless Indian savages, whose known rule of warfare is an undistinguished destruction of all ages, sexes, & conditions of existence:

he has incited treasonable insurrections in our fellow-citizens, with the allurements of forfeiture & confiscation of our property:

he has constrained others taken captive on the high seas to bear arms against their country, to become the executioners of their friends & brethren or to fall themselves by their hands.

he has waged cruel war against human nature itself, violating it's most sacred rights of life & liberty in the persons of distant people who never offended him, captivating & carrying them into slavery in another hemisphere, or to incur miserable death in their transportation thither. this piratical warfare, the opprobrium of *infidel* powers, is the warfare of the CHRISTIAN king of Great Britain. determined to keep open a market where MEN should be bought & sold, he has prostituted his negative for suppressing every legislative attempt to prohibit or to restrain this execrable commerce: and that this assemblange of horrors might want no fact of distinguished die, he is now exciting those very people to rise in arms among us, and to purchase that liberty of which *he* has deprived them, by murdering the people upon whom *he* also obtrude them; thus paying off former crimes committed against the *liberties* of one people, with crimes which he urges them to commit against the *lives* of another.

in every stage of these oppressions we have petitioned for redress in the most humble terms; our repeated petitions have been answered only by repeated injury. a prince whose character is thus marked by every act which may define a tyrant, is unfit to be the ruler of a people who mean to be free. future ages will scarce believe that the hardiness of one man, adventured within the short compass of twelve years only, to build a foundation so broad & undisguised for tyranny over a people fostered & fixed in principles of freedom.

Nor have we been wanting in attentions to our British brethren. we have warned them from time to time of attempts by their legislature to extend a jurisdiction over these our states. we have reminded them of the circumstances of our emigration & settlement here, no one of which could warrant so strange a pretension: that these were effected at the expence of our own blood & treasure, unassisted by the wealth or the strength of Great Britain: that in constituting indeed our several forms of government, we had adopted one common king, thereby laying a foundation for perpetual league & amity with them: but that submission to their parliament was no part of our constitution, nor ever in idea, if history may be credited: and we appealed to their native justice & magnanimity, as well as to the ties of our common kindred to disavow these unsurpations which were likely to interrupt our connection & correspondence. they too have been deaf to the voice of justice & consanguinity, & when occasions have been given them, by the regular course of their laws, of removing from their councils the disturbers of our harmony, they have by their free election re-established them in power. at this very time too they are permitting their chief magistrate to send over not only soldiers of our common blood, but Scotch & foreign mercenaries to invade & destroy us in blood. these facts have given the last stab to agonizing affection and manly spirit bids us to renounce forever these unfeeling brethren. we must endeavor to forget our former love for them, and to hold them as we hold the rest of mankind, enemies in war, in peace friends. we might have been a free & a great people together; but a communication of grandeur & freedom it seems is below their dignity. be it so, since they will have it: the road to happiness & to glory is open to us too; we will climb it apart from them, and acquiesce in the necessity which denounces our separation.

We therefore the representatives of the United States of America in General Congress assembled do, in the name & authority of the good people of these states, reject and renounce all allegiance & subjection to the kings of Great Britain & all others who may hereafter claim by, through, or under them; we utterly dissolve all political connection which may heretofore have subsisted between us & the people or parliament of Great Britain; and finally we do assert and declare these colonies to be free and independent states, and that as free & independant states they have full power to levy war, conclude peace, contract alliances, establish commerce, & to do all other acts and things which independant states may of right do. And for the support of this declaration we mutually pledge to each our lives, our fortunes & our sacred honour.

Jefferson had, as his colleagues on the committee must have remarked, more than adequately fulfilled the assignment Congress had handed him. He had argued America's case on the high ground of moral and legal principles, making it clear the colonists respected authority at the same time they rebuffed its abuse and thus discounting any argument that the new nation should not be welcomed into the world community of nations. He had worked carefully to assure all that America was in the hands of sane leaders and that the Declaration was not designed to promote a democratic revolution. He had produced a document that

developed entirely out of American experience and at the same
time universalized that experience in a way that could appeal to
the world.

While courting sympathy abroad, Jefferson had promoted
unity at home. The catalogue of George III's transgressions
touched on every section of the country. Few colonists could
read the list without feeling that somewhere along the line they
had been directly injured by the King. Arguments that had
ripped apart Congress off and on the past two years—the leveling
tendencies of New England, the aristocratic notions of the South
—had for the most part been successfully avoided. Certain southerners might be irritated by the warm indictment of slavery and
many in the North at casting blame on the British people, but
these were minor flaws that could be easily softened or edited
out by Congress.

Jefferson's Declaration reflected American thought in its optimism and confidence. No hint of doubt nor sense of failure had
insinuated its way into his sentences. We will climb "the road to
happiness & to glory," he said. His words refined those of a Pennsylvania preacher who had said in early 1776 that God watched
over the American cause—"It is usual for the great Jehovah to
interest himself for the enlargement of young and growing states"
—and that eventually America "will extend wider and wider,
until it has reached to the Pacific ocean." America in the Declaration became a land of promise. Separation would bring with it
much more than a mere change of masters. All this Jefferson implied, and with such restraint than no hint of the ludicrous crept
in.

With equal subtlety he abstracted another characteristic of
American thought—the sense of mission the colonists felt about
themselves and their ideals. In suggesting that Americans were
fighting for the rights of all mankind, he expressed a sentiment
that had deep roots. The Puritans had come to New England
convinced they were among God's chosen. William Penn, a half

century later, explained that he, too, had gone thither into the wilderness "to lay the foundation of a free colony for all mankind." Still later a group of "hickory" Quakers, ejected from their meetings for refusing to abide by their sect's pacifistic principles, would put up a plaque on their new meeting house that read: "In the year of our Lord, 1783, of the Empire 8." Tradition has it that someone asked about the meaning of "Empire 8." "I will tell thee, Friend," came the answer, "it is because our country is destined to be the great empire over all this world."

John Adams, like most Americans of the day, would have approved that remark completely. "I always consider the settlement of America with reverence and wonder," he once said, "as the opening of a grand scheme and design in Providence for the illumination and emancipation of the slavish part of mankind all over the earth." Adams, for that matter, approved of nearly all the sentiments—as he understood them—expressed in Jefferson's paper, and yet clearly he could never have written it. For one thing, he lacked Jefferson's controlled style, that "lofty pathos" Carl Becker speaks of. Adams's public writings tended to be either ponderous and dull or inflamed with his easily stirred up passions. (This, from his Novanglus papers, suggests how he might have written the Declaration of Independence: "...a manifest design in the prince, to annul the contract on his part, will annul it on the part of the people. A settled plan to deprive the people of all the benefits, blessings, and ends of the contract, to subvert the fundamentals of the constitution, to deprive them of all share in making and executing laws, will justify a revolution.") The art of writing held little interest for Adams. Jefferson, on the other hand, took great pride in what he wrote. He had, in a sense, been practicing for the Declaration for two years. *A Summary View* might be considered *the* first draft of the Declaration. All the ideas in the later papers are there, and most of the verbosity, the fervent rhetoric, the discursiveness, and the hazy thought have in the meantime been eliminated.

Adams had absorbed Locke as well as Jefferson and could accept the Declaration's version of those ideas with little difficulty. Accepting what one man creates, especially when the creation resembles familiar fare, is something different from oneself creating. If the task had fallen to Adams, he surely would have emphasized other aspects of the natural rights doctrine. His character and New England experience would have forced him to shape the argument in another fashion. The phrase "all men are created equal" would have come slowly, if at all, from his pen. Locke's trio of rights—life, liberty, and property—would have turned up, but "pursuit of happiness," which he could accept easily from another, would hardly have occurred to his fundamentally puritan mind. Rights interested Adams, and he no doubt would have paid attention to them in his paper, but government interested him more and certainly would have received greater emphasis from him.

Adams never really comprehended what Jefferson had done. He later insisted, no doubt in part from jealousy over the acclaim given Jefferson's paper, that the Declaration only repeated ideas that had been aired for many months. But more than jealousy accounts for the sour view. Adams never had a high regard for public papers, tending to dismiss them as of little importance compared to the business of shaping and leading opinion among the elite. He would have approached the writing of the Declaration as a routine if necessary job, and not something close to his heart. The practical work of achieving independence had intrigued him for over a year; once achieved, he cared little how it was publicly declared. He told Jefferson this toward the end of his life. "I never bestowed much Attention on any of those Addresses; which were all but repetitions of the same Things: the same facts and Arguments. Dress and ornament rather than Body, Soul or Substance. My thoughts and cares were nearly monopolized by the Theory of our Rights and Wrongs, by measures for the defence of the country; and the means of governing our Selves."

In spite of Adams's concern with practical affairs and his implied belief that Jefferson dealt with things of less substance, with "dress and ornament," it is notable that throughout their long lives Adams proved the less successful politician. Perhaps Jefferson succeeded mainly because, as Henry Bamford Parkes has observed, "his ideals corresponded more nearly than those of his rivals to the wishes of the majority of the American people." The majority in Congress in 1776, even those strong for independence, tended to think in terms of the European experience. American leaders, Jefferson once said, perhaps with John Adams in mind, inclined "to a submission of true principles to European authorities,...to fears of the people that have been inspired by the populace of their own great cities. . . ." Jefferson's genius, exemplified in his Declaration, was to think in American terms.

To think in American terms does not mean Jefferson expressed the American mind of the day. The strength of his paper was *not* "that it said what everyone was thinking," as Carl Becker considers it, but that it took the American experience—as Jefferson saw it—and "displaced an old god with a new one." He tied American ideals to the matters of daily experience, not to the European experience that so many leaders had imbibed from their readings and blended with their experience in Boston, New York, or Philadelphia. Those who favored the old god accepted only half-heartedly a political philosophy based on liberty, equality, and government by consent of the governed. They saw wealth, property, and class as the basis of political power. The elite should rule. The mob was to be feared, and the mass restrained by effective institutions like a strong government. Jefferson differed from his friends of the day—John Adams in particular—in degree rather than kind. As a liberal Virginian accustomed to an open society—had not his father risen to power in Virginia affairs on his talent—he focused on men rather than institutions. Institutions too often became committed to their own well-being, their own interests, rather than men's. Witness the Church of England's influence on the life of Jefferson's friend Oglivie. Jefferson wished to allow men the freest rein in their pursuit of happiness, and his experience in Virginia offered no reason why they should not be. He was fully committed to all the implications of the words "liberty," "equality," and "consent of the governed."

Jefferson spoke in the language of the day, and this made his new god "bear an astonishing resemblance to the one displaced." Frenchmen, Englishmen, Spaniards could understand him as well as Americans. He used that familiar language so well that when he had finished he had created for America, knowingly or not, an image of itself. America would imagine differently once Jefferson's Declaration of Independence came forth from Congress.

And what was this image of America that Jefferson had shaped? No sure answer is possible, which is one of the reasons, of course, why the Declaration has survived the time it has as a living part of the American tradition. Jefferson certainly meant to picture America as a place where human rights ranked above all others, especially property rights. He also gave prime importance to the doctrine of popular sovereignty and thereby aired without clarifying what was to become the American dilemma: what shall be done when the rights of the individual conflict with popular sovereignty? What if the governed shall give their consent to tread on man's equality?

Jefferson also created an image of America as a nation overflowing with purity and innocence. He had moralized on highly complex issues, creating out of the trouble between Great Britain and the colonies a drama of good and evil. It was, perhaps, hardly possible for him to have done otherwise, but the results of this approach would have unfortunate results in the long run. It would give the people an unrealistic view of politics and power. All the arguments in the June debate on independence had centered, as they do in most political debates, on self-interest.

By completely obscuring the role of self-interest in shaping the colonies' decision, he gave the people an unrealistic picture of how and why political decisions are made.

Clearly, Jefferson's paper had flaws and perhaps Congress would catch them before releasing it to the world. But to an extent the flaws were an excess of the virtues. "We aim above the mark to hit the mark," Emerson once said. "Every act hath some falsehood of exaggeration in it." And the European historian Huizinga added to Emerson's remark: "That reality has constantly given the lie to these high illusions of a pure and noble social life, who would deny? But where should we be, if our thoughts had never transcended the exact limits of the feasible?"

Chapter 6

A Leap in the Dark

✾ ✾ ✾ ✾ ✾ ✾ ✾ ✾ ✾

> Now sir, for your Groans. You and I in the Revolution
> acted from Principle; we did our Duty, as we then believed,
> according to our best Information, Judgment and Con-
> sciences. Shall we now repent of this? God forbid! No! . . .
> Repent? This is impossible: how can a Man repent of his
> virtues?
>
> JOHN ADAMS *to* BENJAMIN RUSH—1808

JEFFERSON'S committee laid the Declaration of Independence
before Congress on Friday, June 28. The document was read
aloud and by a routine vote ordered to lie on the table. This
time Congress determined to follow its rule that no major
paper could be discussed until a day had elapsed after its introduction. Since the Declaration had come before the delegates
on Friday and since Congress had granted itself Saturday as a
regular holiday with the onset of Philadelphia's summer heat,
the members had the entire weekend to plan their comments.
Edward Rutledge took time to write John Jay, still in New
York, urging him to "give your Attendance in Congress Monday next." He complained mightily about the plan for a confederation John Dickinson had drawn. Dickinson contemplated
a strong central government and Rutledge was "resolved to
vest the Congress with no more Power than that is absolutely
necessary. . . ." But it may have been certain sentiments expressed in Jefferson's Declaration as much as Dickinson's pro-

176

posed Articles that led him to rail against the influence of New England in Congress. "I dread their low Cunning, and those levelling Principles which Men without Character and without Fortune in general possess, which are so captivating to the lower class of Mankind, and which still occasion such a fluctuation of Property as to introduce the greatest disorder."

Historians have tried for well over a century to learn exactly what happened in Congress during the first four days of July, 1776. The outline of the story has emerged but the details remain obscure. What follows is the most accurate report that can be developed from the facts that survive.

Monday, July 1, dawned warm and clear. Jefferson appears to have set to work early on another committee assignment. He took notes on an interview with one John Blake, a Montreal merchant, who was airing his views on the Canadian campaign for Congress. Blake seemed to believe, according to Jefferson's notes, that the Canadians were well disposed toward Americans, though the priests and merchants were "in general against us." Jefferson concluded the interview in time to be in his seat at the State House when Congress convened at nine o'clock.

Before Jefferson's paper could be dealt with, the question of independence itself still had to be settled. In the three weeks that had elapsed since Congress had formally discussed the issue, much had occurred. In Pennsylvania, a Provincial Conference had put on record its "willingness to concur in a vote of the Congress declaring the United Colonies free and independent States...." New Jersey had ejected from his seat as Governor, William Franklin, who, to his eminent father's distress, chose to remain loyal to Great Britain. It had also elected new delegates to Congress and given them the right to vote for independence. The Assembly of Delaware had set about creating a new government, free of royal authority, and by implication had given its delegates in Congress a free hand on the question of independence. Caesar Rodney was still absent from Congress, trying to

speed up the transition in Delaware's political affairs. By the
morning of July 1, only New York and Maryland had failed
to permit their delegates to favor a declaration of independence.

Maryland, with a taste for the dramatic, announced its decision as Congress convened that morning. As the delegates were
about to enter on "the great debate," John Adams said in a
letter that day, "the generous and unanimous vote" of the Maryland Convention was brought in. The new instructions permitted the delegation from Maryland to vote for independence.
John Adams was exultant. His gamble on May 15 appeared to
have worked. The rift in the union of the colonies that had
opened with Maryland's abrupt departure from Congress, a departure watched at the time with quiet approval by the other
Middle Colonies, had now been all but closed.

John Adams spoke of the "great debate" Congress was about
to enter upon on July 1, but if his later memory was correct it
is doubtful the delegates expected any lengthy discussion. "In
the morning when Congress met," according to Adams, "we expected the question would be put and carried without any
further Debate; because we knew we had a Majority and thought
that argument had been exhausted on both sides as it indeed was,
for nothing new was ever afterwards advanced on either side."

Adams had not figured on John Dickinson, who remained
adamant against immediate independence and still set to do
what he could to persuade Congress to hold off a decision a
while longer. He had spent the weekend preparing his thoughts,
and not long after Congress convened he rose to speak. For the
past several weeks Dickinson had talked much about his integrity
to friends, and he continued that line now. "My Conduct, this
Day," he said, "I expect will give the finish Blow to my once too
great, and, my Integrity considered now, too diminish'd Popularity." He went on to say he would rather "vote away the Enjoyment of that dazzling display, that pleasing Possession, than
the Blood and Happiness of my Countrymen." He was distressed

that so many of his colleagues, men that up to now he had seen eye to eye with, were now willing "to brave the Storm in a Skiff made of Paper," and he was "alarm'd at this Declaration on being so vehemently presented."

What, Dickinson asked, are the advantages to be obtained from a declaration of independence? It has been argued, he said, that it might "animate the People" and the troops; that it would "Convince foreign Powers of our Strength and Unanimity" and we would receive their "aid in consequence thereof"; that it would assure the union of the colonies; and that the spirit of the colonies requires it. Dickinson saw merit in none of these arguments. "The preservation of Life, Liberty, and Property," he said, using Locke's and not Jefferson's trio of rights, "is sufficient Motive to animate the People. The General Spirit of America is animated." Nor would this Declaration convince foreign powers of anything. They would not rely on words; they would want deeds. "The Event of the Campaign will be the best Evidence of our strength," not a piece of paper. As for unifying the colonies, this Declaration in Dickinson's eyes would in fact achieve the opposite effect. "It may weaken that Union, when the People find themselves engaged in a cause rendered more cruel by such a Declaration without Prospect of an End to their Calamities, by a Continuation of the War." And as for the spirit of the colonies demanding a Declaration, "I Answer that the spirit of the colonies is Not to be relied on."

Dickinson had still more to say, and, while none of his arguments thus far had the merit of novelty, the eloquence of his presentation kept the delegates attentive. There are other disadvantages to making a declaration of independence, he went on. "It is Our Interest to keep Great Britain in the opinion that We mean Reconciliation as long as possible," he said. "Great Britain after one or more successful Campaigns may be induc'd to offer Us such a share of Commerce as would satisfy Us, to appoint Councillors during good Behavior, to withdraw her armies, to

protect our Commerce, Establish our Militias—in short to redress all the Grievances complain'd of in our first Petition." A
belligerent declaration such as this one now before Congress
would only cause the war to be "carried on with more Severity.
The Burning of Towns, the Setting Loose of Indians on our
Frontiers has Not yet been done," Dickinson pointed out, suggesting that some of Jefferson's charges against the King were
not entirely accurate. "Boston might have been burnt, though it
was not," he added.

And what assurance do we have that Europe will take this
Declaration the right way? "People are changeable. In the Bitterness of Soul they may complain against our Rashness & ask
why We did not apply first to foreign Powers, Why We did
not settle Differences among ourselves, why we did not Take
Care to secure unsettled lands for easing their Burthens. . . ."

Dickinson saw a variety of dangers ahead if independence became declared. The possibility of secession haunted his thoughts,
perhaps because he had once threatened to use it against New
England and could thus all the more visualize its use. "A Partition of these Colonies will take Place if Great Britain can't
conquer Us," he said flatly. He went on to add that if independence indeed became a fact he doubted the United States could
survive as one nation. "I should be glad to know whether in
20 or 30 Years this Commonwealth of Colonies may not be
thought too unwieldly, & Hudson's River be a proper Boundary
for a separate Commonwealth to the Northward. I have a strong
Impression on my Mind that this will take Place."

What, then, should America do? "Not only Treaties with
foreign powers but among Ourselves should precede this Declaration." The experience during the past three weeks of working
with twelve other delegates on a constitution for the new nation had disheartened Dickinson about America's future as much
as it had Rutledge, though for different reasons. "We should
know on what Grounds We are to stand with Regard to one

another...the Committee on Confederation dispute almost every Article—Some of Us totally despair of any reasonable Terms of Confederation."

Dickinson's eloquence came with the spoken word, and the abbreviated notes of his speech that survive hardly hint of the deep impress his voice made on Congress. A few weeks earlier a young Philadelphian had heard Dickinson defend his views on independence before an unsympathetic audience. Dickinson's words, the young man wrote, "appeared to be the unpremeditated effusions of the heart. His graceful actions, the emotions of his countenance & a plaintive yet manly voice strongly imposed upon my judgment. He was clearly wrong yet I believed him right. Such were the effects of oratory." Such were the effects, too, to judge by John Adams's recollection, of the July 1 speech on Congress. "He had prepared himself apparently with great labor and ardent zeal," said Adams, "and in a speech of great length, and with all his eloquence, he combined together all that had been said in Congress by himself and others."

When Dickinson finished, silence pervaded the room. Possibly Congress would have proceeded at once to vote on the resolution of independence, but the new delegation from New Jersey wished to have the question discussed further. "We observed to them," Adams recalled long after, "that the Question was so public and had been so long disputed in Pamphlets, NewsPapers, and every Fireside that they could not be uninformed and must have made up their minds. They said it was true. They had been attentive to what had been passing abroad, but they had not heard the arguments in Congress and did not incline to give their opinions until they should hear the sentiments of members there." Richard Stockton, New Jersey's chief justice, "was most particularly importunate." In law both sides present their case before judge or jury hands down a decision, and though Judge Stockton had prejudged this particular "case" he no doubt felt that form should be followed.

As Adams remembered the scene, Edward Rutledge rose from his seat in the midst of the discussion and stepped over to John Adams. "Nobody will speak but you on this subject," he said, smiling. "You have all the topics so ready, that you must satisfy the gentlemen from New Jersey."

Adams gave a forced laugh and, as he recalled, answered "that it had so much the air of exhibiting like an actor or gladiator, for the entertainment of the audience, that I was shamed to repeat what I had said twenty times before, and I thought nothing new could be advanced by me." Nonetheless, he rose and began to speak.

"This is the first time of my life that I have ever wished for the talents and eloquence of the ancient orators of Greece and Rome, for I am very sure that none of them ever had before him a question of more importance to his country and to the world. They would probably, upon less occasions than this, have begun by solemn invocations to their divinities for assistance; but the question before me appears so simple, that I have confidence enough in the plain understanding and common sense that have been given me, to believe that I can answer, to the satisfaction of the House, all the arguments which have been produced, notwithstanding the abilities which have been displayed and the eloquence with which they have been enforced."

"All this to be sure was but a flourish," Adams said later, "and not as I conceive a very bright Exordium: but I felt awkwardly...." Adams went on to give, according to his own and others' judgments, one of the great speeches of his life. "I wish someone had remembered the speech," Adams once remarked, "for it is almost the only one I ever made that I wish was literally preserved." It was the memory of that speech that prompted Jefferson late in life to remark: John Adams was "our colossus on the floor...not graceful nor eloquent, nor remarkably fluent, but he came out occasionally with a power of thought and expression, that moved us from our seats." Richard Stockton, on returning to New Jersey, told friends: "The Man to whom the Country is most indebted for the great measure of Independence is Mr. John Adams of Boston—I call him the Atlas of American Independence—He it was who sustained the debate, and by the force of his reasonings demonstrated not only the justice but the expediency of the measure."

Adams rarely blinked realities, and no doubt in his speech he agreed that many of Dickinson's forebodings about the future would prove true. He addressed men of experience—lawyers, merchants, planters, and politicians—and this sort of frank talk would appeal to such a group. Adams had the talent, however, of making the future seem at once forbidding and yet attractive enough for men to fight for. Certainly something of that lost speech must have slipped into the letter he wrote to a friend that night. "If you imagine that I expect this declaration will ward off calamities from this country, you are much mistaken. A bloody conflict we are destined to endure. This has been my opinion from the beginning. You will certainly remember my declared opinion was at the first Congress when we found that we could not agree upon an immediate non-exportation, that the contest would not be settled without bloodshed; and that if hostilities should once commence, they would terminate in an incurable animosity between the two countries.... If you imagine that I flatter myself with happiness and halcyon days after a separation from Great Britain, you are mistaken again. I do not expect that our new government will be so quiet as I could wish, nor that happy harmony, confidence, and affection between the colonies, that every good American ought to study, labor and pray for, for a long time."

After Adams had finished, little more appears to have been said from the floor. (This statement, however, must be balanced against Jefferson's remark a decade later that the day's debate lasted nine hours, "during which all the powers of the soul had been distended with the magnitude of the object." It is possible that the speeches of Adams and Dickinson occupied most of that time, though this hardly seems likely.) Congress remained in the committee of the whole while an unofficial vote was taken on the question before it in the late afternoon. The result showed nine colonies for independence, two against—Pennsylvania and South Carolina—and one, Delaware, with its delegation down to two men, evenly split. New York abstained from voting. Its delegates, according to Jefferson's notes, "declared they were for it themselves, & were assured their constituents were for it, but that their instructions having been drawn near a twelvemonth before, when reconciliation was still the general object, they were enjoined by them to do nothing which should impede that object. They therefore thought themselves not justifiable in voting on either side, and asked leave to withdraw from the question, which was given them."

No one in Congress—not even John Dickinson—had resisted independence harder than Edward Rutledge. In the three weeks grace period he had managed to wangle from those who favored it, he had seen the tide swing against his view, and now, unlike Dickinson, he decided at the last moment to swing with it as gracefully as possible. (John Adams's earlier sketches of the two men turned out to be strikingly accurate judgments of their characters. He had called Rutledge "a perfect Bob-o-Lincoln... excessively weak, excessively variable and unsteady...." Though Dickinson looked a shadow, "slender as a reed; pale as ashes," Adams saw his strength: "upon a more attentive inspection, he looks as if the springs of life were strong enough to last many years.") After the unofficial vote had been tallied, Rutledge asked that a formal vote be postponed until the next day. He believed he would be able to persuade the recalcitrant member of his delegation to change his mind by then. His request was readily granted, for others hoped that Caesar Rodney, still absent, might be brought up from Delaware in time to break the tie in his delegation. And if sufficient pressure were applied to Pennsylvania, possibly by morning the hesitant members of that delegation might, in view of the voice of the Provincial Conference which had urged immediate independence, have changed their position. Adams hoped, of course, for unanimity the next day, "yet I cannot promise this," he told a friend. "Because one or two gentlemen may possibly be found who will vote point blank against the known and declared sense of the constituents."

The next morning, a Tuesday, the delegates walked through a heavy rain to the State House. Perhaps along the way Philadelphians stopped to congratulate them, for the news that a declaration had passed in the committee of the whole yesterday was, according to one delegate, "well known at the Coffee-House of the city as in Congress." Congress had this time found it impossible to adhere to its oath of secrecy.

Most of the delegates had arrived and unwrapped themselves from their rain garments and entered the meeting room when Caesar Rodney, still in boots and spurs, arrived from his overnight ride up from Delaware. His colleague Thomas McKean met him as he entered the State House, and "after a friendly salutation (without a word on the business) we went into the Hall of Congress together, and found we among the latest: proceedings immediately commenced, and after a few minutes the great question was put."

John Hancock was in the chair now, for this vote would be for the record. Secretary Thomson began the roll call, as usual with New Hampshire, reading off the colonies from north to south. All New England, of course, voted for independence. New York once again abstained. New Jersey voted "aye." A glance at the Pennsylvania delegation indicated that colony would vote in the affirmative, too, for John Dickinson and Robert Morris, another for delaying the break with England, had absented themselves in order that the colony's independent-minded delegates could carry the day. When Thomson called out Delaware, Rodney rose and said: "As I believe the voice of my constituents and of all sensible and honest men is in favor of independence and my own judgment concurs with them, I vote for Independence." (Other delegates may have made similar remarks as they cast their votes, but no record of them has come down.) Thomson continued the roll-call: Virginia, North Carolina, South Carolina, and Georgia—all "aye." The United Colonies had voted unanimously for independence. Charles Thomson now made the following entry in the Journal:

> Resolved, That these United Colonies are, and, of right, ought to be Free and Independent States; that they are absolved from all allegiance to the British crown, and that all political connexion between them and the state of Great Britain is, and ought to be, totally dissolved.

No record survives of how Congress reacted when Thomson had finished the roll call and Hancock announced that the colonies—now states—had officially cut their ties with Great Britain. Perhaps the solemnity of the moment forbade a cheer. Possibly some delegate rose to remind his colleagues that to have committed an act of treason, as they had, gave them nothing to rejoice about. (The treasonable nature of their act caused Congress to delay releasing the names of those who had signed the embossed copy of the Declaration until January of 1777.)

Congress now turned to Jefferson's paper. Apparently some muttering had developed about its contents in the three days the delegates had had to mull over the document since it had been introduced. John Dickinson had already complained of its vehemence. Josiah Bartlett of New Hampshire thought the paper "a pretty good one" but went on to say, as if with the grumblings of others in mind, "I hope it will not be spoiled by canvassing in Congress."

The canvassing began, it would seem, sometime in the early afternoon of July 2, after Congress had agreed to the resolution on independence, and continued through the next two days. At the start it looked as though the document would have an easy time of it. Jefferson's first two paragraphs came through largely as he had turned them in. Congress insisted only on a few changes, most of them minor. If anyone complained about the absence of the word "property," his complaint died on the air. Congress had at least two good reasons for silence on the word. "Their intention to confiscate the large Tory estates implied a distinction between the rights of loyalists and the rights of patriots which could not be honestly described as self-evident and natural," Henry Alonzo Myers notes. Then, the fact that a good number of those in the Continental Army and in the various militias were propertyless offered a convincing reason for keeping the word out of the Declaration in order to widen its appeal.

The phrase "all men are created equal" slid through intact. For nearly all members of Congress it meant simply equality before the law and equality of opportunity. Even plain people of the eighteenth century did not push the idea of equality to the point where they argued that common men with common understanding could or should lead. This, the basic ingredient of the Age of Paine that infuriated John Adams, came later, in part because the Declaration was there as a guide.

The absence of "& independant" that Jefferson had first included made the phrase easier for many, especially southerners, to take. Perhaps Locke, as well as the Bible, had made the sentiment so familiar that it had become an easily swallowed cliché. Perhaps, too, the debate over the phrase in the Virginia Convention helped to smooth things among the southern delegates in Congress. On June 1, Thomas Ludwell Lee had written to his brother Richard Henry that ever since the Virginia Declaration had been reported they had "been stumbling at the threshold...." He went on: "I will tell you plainly that a certain set of aristocrats—for we have such monsters here—finding that their execrable system cannot be reared on such foundations, have to this time kept us at bay on the first line, which declares all men to be born free and independent." Edmund Randolph, also present at the Convention, reported that this opening clause "was opposed by Robert Carter Nicholas, as being the fore-runner or pretext of civil convulsion." Nicholas was a pious and outwardly haughty lawyer who refused to swallow glittering generalities without first examining them. His colleagues, how-ever, were in no mood to listen. He was answered, according to Randolph, "perhaps with too great an indifference to futurity, and not without inconsistency, that with arms in our hands, asserting the general rights of man, we ought not to be too nice and too much restricted in the delineation of them; but that slaves not being constituent members of our society could never pretend to any benefit from such a maxim." In short, the phrase was a pleasant-sounding platitude, more for public consumption than for guiding practical action. No doubt a similar argument was advanced in Congress for anyone brash enough to balk at the phrase in the context Jefferson had given it.

Congress made a few stylistic changes in the introduction. "Inherent & inalienable rights" was changed to "certain un-alienable rights" ("unalienable" was quite likely a typographical error made by the printer and not among the changes Congress made); the word "expunge" became "alter"; "unremitting in-juries" was changed to "repeated injuries." It made several minor excisions, the most important of which occurred in the final sentences, just before the charges commenced:

> The history of the present King of Great Britain is a history of unremitting injuries and usurpations, ~~among which appears no solitary fact to contradict the uniform tenor of the rest~~, all of which have in direct object the establishment of an absolute tyranny over these states. To prove this, let facts be submitted to a candid world, ~~for the truth of which we pledge a faith yet unsullied by falsehood.~~

Congress obviously intended to temper the exuberance that occasionally led Jefferson into mis-statements of fact and unseemly exaggerations. Soon the world would be studying this Declaration, searching for errors; America must not be caught in an indefensible position. Certainly at least once in sixteen years of rule George III had called a halt to his injuries and usurpations, and, if so, at least one solitary fact could be dredged up in his defense. It was equally awkward if not absurd to pretend to the world that America's reputation was completely "unsullied by falsehood," and that sentiment, too, was tossed aside. Wherever possible Congress would try to tone down the saint-like purity with which Jefferson had endowed the colonies.

Congress glided swiftly through these first two paragraphs mainly because they advanced an attitude toward man and government with which all were acquainted and which all for the most part accepted. Also, the delegates considered these paragraphs little more than attractive, if necessary, generalities to build the case against Great Britain. Time would show they took no more literally Jefferson's summary of natural rights than the Virginia Convention did Mason's version. High-sounding sentiments such as these served as ultimate guides, not as guides for immediate, short-run decisions. The delegates were not cynical nor even sceptical about these rights, but as men of affairs the immediately possible concerned them more than ultimate ends. Other parts of the Declaration would receive closer attention from them for that reason.

The end of Jefferson's introduction would have provided an excellent break-off point for the day. If that was the case, when Congress convened the next morning, July 3, and set promptly to work again on the Declaration, it began with the list of charges against the King. No record exists of who made what suggestions for changes in the Declaration, but it would seem that John Adams, for one, shared little in the editing. He spent a good deal of his time on July 3 writing letters to his wife. The first of these may have been written early in the morning. It is a long, leisurely letter, and only after several paragraphs of routine gossip does Adams come round to the heart of the matter:

"Yesterday, the greatest question was decided which ever was debated in America, and a greater, perhaps, never was nor will be decided among men.... You will see in a few days a Declaration setting forth the causes which have impelled us to this mighty revolution, and the reasons which will justify it in the sight of God and man.

"When I look back to the year 1761, and recollect the argument concerning the writs of assistance in the superior court, which I have hitherto considered as the commencement of this controversy between Great Britain and America, and run through the whole period from that time to this, and recollect the series of political events, the chain of causes and effects, I am surprised at the suddenness as well as greatness of this revolution. Britain has been filled with folly, and America with wisdom; at least, this is my judgment. Time must determine. It is the will of Heaven that the two countries should be sundered forever. It may be the will of Heaven that America shall suffer calamities still more wasting, and distresses yet more dreadful. If this is to be the case, it will have this good effect at least. It will inspire us with many virtues which we have not, and correct many errors, follies and vices which threaten to disturb, dishonor, and destroy us. The furnace of affliction produces refinement in states as well as individuals. And the new Governments we are assuming in every part will require a purification from our vices, and augmentation of our virtues, or there will be no blessings. The people will have unbounded power, and the people are extremely addicted to corruption and venality, as well as the great. But I must submit all my hopes and fears to an overruling Providence, in which, unfashionable as the faith may be, I firmly believe."

While Adams wrote, Congress proceeded line by line through Jefferson's paper. There was little bickering over the first thir-

teen charges against the King. Congress insisted on only nine
changes, most of them seeking greater accuracy. "He has
suffered the administration of justice totally to cease in some
of these states..." became "he has obstructed the administration of justice..." for it could be argued that up to now the
King's justice had not totally ceased in the colonies. "He has
erected a multitude of new offices by a self-assumed power..."
displeased some delegates. Congress could offer no legitimate
objection to the King's power; it was the misuse of it that
angered America. The charge was altered to read: "he has
erected a multitude of new offices..." In the next charge, Jefferson had complained about the standing armies and ships of war
kept in America in time of peace. Congress could see the objection to standing armies, but it saw no legitimate reason against
ships of war, which served to protect America's shores and trade
from pirates, and so that phrase was eliminated.

Congress picked Jefferson up on another obvious mis-state-
ment of fact in the fourteenth charge, where he had accused
the King of withdrawing his governors and declaring the colonists "out of his allegiance." The King had done neither. Those
governors who had left the scene had done so to save their
skins; and the King had declared the colonists out of his protection, not his allegiance. The reworded charge, with Congress's
additions in italics, now read:

he has abdicated government here, ~~withdrawing his government &~~ *by* declaring us out of his ~~allegiance and~~ protection
and waging war against us.

The sixteenth charge dealt with the use of foreign troops, and
here, for the first time, Congress felt the need to shore up Jefferson's prose. To underscore the cruelty and perfidy of this act
they added that it was "*scarcely paralleled in the most barbarous
ages and totally* unworthy of the head of a civilized nation."

Congress had by now covered over half of Jefferson's handiwork. The relatively minor alterations introduced should have provoked no complaint from the most sensitive author, and Jefferson had probably managed to endure the ordeal thus far with few tremors. While Congress discussed, he passed away at least part of his time on July 3 making copies of the Declaration for his absent friends George Wythe and Richard Henry Lee. He must have been distracted from that task, or whatever occupied him at the moment, when Congress came to the last of his charges, in which the King was accused as the sole cause of slavery in America. Here Jefferson had exposed with feeling his belief, as Myers puts it, "that independence demanded in the name of equality could not long keep company with human bondage." Congress eliminated the entire charge. The delegates could have thrown it out on the ground that once again Jefferson had exceeded the limits of accuracy, but as Jefferson reported the event in his notes at the time, they found other reasons. It was struck out, he said, "in complaisance to South Carolina & Georgia, who had never attempted to restrain the importation of slaves, and who on the contrary still wished to continue it. Our Northern brethren also I believe felt a little tender under those censures; for tho' their people have very few slaves themselves yet they had been pretty considerable carriers of them to others."

The debate over this last charge must have been long and rancorous. John Adams's great battle for independence was behind him, and possibly while this one raged around him he idled away the time writing a second letter to his wife, enlarging on some points he had overlooked in the earlier one. A residue of bitterness pervaded the opening paragraphs:

"Had a Declaration of Independency been made seven months ago, it would have been attended with many great and glorious effects. We might, before this hour, have formed alliances with foreign states. We should have mastered Quebec, and been in possession of Canada. You will perhaps wonder how such a declaration would have influenced our affairs in Canada, but if I could write with freedom, I could easily convince you that it would, and explain to you the manner how. Many gentlemen in high station, and of great influence, have been duped by the ministerial bubble of Commissioners to treat. And in real, sincere expectation of the event which they so fondly wished, they have been slow and languid in promoting measures for the reduction of that province. Others there are in the Colonies who really wished that our enterprise in Canada would be defeated, that the Colonies might be brought into danger and distress between two fires, and be thus induced to submit. Others really wished to defeat the expedition to Canada, lest the conquest of it should elevate the minds of the people too much to hearken to those terms of reconciliation which, they believed, would be offered us. These jarring views, wishes, and designs occasioned an opposition to many salutary measures which were proposed for the support of that expedition, and caused obstructions, embarrassments, and studied delays, which have finally lost us the province.

"All of these causes, however, in conjunction would not have disappointed us, if it had not been for a misfortune which could not be foreseen and perhaps could not have been prevented; I mean the prevalence of the small-pox among our troops. This fatal pestilence completed our destruction. It is a frown of Providence upon us, which we ought to lay to heart."

Adams had now disposed of his anger and continued on in another vein: "But, on the other hand, the delay of this Declaration to this time has many great advantages attending it. The hopes of reconciliation which were fondly entertained by multitudes of honest and well-meaning, though weak and mistaken people, have been gradually, and at last totally extinguished. Time has been given for the whole people maturely to consider the great question of independence, and to ripen their judgment, dissipate their fears, and allure their hopes, by discussing it in newspapers and pamphlets, by debating it in assemblies, conventions, committees of safety and inspection, in town and county meetings, as well as in private conversations, so that the whole people, in every colony of the thirteen, have now adopted it as their own act. This will cement the union, and avoid those heats and perhaps convulsions, which might have been occasioned by such a Declaration six months ago.

"But the day is past. The second of July, 1776, will be the most memorable epocha in the history of America. I am apt to believe that it will be celebrated by succeeding generations as the great anniversary festival. It ought to be commemorated, as the day of deliverance, by solemn acts of devotion to God Almighty. It ought to be solemnized with pomp and parade, with shows, games, sports, guns, bells, bonfires, and illuminations, from one end of this continent to the other, from this time forward forevermore."

Two months earlier a writer in the *Pennsylvania Gazette* had said that those for immediate independence were rushing America "into a scene of anarchy," and that the "scheme of independence is visionary; they know not themselves what they mean by it." To break the ties with England, he said, was to "leap in the dark." Adams ended his second letter to his wife explaining what that leap meant to him:

"You will think me transported with enthusiasm, but I am not. I am well aware of the toil and blood and treasure that it will cost us to maintain this Declaration and support and defend these States. Yet, through all the gloom, I can see the rays of ravishing light and glory. I can see that the end is more than worth all the means. And that posterity will triumph in that day's transaction, even although we should rue it, which I trust in God we shall not."

If it seems reasonable to assume that Congress wound up its discussions on July 3 by eliminating the paragraph on slavery and that it dealt with the concluding section of the Declaration on Thursday, then it seems safe to say that July 4, 1776, was among the unhappiest of Jefferson's life. Both he and his paper suffered most on this day. The concluding section fared badly from the start. Jefferson up to now had attacked George III in his official capacity. When, however, near the start of the Declaration's concluding section he wrote that

> future ages will scarce believe that the hardiness of one man adventured within the short compass of twelve years only to build a foundation, so broad and undistinguished, for tyranny over a people fostered and fixed in principles of freedom

he was censuring George as an individual. John Adams, though he had left the passage unaltered, had not liked it. "I thought this too personal; for I never believed George to be a tyrant in disposition and in nature," he told a friend many years later. "I always believed him to be deceived by his courtiers on both sides of the Atlantic, and in his official capacity only cruel. I thought the expression too passionate, and too much like scolding, for so grave and solemn a document; but as Franklin and Sherman were to inspect it afterwards, I thought it would not become me to strike it out." Franklin and Sherman had left the passage as it stood, but Congress struck it out completely.

Jefferson's run of bad luck continued:

> Nor have we been wanting in attentions to our British brethren. we have warned them from time to time of attempts by their legislature to extend *an unwarrantable* jurisdiction over ~~these our states~~ *us.* we have reminded them of the circumstances of our emigration & settlement here, ~~no one of which could warrant so strange a pretension: that these were effected at the expence of our own blood and treasure, unassisted by the wealth or the strength of Great-Britain: that in constituting indeed our several forms of government, we had adopted one common king, thereby laying a foundation for perpetual league and amity with them: but that submission to their parliament was no part of our constitution, nor ever in idea, if history may be credited:~~

Congress obviously felt that, despite Jefferson's skillful explanation of the original migration to America, the issue could best be handled by ignoring it. A majority also believed Congress would be leaving itself open to justified criticism if it said that "submission to their parliament was no part of our constitution, nor ever in idea, if history may be credited." The dominion theory of empire had been developed too recently to become a fixed part of American tradition. There were too many instances in the past of America's accepting Parliamentary jurisdiction without complaint. Congress faced this problem, too, by ignoring it.

Momentarily things got better for Jefferson. His next sentence escaped with a few stylistic changes only. Then came the severest blow since Congress began editing his paper.

> ~~and when occasions have been given them, by the regular course of their laws, of removing from their councils the disturbers of our harmony, they have by their free election reestablished them in power. at this very time too, they are permitting~~ ...

and thus up to the Declaration's concluding paragraph. All but a single sentence of the peroration he had worked over with care was eliminated. Some of Jefferson's happiest phrases—"the road to happiness & glory is open to us too; we will climb it apart from them"—went by the board. Congress apparently made the cuts reluctantly. It tried first to amend the passage to suit the needs of all. The word "Scotch" in the phrase "Scotch & foreign mercenaries" was scratched out at one point, clearly to please the Scotsmen in Congress, such as James Wilson and Dr. Witherspoon. Eventually, however, it became clear that the sentiments of the entire passage were unacceptable. It concentrated too much on the perfidies of the British people. "The pusillanimous idea that we had friends in England worth keeping terms with, still haunted the minds of many," Jefferson said on this excision; "for this reason those passages which conveyed censures on the people of England were struck out, lest they should give them offence." There were sounder reasons than this for the cut. America was breaking its ties with Great Britain not because of the iniquities of the British people but because of the King's crimes against America. Once the United States had won their independence, they would want to trade again with the people of that island. Common sense demanded that the passage must go.

The loss of this passage that he had worked over so hard must have hurt deeply. Possibly it was somewhere along in here that Benjamin Franklin, "who perceived that I was not insensible to these mutilations," leaned over from his seat next to Jefferson and tried to divert his mind with a story.

"I have made it a rule," Franklin said, according to Jefferson's memory, "whenever in my power, to avoid becoming a draughtsman of papers to be reviewed by a public body. I took my lesson from an incident which I will relate to you. When I was a journeyman printer one of my companions, an apprentice Hatter, having served out his time, was about to open shop for himself. His first concern was to have a handsome signboard, with a proper inscription. He composed it in these words:

> John Thompson, Hatter
> makes and sells hats for ready money

with a figure of a hat subjoined. But he thought he would submit it to his friends for their amendments. The first he shewed it to thought the word 'hatter' tautologous, because followed by the words 'makes hats' which shew he was a hatter. It was struck out. The next observed that the word 'makes' might as well be omitted, because the customers would not care who made the hats. If good and to their mind, they would buy, by whomever made. He struck it out. A third said he thought the words 'for ready money' were useless, as it was not the custom of the place to sell on credit. Everyone who purchased expected to pay. They were parted with, and the inscription now stood:

> John Thompson
> sells hats

'*Sells* hats' says his next friend. 'Why nobody will expect you to give them away. What then is the use of that word?' It was stricken out, and 'hats' followed it, the rather, as there was one painted on the board. So his inscription was reduced ultimately to

> John Thompson

with the figure of a hat subjoined."

Congress had neared the end. The final paragraph was reworked to include the original wording of the Lee resolution of June 7. Several of the delegates apparently felt Jefferson had been remiss in his references to God. Two more were added to the last paragraph. One noted that Congress, in doing what it did, was "appealing to the supreme judge of the world for the rectitude of our intentions." And Jefferson's final sentence was now changed to read:

> And for the support of this declaration *with a firm reliance on the protection of divine providence,* we mutually pledge to each our lives, our fortunes & our sacred honor.

Congress completed its revision in the early evening of July 4. "The president resumed the chair," the Journal notes. "Mr. Harrison reported, that the committee of the whole Congress have agreed to a Declaration, which he delivered in. The Declaration being read, was agreed to as follows:"—here, glued into the Journal, was a broadside copy of the document which had been printed by John Dunlap of Philadelphia.

IN CONGRESS, JULY 4, 1776.
A DECLARATION
BY THE REPRESENTATIVES OF THE
UNITED STATES OF AMERICA
IN GENERAL CONGRESS ASSEMBLED.

When in the Course of human Events, it becomes necessary for one People to dissolve the Political Bands which have connected them with another, and to assume among the Powers of the Earth, the separate and equal Station to which the Laws of Nature and of Nature's God entitle them, a decent Respect to the Opinions of Mankind requires that they should declare the causes which impel them to the Separation.

We hold these Truths to be self-evident, that all Men are created equal, that they are endowed by their Creator with certain unalienable Rights, that among these are Life, Liberty, and the Pursuit of Happiness—That to secure these Rights, Governments are instituted among Men, deriving their just Powers from the Consent of the Governed, that whenever any Form of Government becomes destructive of these Ends, it is the Right of the People to alter or to abolish it, and to institute new Government, laying its Foundation on such Principles, and organizing its Powers in such Form, as to them shall seem most likely to effect their Safety and Happiness. Prudence, indeed, will dictate that Governments long established should not be changed for light and transient Causes; and accordingly all Experience hath shewn, that Mankind are more disposed to suffer, while Evils are sufferable, than to right themselves by abolishing the Forms to which they are accustomed. But when a long Train of Abuses and Usurpations, pursuing invariably the same Object, evinces a Design to reduce them under absolute Despotism, it is their Right, it is their Duty, to throw off such Government, and to provide new Guards for their future Security. Such has been the patient Sufferance of these Colonies; and such is now the Necessity which constrains them to alter their former Systems of

Government. The History of the present King of Great-Britain is a History of repeated Injuries and Usurpations, all having in direct Object the Establishment of an absolute Tyranny over these States. To prove this, let Facts be submitted to a candid World.

HE has refused his Assent to Laws, the most wholesome and necessary for the public Good.

HE has forbidden his Governors to pass Laws of immediate and pressing Importance, unless suspended in their Operation till his Assent should be obtained; and when so suspended, he has utterly neglected to attend to them.

HE has refused to pass other Laws for the Accommodation of large Districts of People, unless those People would relinquish the Right of Representation in the Legislature, a Right inestimable to them, and formidable to Tyrants only.

HE has called together Legislative Bodies at Places unusual, uncomfortable, and distant from the Depository of their public Records, for the sole Purpose of fatiguing them into Compliance with his Measures.

HE has dissolved Representative Houses repeatedly, for opposing with manly Firmness his Invasions on the Rights of the People.

HE has refused for a long Time, after such Dissolutions, to cause others to be elected; whereby the Legislative Powers, incapable of Annihilation, have returned to the People at large for their exercise; the State remaining in the mean time exposed to all the Dangers of Invasion from without, and Convulsions within.

HE has endeavoured to prevent the Population of these States; for that Purpose obstructing the Laws for Naturalization of Foreigners; refusing to pass others to encourage their Migrations hither, and raising the Conditions of new Appropriations of Lands.

HE has obstructed the Administration of Justice, by refusing his Assent to Laws for establishing Judiciary Powers.

HE has made Judges dependent on his Will alone, for the

Tenure of their Offices, and the Amount and Payment of their Salaries.

HE has erected a Multitude of new Offices, and sent hither Swarms of Officers to harrass our People, and eat out their Substance.

HE has kept among us, in Times of Peace, Standing Armies, without the consent of our Legislatures.

HE has affected to render the Military independent of and superior to the Civil Power.

HE has combined with others to subject us to a Jurisdiction foreign to our Constitution, and unacknowledged by our Laws; giving his Assent to their Acts of pretended Legislation:

FOR quartering large Bodies of Armed Troops among us:

FOR protecting them, by a mock Trial, from Punishment for any Murders which they should commit on the Inhabitants of these States:

FOR cutting off our Trade with all Parts of the World:

FOR imposing Taxes on us without our Consent:

FOR depriving us, in many Cases, of the Benefits of Trial by Jury:

FOR transporting us beyond Seas to be tried for pretended Offences:

FOR abolishing the free System of English Laws in a neighbouring Province, establishing therein an arbitrary Government, and enlarging its Boundaries, so as to render it at once an Example and fit Instrument for introducing the same absolute Rule into these Colonies:

FOR taking away our Charters, abolishing our most valuable Laws, and altering fundamentally the Forms of our Governments:

FOR suspending our own Legislatures, and declaring themselves invested with Power to legislate for us in all Cases whatsoever.

HE has abdicated Government here, by declaring us out of his Protection and waging War against us.

HE has plundered our Seas, ravaged our Coasts, burnt our Towns, and destroyed the Lives of our People.

HE is, at this Time, transporting large Armies of foreign Mercenaries to compleat the Works of Death, Desolation, and Tyranny, already begun with circumstances of Cruelty and Perfidy, scarcely paralleled in the most barbarous Ages, and totally unworthy the Head of a civilized Nation.

HE has constrained our fellow Citizens taken Captive on the high Seas to bear Arms against their Country, to become the Executioners of their Friends and Brethren, or to fall themselves by their Hands.

HE has excited domestic Insurrections amongst us, and has endeavoured to bring on the Inhabitants of our Frontiers, the merciless Indian Savages, whose known Rule of Warfare, is an undistinguished Destruction, of all Ages, Sexes and Conditions.

IN every stage of these Oppressions we have Petitioned for Redress in the most humble Terms: Our repeated Petitions have been answered only by repeated Injury. A Prince whose Character is thus marked by every act which may define a Tyrant, is unfit to be the Ruler of a free People.

NOR have we been wanting in Attentions to our British Brethren. We have warned them from Time to Time of Attempts by their Legislature to extend an unwarrantable Jurisdiction over us. We have reminded them of the Circumstances of our Emigration and Settlement here. We have appealed to their native Justice and Magnanimity, and we have conjured them by the Ties of our common Kindred to disavow these Usurpations, which, would inevitably interrupt our Connections and Correspondence. They too have been deaf to the Voice of Justice and of Consanguinity. We must, therefore, acquiesce in the Necessity, which denounces our Separation, and hold them, as we hold the rest of Mankind, Enemies in War, in Peace, Friends.

WE, therefore, the Representatives of the UNITED STATES OF AMERICA, in GENERAL CONGRESS, Assembled, appealing to the Supreme Judge of the World for the Rectitude of our Intentions, do, in the Name, and by the Authority of the good People of these Colonies, solemnly

Publish and Declare, That these United Colonies are, and of Right ought to be, FREE AND INDEPENDENT STATES; that they are absolved from all Allegiance to the British Crown, and that all political Connection between them and the State of Great-Britain, is and ought to be totally dissolved; and that as FREE AND INDEPENDENT STATES, they have full Power to levy War, conclude Peace, contract Alliances, establish Commerce, and to do all other Acts and Things which INDEPENDENT STATES may of right do. And for the support of this Declaration, with a firm Reliance on the Protection of divine Providence, we mutually pledge to each other our Lives, our Fortunes, and our sacred Honor.

Signed by ORDER *and in* BEHALF *of the* CONGRESS

JOHN HANCOCK, PRESIDENT

ATTEST.
CHARLES THOMSON, SECRETARY

PHILADELPHIA: PRINTED BY JOHN DUNLAP

Jefferson's Declaration had passed the scrutiny of some fifty conservative gentlemen who had wanted old and tested ideas to justify their "great revolution," and they had wanted nothing more. Old and tested ideas, apparently, are what Jefferson had handed them. Certainly they did not think they had approved a paper that opened the door to a democratic revolution. They had no awareness that an "old god" had been displaced, or that the Declaration would ever be used to promote ideas they frowned on. If they had, John Adams for one, despite his affection for Jefferson, would have been on his feet in an instant protesting these "innovations," these "leveling principles."

What, then, had the delegates done in the two and a half days spent revising and editing Jefferson's paper? They had, in spite of some forty additions and extensive excisions that cut the length by one-quarter, left the document pretty much intact, especially that part of it that would appeal to future generations. Jefferson said years later that the Declaration's "authority rests ...on the harmonizing sentiments of the day," and so far as pointing up those sentiments went, Congress improved Jefferson's paper at every point. It eliminated the diatribe against slavery; it omitted a remark that would have jarred the sensibilities of an ethnic group, the Scotch; and it inserted additional references to God to satisfy the devout in Congress and out. The Declaration of Independence as it came from Congress was more than the first public document of the new United States; it was in a real sense also the first product of the demand for conformity in the new nation. But this pressure for conformity operated within a generous and tolerant tradition. It aimed at promoting unity within the new nation, not at infringing on the privacy or liberties of individuals.

The process of making Jefferson's Declaration into an American Declaration did more than improve the paper. It revealed that, despite strong divisive forces within the new nation, there appeared to exist a solid ideological basis for unity. Thirteen states, whose representatives only two years earlier had first met in Philadelphia and been appalled at the diversity of customs, laws, and traditions among the colonies, and who only three weeks earlier had been at loggerheads over the practical question of independence, had with little difficulty been able to agree on a set of fundamental political beliefs. That unity was not, of course, as solid as it seemed. The South and North did not really understand how far their ideals diverged. Nor did they seem to sense that men speaking the same language can nonetheless use identical words without realizing they comprehend those words differently. It would take the French Revolution to make them aware of how far apart they had been in July of 1776.

Still, the clocks had been timed to strike as one, and also to strike the same tone. This, as the delegates knew, was among the remarkable things about the Declaration of Independence as it left their chamber. Like the Constitution that would come a few years later, there may have been much in Jefferson's paper that dissatisfied or perturbed the more perceptive delegates. Quite likely they voiced their complaints to the end, but when it seemed apparent that this was the best that could be produced to satisfy thirteen distinctly various colonies, defeat was accepted with the same grace, in the same spirit of realistic compromise with which it had been accepted when independence itself, horrifying as it was to many of the delegates, became inevitable.

Both Jefferson and Congress, then, could be equally pleased with their joint handiwork. Now, the delegates might have begun to ask themselves, how would America, and the world, too, for that matter, react to this skiff made of paper? "We are now Sir," Abraham Clark of New Jersey wrote the morning of July 4, before revisions on the Declaration were completed, "embarked on a most Tempestious Sea; Life very uncertain, Deceiving danger, Scattered thick around us, Plots against the military and it is whispered against the Senate. Let us prepare for the worst, we can die but once...."

The practical dangers ahead preoccupied Congress so much, no one apparently sensed that a new idea—equality—had been so powerfully expressed it would eventually become "at once a gadfly, irritating, and beacon luring, the victims among whom it dwelled." Alfred North Whitehead has explained what had and would happen. "There will be a general idea in the background flittingly, waveringly realized by the few in its full generality—or perhaps never expressed in any adequate universal form with persuasive force. Such persuasive expression depends on the accidents of genius." The idea of equality had chanced upon its genius unbeknownst to the members of Congress. They had looked lightly at the glittering generalities of Jefferson's paper and concentrated on the "facts" being submitted to a candid world. They would regret their action, for in time this idea would embody "itself in special expression after special expression," losing some of its magnificence, perhaps, but becoming "a hidden driving force, haunting humanity, and ever appearing in specialized guise as compulsory on action by reason of its appeal to the uneasy conscience of the age." All this, John Adams for one, would see only after the skiff had been at sea several years.

Chapter 7

The Skiff Sets Sail

❋ ❋ ❋ ❋ ❋ ❋ ❋ ❋

"You and I ought not to die, before We have explained our
selves to each other."

ADAMS *to* JEFFERSON—1813

CONGRESS sat until early evening on July 4 revising Jefferson's
Declaration. After the document had for the final time been
read aloud and at last approved by the members present, the committee of five was ordered to superintend the printing of it. The
committee, which might have been expected to be somewhat
elated, may have given only perfunctory attention to its proof-
reading duties. The word "unalienable" slipped into Dunlap's
broadside, rather than the "inalienable" Jefferson had written,
possibly through a printer's error. The Pattern of Capitalization,
always Haphazard in the eighteenth Century, seems to have been
based on the Printer's whim rather than the committee's Direction. Dunlap was allowed to use the date July 4 at the top of his
broadside, thus implying that America had declared her independence on that day rather than on July 2, the day John Adams
had expected would be celebrated with great pomp and ceremony.

The first celebration of the event occurred on neither of these
days. It was delayed until July 8 in order to give Philadelphia
time to prepare a suitable ceremony. At eleven in the morning on
that day, nearly all the one hundred members of the city's Committee of Inspection and Observation gathered in the warm sun

outside the Philosophical Hall. The Committee of Safety joined them there, then the two groups walked over to the State House yard. There, "in the presence of a great concourse of people," the Declaration of Independence was read by John Nixon, a member of Pennsylvania's Committee of Safety. The crowd gave three huzzas, shouting with each, "God bless the Free States of North America!" Nine Pennsylvania soldiers chosen especially for the honor ripped down the King's arms over the entrance to the State House and carried them over to the London Coffee House.

After the multitude had dispersed, several of the city Committee went over to Armitage's Tavern to celebrate the occasion with refreshment. In the afternoon, the city's five battalions paraded on the city commons "and gave us," wrote John Adams, "the *feu de joie*, notwithstanding the scarcity of powder." The sound of clanging bells filled the cool evening air—"the bells rang all day and almost all night," reported Adams—and bonfires flickered throughout the city. The high point of the celebration came in the evening at the Coffee House. There, as the great crowd cheered, the Kings arms were heaved onto a mound of flaming wooden casks and the symbol of royal authority in Philadelphia swiftly vanished in fire. With these and "other great Demonstrations of joy" Philadelphia celebrated the declaration of America's independence.

Other changes wrought by the Declaration had already begun before the Kings arms had been burned. The vestry of Christ Church had met and agreed it would now "be proper to omit those petitions in the liturgy wherein the King of Great Britain is prayed for." Writs were no longer being issued in the King's name, and where the courts were open the King's justice was being practiced no more.

"We have lived to see a Period which a few years ago no human forecast could have imagined," William Ellery wrote and then went on to temper his joy. "We have lived to see these

Colonies shake off, or rather declare themselves independent of a State which they once gloried to call their Parent—I said *declare* themselves independent for it is one Thing for Colonies to declare themselves independent and another to establish themselves in Independency...."

On July 9 Philadelphia and Congress turned back to the job of establishing themselves in independency. Philadelphia's battalions made ready to march for New York, where Washington was assembling all available troops to repel the expected British invasion there. All through July Associators from the Pennsylvania backcountry poured into Philadelphia, paused for a few days at the city barracks to rest and reorganize, pick up equipment and supplies, then move on. Some two thousand had passed through by the end of the month, and "the cry of them all is for BATTLE."

In August, as the preparation for war continued, Congress paused one morning for all the delegates present to sign the engrossed vellum copy of the Declaration. "Do you recollect," Benjamin Rush asked Adams years later, "the pensive and awful silence which pervaded the house when we were called up, one after another, to the table of the President of Congress to subscribe what was believed by many at that time to be our own death warrants?" The "silence and gloom" of that morning were broken only once. Stout Benjamin Harrison, whose jocularity had often irritated John Adams, was standing at the table with Elbridge Gerry. He said: "I shall have a great advantage over you, Mr. Gerry, when we are all hung for what we are now doing. From the size and weight of my body I shall die in a few minutes, but from the lightness of your body you will dance in the air an hour or two before you are dead." Rush recalled that "this speech procured a transient smile, but it was soon succeeded by the solemnity with which the whole business was conducted."

The first year is a hard one for all newborns, and that of the United States proved no exception. The battle for New York went badly, and though Washington saved his army he lost the city to the British. Successes were few. As 1776 merged into 1777, Americans had only Washington's midnight raid across the Delaware into Trenton to cheer about. For want of more, that casual exploit was blown into a full-scale victory. Tom Paine, now traveling with Washington's troops, summed up the dismal state of things in the opening line of his latest pamphlet—"These are the times that try men's souls."

The nation still had little to rejoice about when summer appeared again. Nonetheless, Philadelphia, as the unofficial capital of the new nation, had planned an auspicious celebration for the United States' first Independence Day. The day was to be commemorated much as John Adams had hoped—"with pomp and parade, with shows, games, guns, bells, bonfires, and illuminations ..."—and it would set the pattern for the future. "Perhaps some disorders may happen," one man said apprehensively, "but we were willing to give the idea of rejoicing its swing. The spirits of the whigs must be kept up." The Philadelphia city council worried that the festivities would lead to riots and decided to hold the elaborate fireworks display, planned as a climax to the day-long celebration, on the outskirts of the city—to "draw many disorderly persons out of town after dark."

The celebration began officially at noon when all the armed ships in the Delaware were drawn up before the city. "They were dressed in the gayest manner," reported the *Evening Post*, "with the colours of the United States and streamers displayed. At one o'clock, the yards being properly manned, they began the celebration of the day by a discharge of thirteen cannon from each of the ships...." There was an "elegant" banquet in the afternoon at Smith's City Tavern and after the banquet, the *Post* noted, "a number of toasts were drank, all breathing independence and a generous love of liberty...." Each of the toasts was followed by a salute outside the tavern from a company of British "deserts" now serving with the Georgia troops, and then by a rendition from a Hessian band which had been captured during Washington's Christmas foray into Trenton. The pleasure of having the band present, a visitor explained, was "heightened by the reflection that they were hired by the British Court for purposes very different from those to which they were applied." Late in the afternoon, while "huzzas resounded from street to street through the city," a thousand North Carolinians, a company of Maryland lighthorse, and a corps of artillery were reviewed by Congress and Generals Horatio Gates and Benedict Arnold.

The celebration continued unabated into the night. Perhaps the single unhappy soul in the city was William Williams, a dour member of Congress from Connecticut, who noted with an air of resentment that "a great Expenditure of Liquor, powder, etc. took up the Day." John Adams, on the other hand, expressed nothing but satisfaction. Adams, who had remained in Congress to implement the eloquence of the Declaration with action, while Jefferson had returned to his "country" to serve out the war in Virginia's government, found "the whole city lighting up their candles at the windows. I walked most of the evening and I think it was the most splendid illumination I ever saw; a few surly houses were dark, but the lights were very universal."

Those "few surly houses"—Tories still opposed to independence and Quakers attempting to remain neutral—had led the city council to fear riots. Two days earlier the council had pleaded for "moderation and forebearance towards persons who might not illuminate," and then, as a further precaution, had advised the city's justices of peace to warn "by bellmen, by note at the Coffee House, and otherwise every Inhabitant who sets up lights to extinguish them, at eleven o'clock precisely." These precautions, backed up by two hundred soldiers assigned to patrol the streets, were effective, "Everything was conducted with the greatest order and decorum," according to the *Evening Post*.

The day ended with a final, splendid burst of fireworks—thirteen blazing rockets zooming into the sky—and then the thousands of exhausted citizens trudged back to their homes, ready for another year of war. "Thus," the *Evening Post* said, "may the fourth of July, that glorious and ever memorable day, be celebrated through America, by the sons of freedom, from age to age, till time shall be no more. Amen and Amen."

The Fourth became, of course, that "glorious and memorable day" the *Evening Post* hoped it would. But the notable thing about the first anniversary celebration of the day was the absence of Jefferson's Declaration from the festivities. The ceremonies centered entirely on the act of declaring independence; the paper explaining and justifying that act went ignored. The fact that only fifteen copies have survived of what must have been a large printing of Dunlap's broadside suggests that Jefferson's paper was not something instantly treasured by Americans. Even those who had shared in its creation were slow to accept it as a touchstone of American ideals. James Wilson told a Philadelphia audience in 1791 that the unifying theme in American history was found in the adherence of the people to a common body of principle. He talked about the Mayflower Compact and about Lord Baltimore's statute of religious liberty. He did not mention the Declaration of Independence.

Perhaps Americans ignored the Declaration in its early years of existence because it expressed so well the obvious, the commonplace, sentiments so in tune with the facts that it merited little comment. Europe saw the radical implications of the Declaration much sooner than America, for there the assumptions clear to Americans were not self-evident. Charles Pinckney of South Carolina perceived this distinction and tried to impress it on his colleagues at the Constitutional Convention in 1787. Too many of the delegates, he said, were trying to draw up a constitution in terms of European experience, and he insisted that "we cannot draw any useful lessons from the example of any of the European states or kingdoms." The United States was unique in that "there is more equality of rank and fortune in America than in any other country under the sun; and this is likely to continue as long as the unappropriated western lands remain unsettled.... Where are the riches and wealth whose representation and protection is the peculiar province of this present body? Are they in the hands of the few who may be called rich; in the possession of less than a hundred citizens? Certainly not. They are in the general body of the people, among whom there are no men of wealth, and very few of real poverty." And, he went on, "this equality is likely to continue, because in a new country, possessing immense tracts of uncultivated lands, where every temptation is offered to emigration and where industry must be rewarded with competency, there will be few poor, and few dependent.... We have unwisely considered ourselves as the inhabitants of an old instead of a new country."

Although Americans enjoyed considerably more material equality than Europeans, they preserved one form of European heritage. They continued to elect to public office men of distinguished background. The common people never dreamed of rising from their modest stations to a high level in politics. This was a preserve of the well-to-do and the well-trained. The plain people deferred to the elite. "Although it be granted, on all hands," a letter-writer to the *Evening Post* wrote in July of 1776, "that all power originates from the people; yet it is plain, that in those colonies where the government has, from the beginning, been in the hands of a very few rich men, the ideas of government both in the minds of those rich men, and of the common people, are rather aristocratical than popular. The rich, having been used to govern, seem to think it is their right; and the poorer commonalty, having hitherto had little or no hand in government, seem to think it does not belong to them to have any."

John Adams complained about nothing in the Declaration as long as the plain people continued to acknowledge his beliefs about man and government. A decade would pass before the people and events would incite Adams to argue over the meaning of certain words in the Declaration. During that decade the friendship between Adams and Jefferson grew stronger than ever. Mrs. Adams told Jefferson he was "the only person with whom my Companion could associate with perfect freedom, and unreserve." Jefferson, for his part, told a friend that after several months close association with Adams in France he found him "so amiable, ... I pronounce you will love him if ever you become acquainted with him." The friendship that had ripened in Paris continued through letters after Adams went to London as ambassador to the Court of St. James and Jefferson remained in Paris as ambassador to France.

In the early part of these years abroad, Adams, who often had to restrain gently a young man eager to remake the world overnight, played something akin to the role Wythe, Dr. Small, and Randolph had held in Jefferson's youth. Jefferson's cautious boldness first came forward in the draft of a treaty wherein he proposed reciprocal rights for citizens of one nation traveling in another. What better way, he seemed to say, could be devised to spread American ideas quickly throughout Europe? "If successfully carried out," Julian Boyd has remarked, "it would have altered the very nature of the union and of the society of nations." Adams dampened Jefferson's enthusiasm promptly but kindly. "We must not, my Friend, be the Bubbles of our own Liberal Sentiments," he wrote from London, attempting to make clear the United States must work within the accepted pattern of international relations and not try to form a new pattern at once. "If We cannot obtain reciprocal Liberality, We must adopt reciprocal Prohibitions, Exclusions, Monopolies, and Imposts. Our offers have been fair, more than fair. If they are rejected, we must not be the Dupes."

The idea remained fixed with Jefferson that America must set a model example for western civilization. The Barbary Pirates offered the next opportunity to practice what he preached. The rulers of several Mediterranean coastal states were demanding from the United States, as they had been demanding and receiving from most of Europe, bribery money for safe conduct through the Mediterranean. John Adams worried about the practical side of the problem. "I conclude it to be wisest for Us to negotiate and pay the necessary Sum, without Loss of Time," he wrote. "At present we are Sacrificing a Million, annually to Save one Gift of two hundred Thousand Pounds. This is not good Oeconomy."

"The same facts," Jefferson answered in a sentence that would explain their differences for years to come, "impress us differently." Jefferson hated the idea America had to "buy a peace." He preferred war. He thought justice and honor favored this view; also "it will procure us respect in Europe" and strengthen the "federal head." Adams replied he had no objections to war, but Jefferson should consider that the Barbary States were stronger and America weaker than he had calculated. Wars must be fought with vigor, and "Congress will never, or at least not for years, take any such Resolution, and in the meantime our Trade and Honour suffers beyond Calculation." Then, with a realism Jefferson accepted with reluctance, he said: "Our States are so backward that they will do nothing for some years." Principles dominated Jefferson's thought as his eye strayed over the "decadent" European scene; principles backed by power concerned Adams.

Shays's Rebellion in Massachusetts highlighted even more the way they looked at the same facts differently." "Dont be allarmed at the late Turbulence in New England," Adams wrote calmly at first. "The Massachusetts Assembly had, in its Zeal to get the better of their Debt, laid on a Tax, rather heavier than the People could bear; but all will be well, and this Commotion will terminate in additional Strength to Government." Jefferson said of course he had not been alarmed: "I can never fear that things will go far wrong where common sense has fair play." And to

Mrs. Adams he added: "I like to see the people awake and alert."

Later news revealed the people had been too alert for the Adamses. "Ignorant, wrestless desperadoes, without conscience or principals, have led a deluded multitude to follow their standard," Mrs. Adams reported with all her husband's verve. "Instead of that laudible spirit which you approve, which makes a people watchfull over their Liberties and alert in the defence of them, these mobish insurgents are for sapping the foundation, and destroying the whole fabrick at once." Jefferson replied in a manner that only the distressed Adamses' deepest affection made possible to overlook. "I like a little rebellion now and then," he said. "It is like a storm in the Atmosphere."

The trend of events in America and France had meanwhile led Adams into writing what eventually turned out to be a three-volume "essay" called *A Defence of the Constitutions of the United States of America*. He sought to make clear to Europe as well as to America the merits of the American system of balanced government. By "balanced" he meant, as Zoltán Haraszti has pointed out, "not the separation of the legislative, executive, and judiciary functions but the equilibrium of the democratic, aristocratic, and monarchic elements." Self-interest was the mainspring of human activity and the cause of human strife. Only effectively balanced governments could check this natural tendency toward anarchy and at the same time preserve men's natural rights. Adams called his book the American Boudoir, "in which our dear United States may contemplate themselves and their own defects as well as beauties." Though the first volume displayed Adams's political philosophy in full, Jefferson found little in it to argue about. He told Adams he was arranging for a translation and publication of the book in France.

The *Defence* appeared in America about the time delegates were assembling for the Constitutional Convention in Philadelphia. Rumors drifted back that the volume had helped shape the Constitution as it emerged from the Convention in September.

Adams, understandably, liked the Constitution. "It seems to be admirably fitted to preserve the Union, to increase Affection, and to bring us all to the same mode of thinking," he told Jefferson. "I think that Senates and Assemblies should have nothing to do with executive Power. But still I hope the Constitution will be adopted, and Amendments be made at a more convenient opportunity."

Jefferson confessed, before he had heard from Adams, that "there are things in it which stagger all my dispositions." It seemed to him that the House of Representatives would "not be adequate to the management of affairs either foreign or federal," that the "President seems a bad edition of a Polish king," in that "he may be reelected from 4. years to 4. years for life." He was not certain that the Articles of Confederation merited such complete dismissal. "Indeed, I think all the good of this new constitution might have been couched in three or four new articles to be added to the good, old, and venerable fabrick, which should have been preserved even as a religious relique."

Now the differences between the two men were becoming clearer. "You are afraid of the one—I, of the few," Adams replied. "You are Apprehensive of Monarchy; I, of Aristocracy. I would therefore have given more Power to the President and less to the Senate. The Nomination and Appointment of all offices I would have given to the President.... You are apprehensive the President when once chosen, will be chosen again and again as long as he lives. So much the better as it appears to me.... The less frequently they [elections] happen the less danger.... Elections, my dear sir, Elections to offices which are great objects of Ambition, I look at with terror. Experiments of this kind have been so often tryed, and so universally found productive of Horrors, that there is great Reason to dread them."

The early rumblings of the French Revolution pointed up the differences between them even more. Jefferson was convinced that the people had only to overthrow the government, establish one of their own choosing, and all would be well. Adams had doubts. "The world will be entertained with noble sentiments and enchanting Eloquence, but will not essential Ideas be sometimes forgotten, in the anxious study of brilliant Phrases?" New, more liberal institutions needed to be devised before France could succeed. For all his doubts, Adams told his friend he was departing from Europe leaving behind "the most fervent good Wishes for the Safety and Prosperity of all who have the Cause of Humanity, Equity, Equality and Liberty at heart."

After a brief hiatus the two men renewed their friendship as members of Washington's government—Jefferson as Secretary of State, Adams as Vice-President. The developing violence of the French Revolution forced them intellectually farther apart. The distance widened in 1790 when Adams published *Discourses on Davila*, which originally appeared as a series of thirty-two newspaper articles. He was obsessed with the misuse of the word "equality." Again and again he sought to limit its meaning. "Although, among men, all are subject by nature to *equal laws* of morality, and in society have a right to *equal laws* for their government, yet no two men are perfectly equal in person, property, understanding, activity, and virtue, or ever can be made so by any power less than that which created them." When he searched for fundamental American principles, he found them not in Jefferson's Declaration, which he studiously avoided mentioning now, but in the Declaration of Resolves put forth by the First Continental Congress—and written by "little John Adams," as he noted deprecatingly. That Declaration entitled Americans to "life, liberty, and property." No mention of the word "equality" occurred.

Jefferson referred to the *Discourses* as "political heresies." When he learned the phrase had reached his old friend, he hastened to write Adams that this should not be the cause of ending their warm relationship, for it had long been known "that You and I differ in our Ideas of the best form of Government, . . . but we have differed as friends should so, respecting the purity of each other's motives...." Adams answered with an unconscious bow to Jefferson's circumspect personality. "I know not what your Idea is of the best form of Government. You and I have never had a serious conversation together that I can recollect concerning the nature of Government."

Jefferson, without really attempting to understand Adams's political philosophy, helped spread the word that the Vice-President was attached to monarchy and had abandoned all his republican principles. Adams had abandoned nothing; he was airing views long held. The views he had held on popular sovereignty in 1776 had only been refined, not changed, when he spoke to Benjamin Rush in mid-1789. "Whenever I use the word republic with approbation, I mean a government in which the people have collectively, or by representation, an essential share in the sovereignty." He sees popular sovereignty limited to some extent by the power the people have given their representatives, something quite different from Jefferson's literal interpretation of the phrase.

Liberty, which Adams had always seen as something limited, he now defines as "being subject to equal laws only." Talk from his old friend Sam Adams about the love of liberty being interwoven in the soul of man infuriated him. He reminded his cousin it was also embedded in the soul of the wolf. "We must not then depend alone upon the love of liberty in the soul of man for its preservation," he went on. "Some political institutions must be prepared, to assist this love against its enemies. Without these, the struggle will ever end only in a change of impostors."

As the Age of Paine, to use Adams's title, began to become a reality, Adams fought all the harder to hold it back. What incensed him most was that a sound maxim like "men are born free and equal" had been "perverted by knaves and fools." Men may have equal rights, Adams granted, "but they cannot, ought not to have equal power," and this was what Jefferson and his followers were suggesting. When equality comes to be interpreted as equality of power, that leads to majority rule and, implied Adams, America is right back to the principle that all Europe has acted on—"that Power was Right." "Power always sincerely, conscientiously,... believes itself Right," Adams told Jefferson toward the end of their lives. "Power always thinks it has a great Soul, and vast Views, beyond the Comprehension of the Weak; and that it is doing God Service, when it is violating all his Laws.... And I may be deceived as much as any of them, when I say, that Power must never be trusted without a Check."

A new idea—a living thing—was forcing itself through, and Adams stood by protesting its birth but helpless to prevent it. Saddest of all, his closest friends were certain he was "devoted to monarchy in all its forms and consequences." Birth of the new age, however, came slowly enough not to prevent his election to the Presidency in 1796 by a slim majority over Jefferson. And the friendship with Jefferson had not yet deteriorated completely. Through Benjamin Rush, Jefferson heard that Adams had spoken "with pleasure of the prospect of administering the government in a connection with you." But the old intimacy was gone.

Four years passed, another election was held, and soon afterward the man Adams had regarded as a mere youngster in 1776 came to call upon him as President-Elect. "Mr. Adams advanced to him in a hurried and agitated step," a friend long later remembered Jefferson telling him, "and with a tremulous voice, said 'You have turned me out, you have turned me out!'" Now it was Jefferson's turn for kindliness, and soon he had calmed John Adams's anger. The two spent the remainder of the morning chatting and saw no more of each other the rest of their lives.

Jefferson's two terms in the White House passed, and silence continued between the men. Mrs. Adams carried on a brief, stilted correspondence with Jefferson without her husband's knowledge. Jefferson explained that both parties had the public good in mind, but "one fears most the ignorance of the people: the other the selfishness of rulers independant of them. Which is right, time and experience will prove." The rift continued for nearly a decade more, then Benjamin Rush forced the old friendship alive again. During the "negotiations" Jefferson said something to Rush that had been obscured in 1776 but that time had made apparent. "Our different views of the same subjects are the results of the difference in our organization and experience." Later he amplified that remark to Adams directly: "It is probable that our difference of opinion may in some measure be produced by a difference of character in those among whom we live."

Old age helped to dampen the heat of those differences. More important, America had changed so much in their lifetimes, that they, men of another era, had more in common now, for all their differences, than the new generation arisen. They were men of the eighteenth century, and that in 1812, when they began to correspond once again, overrode all the distinctions between the South and New England. Adams spoke the pride of both when he wrote of the past they shared: "We may say that the Eighteenth Century, notwithstanding its Errors and Vices has been, of all that are past, the most honourable to human Nature. Knowledge and Virtues were increased and diffused, Arts, Sciences useful to Men, ameliorating their condition, were improved, more than in any former equal Period."

From the beginning of the friendship's renewal, the two men sought to explain themselves to one another. At first they discussed specific issues they had disagreed over—non-importation and non-intercourse; the role of the judiciary in the national government; "neglect of the Navy"; the Alien and Sedition laws. Soon they ventured into more general matters. Adams raised the question of the role of aristocrats in society. "Who are these 'aristocrats'? Who shall judge? Who shall select these choice Spirits from the rest of the Congregation? Themselves?" Jefferson answered that there was a natural aristocracy among men based on virtue and talents, that there was an artificial aristocracy grounded on wealth and birth. "The artificial aristocracy is a mischievous ingredient in government, and provision should be made to prevent it's ascendancy," he said. "On the question, What is the best provision, you and I differ.... *You* think it best to put the Pseudo-aristoi into a separate chamber of legislation where they may be hindered from doing mischief.... *I* think the best remedy is exactly that provided by all our constitutions, to leave to the citizens the free election and separation of the aristoi from the pseudo-aristoi, of the wheat from the chaff. In general they will elect the real good and wise. In some instances, wealth may corrupt, and birth blind them; but not in sufficient degree to endanger the society."

That reply raised more questions than it answered for Adams's still sharp mind. What did Jefferson mean by talents? Fashion had stretched the word out of shape. "Education, Wealth, Strength, Beauty, Stature, Birth, Marriage, graceful Attitudes and Motions, Gait, Air, Complexion, Physiognomy, are Talents, as well as Genius and Science, and Learning. Any one of these Talents, that in fact commands or influences true Votes in Society, gives to the Man who possesses it, the Character of an Aristocrat, in my Sense of the Word."

Jefferson's optimism that the people would "elect the real good and wise" still remained so far from Adams's doubts that they dropped the subject of aristocracy. The French Revolution kept turning up again and again in their letters. "Let me now ask you, very seriously my Friend," Adams wrote, "Where are now in 1813, the Perfection and perfectability of human Nature? Where is now, the progress of the human Mind? Where is the Amelioration of Society? Where the Augmentations of human Comforts?" Later Adams recalled with subdued satisfaction his prophecy that a million humans would die in the French Revolution. Jefferson acknowledged Adams's rightness but refused to give up hope. "That same light from our West seems to have spread and illuminated the very engines employed to extinguish it. It has given them a glimmering of their rights and their power. The idea of representative government has taken root and growth among them." The strength of Jefferson's faith in that Revolution continued to puzzle and intrigue Adams to the end of their correspondence. "The object is worth rivers of blood, and years of desolation for what inheritance so valuable can man leave to his posterity?" Jefferson wrote in 1823, and Adams agreed. He had never said it was not; he had only insisted in 1789 not to expect too much too soon from people accustomed to bigotry, ignorance, and tyranny.

As eighteenth century gentlemen, they found themselves in agreement on many matters. Jefferson spoke for both when he said that the moral sense was innate in men, "as much a part of our constitution as that of feeling, seeing, or hearing." They agreed that whatever affects the happiness of men is virtuous. Jefferson had edged closer to Adams's view on the tyranny of the majority when he wrote in 1821: "The inquisition of public opinion overwhelms in practice the freedom asserted by the laws in theory." And both feared for the Union. "Aye! there's the rub!" said Adams, and Jefferson no doubt nodded in agreement as he read the words. "I fear there will be greater difficulties to preserve our Union, than You and I, our Fathers Brothers Friends Disciples and Sons have had to form it."

The turmoil in Missouri over the question of slavery tormented these two old men and made them doubt the durability of all they had built. "From the battle of Bunker's hill to the treaty of Paris we never had so ominous a question," wrote Jefferson. "I thank god that I shall not live to witness it's issue." Adams matched Jefferson's pessimism perfectly in his answer: "The Missouri question I hope will follow the other Waves under the Ship and do no harm. I know it is high treason to express a doubt of the perpetual duration of our vast American Empire, and our free Institution[s],... but I am sometimes Cassandra enough to dream that another Hamilton, another Burr might rend this mighty Fabric in twain, or perhaps into a leash, and a few more choice Spirits of the same Stamp, might produce as many Nations in North America as there are in Europe."

More and more it was apparent an old way of life was swiftly being superceded by a new and strange one. It must have seemed odd to these two old gentlemen who, after a friendship of nearly a half century, still addressed one another as "Dear Sir," to see now on the political scene a candidate for the President of the United States who was known everywhere as "Andy" Jackson. Jackson did not change America into something new; he mirrored changes that had come about in the twilight of Jefferson's and Adams's lives, changes that to some extent Jefferson's Declaration had served as guide for and that Adams had fought bitterly from the moment he had seen them on the horizon. Jackson's nickname heralded more than the arrival of informality in American life. It was the people's way of bringing their leader down to their level. The thing Adams had feared and Jefferson had never meant to be taken literally—all men are equal in every way —had come to pass.

The new age had taken other words from the Declaration and warped them to their needs. America was now the "bedollared nation," according to Benjamin Rush. With the new emphasis on material things, the age had created a new definition of happiness. Gone was Jefferson's and Adams's understanding of the word as the achievement of virtue or moral perfection. Happiness was now synonymous with material success. The word "liberty," too, had undergone a change. Freedom for the eighteenth century had carried with it obligations to society that restricted the right. Men in that era had duties as well as rights. Now liberty, or *laissez faire* as it came to be called, carried no duty to act only in the best interests of society. The acquisitive instinct had free play, untrammeled by obligations to anything but self-interest.

The nineteenth century might twist Jefferson's words into

new meanings; it nonetheless *thought* it listened to him. It knew it did not listen to John Adams. Jefferson had the best of the future—for a time. Only when American society took on some of the complexity that Adams had always envisioned it would, did he begin to receive a hearing. Neither Jefferson nor the early nineteenth century understood when Adams remarked: "I think a free government is necessarily a complicated Piece of Machinery, the nice and exact Adjustment of whose Springs Wheels and Weights are not yet well comprehended by the Artists of the Age and still less by the People." Jefferson had throughout a long life in politics found no reason to amend his remark of 1774 that "the whole art of government consists in the art of being honest," a remark implicit throughout the Declaration and, despite Adams's blistering comments to the contrary, one that would mislead the people for over a century, if not longer. It would take the twentieth century to at least begin to appreciate Adams's insight.

In time Adams's interpretation of the Declaration's "glittering generalities" would receive a more favorable hearing. In time, too, after enduring a decade and more of Nazism, the twentieth century would accept more easily Adams's low view of mankind, his awareness that the evil in man could be restrained only by effective institutions that checked and balanced it, not by innocent faith in man's capacity for good. "The vast prospect of Mankind...," Adams wrote in 1817, "has sickened my very Soul; and almost reconciled me to Swifts Travels among The Yahoo's." That sentence appeals so much to the cynical twentieth century that the thought Adams followed it up with is often overlooked. "Yet I never can be a Misanthrope. *Homo Sum* ["I am a man"]. I must hate myself before I can hate my Fellow Men: and that I cannot and will not do. No! I will not hate any of them, base, brutal and devilish as some of them have been to me."

Perhaps the wheel has turned too far in Adams's favor. Will America repeat the obverse of its mistake of the nineteenth century? Then it had listened almost solely to Thomas Jefferson; now it appears to be giving its fullest attention to John Adams. Will the nation forget that just as it needed both men in 1776 to give it the Declaration of Independence, it still needs both men in the twentieth century—one man with his eye on the mark, the other with his eye above the mark?

For all their differences the two marksmen were not too far apart at the end. "My temperament is sanguine," Jefferson wrote in 1816. "I steer my bark with Hope in the head, leaving Fear astern. My hopes indeed sometimes fail; but not oftener than the forebodings of the gloomy." Adams answered this way: "I admire your Navigation and should like to sail with you, either in your Bark or in my own, along side of yours; Hope, with her gay Ensigns displayed at the Prow; fear with her Hobgoblins behind the Stern."

An Epilogue:

A Salad of Illusions?

❋ ❋ ❋ ❋ ❋ ❋ ❋ ❋

Ideas won't keep. Something must be done about them. The idea must constantly be seen in some new aspect. Some element of novelty must be brought into it freshly from time to time.

ALFRED NORTH WHITEHEAD

JOHN ADAMS and Thomas Jefferson died within a few hours of each other on July 4, 1826. For weeks the press was filled with comment on this coincidence, so extraordinary to many that it seemed to reveal God's hand guiding the American experiment. Soon, however, the noise died down, as Adams might have predicted. John Adams had never expected the future to hand him many honors. "Mausoleums, statues, monuments will never be erected to me," he once said, "nor flattering orations spoken to transmit me to posterity in brilliant colors." He was right, as so often before. Jefferson had a right to count on more, yet within a few years lovely Monticello had become a storehouse for a farmer's grain, and southerners were saying that the principles embedded in the Declaration's preamble were "false, sophistical or unmeaning."

Even in the North those principles no longer won uncritical praise, especially among the intellectuals. Jarvis Gregg, a tutor in Dartmouth College, said in 1834 that while the Declaration was "the apple of the public eye," that eye was covered by a cataract. That document, he said, overlooks the fact that God

227

has established natural inequalities and distinctions. "But why labor a point that is so plain? Because there is a spirit of radicalism pervading a portion of the public mind, of which this principle is the root." The abolitionists, who were just beginning to propagate their gospel, expressed that spirit. Gregg, who favored gradual emancipation of the slaves, developed an elaborate and scholarly argument, much along the lines southerners were devising at this point, to prove the natural rights philosophy false. The abolitionists not only held to an indefensible philosophy, their approach to the slavery question was ill-mannered and foolhardy. "Indiscriminate invective will only provoke defiance," Gregg said, then went on to conclude: ". . . let the principles of the abolitionists extensively prevail among us...and not only every advocate of perpetual bondage, but every friend of gradual and ultimate emancipation at the south will be against us...If they [these doctrines] become general in New England and the non-slaveholding States, the horrors of a civil war must be the inevitable result."

From this point, until Gregg's prediction came true, the divergent views toward the Declaration never altered. One side, led in the beginning by William Lloyd Garrison, said that the principles in Jefferson's paper were absolute and unchanging, and had the force of moral law. The other, led by Calhoun, denied the validity of the natural rights doctrine. By the 1850's northern leaders were accepting the southern interpretation in the hope they could save the union. Rufus Choate condemned the newly formed Republican party by calling "its constitution the glittering and sounding generalities of the Declaration of Independence." A year later the Supreme Court said in the Dred Scott decision that "the legislation and histories of the times, and the language used in the Declaration of Independence, show, that neither the class of persons who had been imported as slaves, nor their descendants, whether they had become free or not, were then acknowledged as a part of the people, nor intended to be included in the general words used in that memorable instrument...." The court, of course, was right. The Declaration as Jefferson had written it clearly intended to include the Negro among "all men." As amended by Congress that "memorable instrument" was intended to exclude the Negro from the rights natural to other men. But the reformers of the generation before the Civil War were no more interested in an accurate interpretation of the past than Jefferson and *his* generation had been when they concocted the Declaration of Independence. They wished to use the past to shape the present as they desired it.

The court's decision and its use of the Declaration—"that electric cord...that links the hearts of patriotic and liberty-loving men together," Lincoln called it—prompted Lincoln to challenge Stephen Douglas for his Senate seat in 1858. The Declaration provided one of the themes in the debates of the ensuing campaign. At the start Lincoln tended to be more clever than sincere. "Now, sirs," he said at Chicago, "....we have Judge Douglas giving his exposition of what the Declaration of Independence means, and we have him saying that the people of America are equal to the people of England. According to his construction, you Germans are not connected with it.... I should like to know if taking this old Declaration of Independence, which declares that all men are equal upon principle and making exceptions to it where will it stop. If one man says it does not mean a negro, why not another say it does not mean some other man? If that declaration is not the truth, let us get the Statute book, in which we find it and tear it out! Who is so bold as to do it [Voices—"me," "no one," &c]? If it is not true let us tear it out! [cries of "no, no"] let us stick to it then, [cheers] let us stand firmly by it then [applause]."

Douglas amplified his earlier remarks by saying he had "intended to allude...to men of European birth or descent, being white men." He then went on: "I am not only opposed to negro equality, but I am opposed to Indian equality. I am opposed to putting the coolies, now importing into this country, on an equality with us ... I hold that the white race, the European race, I care not whether Irish, German, French, Scotch, English or to what nation they belong, so they are the white race to be our equals."

Lincoln soon after discarded tricks of rhetoric and appeals to the audience. "My declarations upon this subject of negro slavery may be mis-represented, but can not be misunderstood," he said at Springfield. "I have said that I do not understand the Declaration to mean that all men were created equal in all respects. They are not our equal in color; but I suppose that it does mean to declare that all men are equal in some respects; they are equal in their right to 'life, liberty, and the pursuit of happiness.' Certainly the negro is not our equal in color—perhaps not in many other respects; still, in the right to put into his mouth the bread that his own hands have earned, he is the equal of every other man, white or black. In pointing out that more has been given you, you can not be justified in taking away the little which has been given him. All I ask for the negro is that if you do not like him, let him alone. If God gave him little, that little let him enjoy."

Two years later the Republican Party platform opened with the statement "That the maintenance of the principles promulgated in the Declaration of Independence and embodied in the Federal Constitution . . . is essential to the preservation of our Republican institutions. . . ." It was hissed but slipped through with a bare majority. Lincoln was nominated and elected. The war came. It ended. Northern leaders set out to implement the ideals of the Declaration in the South. Sincere attempts were made to give the Negro equality, liberty, and the chance to pursue happiness unmolested. The efforts ended when the South convinced the North to let the "problem" be settled on southern terms. The Declaration again became the document as Douglas had interpreted it—a white man's Declaration that implicitly excluded Negroes.

A few southerners, like George W. Cable, refused to accept this emasculated version. "As to my pen," he wrote in 1888, "I dedicate it to that great question—not of party exigency but of political ethics—on which I can best speak and write, to which as a native Louisianian and 'ex-Confederate' I am duty bound, and which is still the most serious and urgent question before the nation: a peaceable renaissance of the southern states upon the political foundations laid by the nation's fathers, northern and southern, when they rose above the dictates of established order, the temptations of the moment's comfort, and the fear to take risks for the right, and gave to their children and the world the Declaration of Independence as an ultimate ideal to be daily and yearly striven toward with faith, diligence, and courage."

Once Americans had decided, for the time being at least, that the Declaration did not apply to the Negro, the country turned to the question of economic inequality. Since the Civil War the disparity between rich and poor had increased, but in the meantime the defenders of vested interests had come upon a weapon to rebuff those who demanded economic equality. Charles Darwin's *Origin of Species* and the phrase "survival of the fittest" buried within that volume had given them a scientific answer to Jefferson's statement that all men were created equal. Abbott Lawrence could now say with confidence in 1889 in his *Essays in Government* that the natural rights theory was "exploded doctrine." For Nicholas Murray Butler, "the corner-stone of democracy is natural inequality, its ideal the selection of the most fit." "The doctrine that all men are equal is being gradually dropped, from its inherent absurdity..." William Graham Sumner remarked in *Folkways*.

Sumner was wrong. Darwin's ideas, like Newton's three centuries earlier, could be a double-edged weapon. Edward Bellamy, for instance, argued in *Equality* that democracy—and "equality is the vital principle of democracy"—was an evolutionary process. The Declaration had simply stated the ideal toward which society was evolving. But most of those who favored Jefferson's ideas answered the Darwinians by ignoring them. Henry George, for instance, paid no attention to the findings of science in *Progress and Poverty*. "The reform I have proposed," he wrote, "accords with all that is politically, socially, or morally desirable. It has the qualities of a true reform, for it will make all other reforms easier. What is it but the carrying out in letter and spirit of the truth enunciated in the Declaration of Independence? ... Political liberty, when the equal right to land is denied, becomes, as population increases and invention goes on, merely the liberty to compete for employment at starvation wages."

The Populists paid little attention to George's specific proposals, but they shared his affection for the Declaration. Their party was conceived on July 4, 1892, and their first platform came forth as a "declaration of principles" similar in form and content to Jefferson's. (About the time the Populists were using the Declaration as their political text, Julia Ward Howe, mirroring the genteel attitude of the day, wrote an article on "How the Fourth of July Should be Celebrated." Her ideal Fourth would abolish fireworks and liquor and center on "a Spartan feast, wholesome and simple," and a pledge of good citizenship. She found no spot to commemorate the Declaration of Independence in this antiseptic day of hers.) When Bryan carried the Populists into the Democratic party in 1896, he played down their demand for economic equality. We believe, he said in his appeal for the votes of New Yorkers, "as asserted in the Declaration of Independence, that all men are created equal; but that does not mean that all men are or can be equal in possessions, in ability, or in merit; it simply means that all shall stand equal before the law...." The Declaration had come, of course, to mean much more, and all Bryan's rhetoric was not going to alter the fact.

The Spanish-American War temporarily distracted Americans

from concern with equality and turned them to another phrase in the Declaration—"consent of the governed." "We regret that it has become necessary in the land of Washington and Lincoln [not the land of Jefferson] to reaffirm that all men, of whatever race or color, are entitled to life, liberty, and the pursuit of happiness," ran the platform of the American Anti-Imperialist League of 1899. "We maintain that governments derive their just powers from the consent of the governed.... We earnestly condemn the policy of the present national administration in the Philippines. It seeks to extinguish the spirit of 1776 in those islands."

The Anti-Imperialists were answered by Amos K. Fiske, who believed the Declaration "consecrated to perpetuity some of the most obvious fallacies that were ever promulgated . . ." Men have no natural rights. "Rights, in the political sense and in the social sense, are acquired, or conceded, as society and policy develop.... Rights, when once acquired, are not inalienable." The right of the people of Cuba to self-government, then, depended on their ability to exercise it. And, asked Ames, must the lack of the consent of the people of the Philippines, "even though induced by ignorance or incapacity of judgment, stand against a better judgment of what is for the well-being of the islands and their people; stand against the interests of the United States in that part of the world, however important they may be...?"

The argument lingered on into the Progressive period. When in 1902 Senator Spooner referred to the phrase all men are created equal as "a living lie in this land for seventy years," Samuel C. Parks published in the now dying Populist magazine *Arena* "A Defence of the Declaration of Independence." He argued warmly that "the right of self-government follows logically and inevitably from the right to life and liberty." He censured as "the *doctrine of thrones*" the patronizing assumption that the United States had the right to govern the Filipinos. Spooner claimed that the Filipinos were uncivilized, yet in America three Presidents had been assassinated, the nation had endured a civil war that took nearly a million lives and "filled the land with widows and orphans," and, added Parks with heavy emphasis, "*the United States is the only country in the Christian world where human beings are roasted alive.*"

The Progressives, like those who had gone before, found in the Declaration exactly what the times led them to find. "We think of it as a highly theoretical document," Woodrow Wilson wrote in 1908, "but except for its assertion that all men are equal it is not. It is intensely practical, even upon the question of liberty.... Its chief justification of the right of the colonists to break with the mother country is the assertion that men have always the right to determine for themselves by their own preferences and their own circumstances whether the government they live under is based upon such principles or administered according to such forms as are likely to effect their safety and happiness. In brief, political liberty is the right of those who are governed to adjust government to their own needs and interests."

B. O. Flower described Jefferson in the *Arena* as "the leader and the very life of the progressive or reform element," and William Allen White said much the same thing about Jefferson's paper when he wrote of the Progressives' achievements in 1910: "Each of these innovations, the secret ballot, the primary, and the reformed party, is a step toward democracy—a step toward the Declaration of Independence and away from the Constitution, which so feared majority rule that the majority was hedged about with checks and balances at every possible point."

Most of the Progressive leaders came from middle-class backgrounds and were less concerned with economic than political abuse. They sought generally to take government out of the hands of vested interests—big business and political bosses—and thus they tended to see the Declaration in terms of political rights. "The whole document," George Harvey wrote in 1915, "was a complaint of and a protest against bad government, and conversely a practical pledge to establish and to maintain good government... That was the end for which independence was only a means. Good Government, and again, Good Government; and yet again, Good Government."

With the onset of World War I, the sense of American mission embedded in the Declaration became usable once again. Up to now the prevailing notion had been that American institutions were distinctive and it was hoped the rest of the world would soon copy them. This was Lincoln's belief and it was the one expressed by Hayne Davis in the *Independent* in 1903 when he wrote: "In this Americanization of the world America's part is simply to let her light so shine, by wise conduct of her own home affairs, that other nations may see her good works and adopt the political principle which has been her source of power." Wilson transformed this passive belief into a fighting faith when he urged Americans in 1918 to be "citizens of the world" and to make "the world safe for democracy."

When World War I ended, the Declaration did not escape the scepticism that crept into America. The remark of one writer, that "the signers of the Declaration of Independence themselves can hardly have meant what they said to be taken literally," was typical of the times. Mencken's work of the period is shot through with contempt for Jefferson's paper and the ideas put forth in it. Carl Becker found, after a close study of the Declaration, that it "was founded upon a superficial knowledge of history ... and upon a naïve faith in the instinctive virtues of human kind." This faith could not survive the realities of the twentieth century, where nationalism and industrialism "provided an atmosphere in which faith in Humanity could only gasp for breath." In his *coup de grâce* to that faith, Becker steered clear of cynicism. He mourned the passing of this age of innocence, for the sentiments expressed in the Declaration were those of "a humane and engaging faith." He went on: "At its best it preached toleration in place of persecution, goodwill in place of hate, peace in place of war. It taught that beneath all local and temporary diversity, beneath the superficial traits and talents that distinguish men and nations, all men are equal in the possession of a common humanity; and to the end that concord might prevail on the earth instead of strife, it invited men to promote in themselves the humanity which bound them to their fellows and to shape their conduct and their institutions in harmony with it." No faith could have asked for a more eloquent burial.

But Becker's burial, while it expressed the thoughts of a large part of intellectual America, was not accepted by all. Vernon Parrington, for one, still found much in the old faith. "The humanitarian idealism of the Declaration has always echoed as a battle-cry in the hearts of those who dream of an America dedicated to democratic ends," he wrote in the 1920's, about the time Becker published *The Declaration of Independence.* "It cannot be long ignored or repudiated, for sooner or later it returns to plague the council of practical politics. It is constantly breaking out in fresh revolt....Without its freshening influence our political history would have been much more sordid and materialistic."

The depression of the 1930's would seem to have revived respect for the Declaration. Franklin D. Roosevelt referred to it in his first inaugural. "The first term of the high contract was for liberty and the pursuit of happiness," he said. He continued in an ominous vein, so far as those who resisted change were concerned. "We have learned a great deal of both in the past century. We know that individual liberty and individual happiness mean nothing unless both are ordered in the sense that one man's meat is not another man's poison....Faith in America in our tradition of personal responsibility, faith in our institutions, faith in ourselves demands that we recognize the new terms of the old social contract."

Exactly what the new terms were only appeared when the New Deal unfolded. But in the unfolding the public prints re-

mained chary of the Declaration. The *National Republic*—
"a Magazine of Fundamental Patriotism," according to its mast-
head—printed a routine piece about the parchment copy of the
Declaration and its travels about the country. Otherwise, there
was little comment about the document. It was as if the American
press now feared to comment about a document which not too
long ago had justified a revolution. Its fears seemed justified, for
during the depression all liberal and radical organizations at one
time or another exhibited Jefferson's paper as the touchstone
of their ideals. The socialists, for example, according to Harry W.
Laidler in 1937, believed "that government should be instituted
to advance life, liberty, and the pursuit of happiness."

The depression went and Hitler came and men began to forget
they had decried the idea of natural rights. Carl Becker now
wrote an article entitled "What Is Still Living in the Philosophy
of Thomas Jefferson?" This time he found a great deal. Henry
Alonzo Myers asked in 1945 *Are Men Equal?* and found that
"the proposition of equality is true because it is useful." He concluded that "the history of the United States shows conclusively
that the proposition of equality works. It unites men, making
society possible."

But the skiff made of paper, it would seem, had ended its
sail. In the America of the late 1940's and '50's, less and less
attention was paid to the Declaration. Some said the less the
better. "Our age is involved in irony because so many dreams of
our nation have been so cruelly refuted by history," Reinhold
Niebuhr has remarked. "It is necessary to be wiser than our creed
if we would survive in the struggle against communism."

It has been effectively argued in recent years that the Declaration of Independence has outlived its usefulness. More than that,
some say that what life it still has does more to lead Americans
astray than toward a sane and reasonable goal. Much can be said
for this view of the Declaration.

For one thing, America had achieved the firm union that "the Unanimous Declaration of the Thirteen United States of America" pretended existed in 1776. The Declaration had eased its way into the American conscience about the time the loosely knit United States began to be concerned with the problem of unity. James Madison had recorded an exchange between Luther Martin of Maryland and James Wilson in the Constitutional Convention in 1787, in which Mr. Martin "said he considered that the separation from G[reat] B[ritain] placed the 13 States in a state of Nature towards each other." Mr. Wilson refused to admit that. "He read the declaration of Independence, observing thereon that the *United Colonies* were declared to be free & independent States; and inferring that they were independent, not *individually* but *Unitedly* and that they were confederated as they were independent States."

Use of the Declaration to clarify the nature of the union continued down to the Civil War. The South's political philosopher John Taylor of Caroline said in 1823: "A people of each state [was] created by the declaration of independence, invested with sovereignty, and therefore entitled to unite or not." About the same time, John Quincy Adams was contending in the North that when the American people revolted they did so as one people, not thirteen separate peoples. He called the constitution a return from the disunity of the Articles of Confederation, a return to the theory of the Declaration of Independence. The final statement of the North's view was made by Lincoln just before the war that settled the question broke out. "The Union is much older than the Constitution," he said in his inaugural address. "It was formed, in fact, by the Articles of Association in 1774. It was further matured, and the faith of all the then thirteen States expressly plighted and engaged that it should be perpetual, by the Articles of Confederation in 1776. And finally, in 1787, one of the declared objects for ordaining and establishing the Constitution was '*to form a more perfect Union.*'"

It required a long civil war, a century of industrial and technological development, and a revolution in communications to bring about the unity that James Wilson, John Quincy Adams, and Abraham Lincoln talked about. The Declaration shared in the achievement to the extent that the ideal of union it embodied came through the years to serve as a moral imperative to these men. Once the union had become forever fixed, the Declaration had lost one of its reasons for surviving.

Meanwhile, the sentiments embedded in Jefferson's preamble had lost most of their driving power for the majority of Americans. The belief that all men are created equal became an efficacious slogan only when it ceased to be a self-evident fact. Its effectiveness today, considering the past, is slight for all save Negroes. This is not said to minimize the plight of the Negro but to point up the fact that America now has more equality than any nation in the history of mankind. The extremes of wealth so apparent in the nineteenth century have all but disappeared in the postwar prosperity of the 1950's and '60's. With the disappearance, much of the tension in the old social problem has evaporated. "To all intents and purposes," says Father R. L. Bruckberger, a recent visitor from France, "you Americans have solved [the social problem]. You no longer have that bitter obdurate antagonism between rich and poor which for so long has characterized it."

Despite the incantations of the sociologists who picture America as a class-ridden society filled with status seekers, equality—be it political, economic, or even social—remains a persistent fact. Minority groups—again, except for the Negro—that once turned to the Declaration for spiritual sustenance no longer find the need. Prejudice persists, of course, but only in an attenuated form. Ethnic and religious groups once excluded from positions of power in politics and business have infiltrated the Anglo-Saxon ranks everywhere. Equality, whether it be judged a virtue or vice of American life, must be accepted as an ideal all but fully realized. "When I say that we value Equality," Seymour Martin Lipset has written, "I mean that we believe all persons must be given respect simply because they are human beings; we believe that the differences between high- and low-status people reflect accidental, and perhaps temporary, variations in position—differences which should not be stressed in social relationships."

The phrase "pursuit of happiness" has also lost much of its power to move men in contemporary America. While happiness itself may remain a flimsy hope for many, few feel they are actively restrained from pursuing it. What force remains in the phrase for Americans strikes some as a force for evil. "The final vulgarity is to equate the ultimate ends of life with the dubious goals of 'happiness' and to equate happiness with creature comforts," Reinhold Niebuhr says. "Our nation, despite its so-called religious revival, is today threatened by this kind of vulgarity. It is what creates the ironic similarity between the technocratic approach to life, despite the emphasis we place on the dignity of the individual in our culture and the absence of such an emphasis in the communist culture."

Niebuhr reflects the currently fashionable attitude toward the Declaration. This view, if it does not date from George Santayana, at least received one of its most effective statements from him. Santayana believed that the Declaration and the sentiments it contained had acted as a baleful influence on American thought and that the influence was powerful enough to affect the views of so perceptive an American as William James. At the start of the Spanish-American War, says Santayana, James "cried disconsolately that he had lost his country, when his country, just beginning to play its part in the history of the world, appeared to ignore an ideal that he had innocently expected would always guide it, because this ideal had been eloquently expressed in the Declaration of Independence.

"But the Declaration of Independence was a piece of literature, a salad of illusions," Santayana continues. "Admiration for the noble savage, for the ancient Romans (whose republic was founded on slavery and war) mixed with the quietistic maxims of the Sermon on the Mount, may inspire a Rousseau but it cannot guide a government. The American Colonies were rehearsing independence and were ready for it. That was what gave to the Declaration of Independence its timeliness and political weight.

"In 1898 the United States were rehearsing domination over tropical America and were ready to organize and legalize it; it served their commercial and military interests and their imaginative passions. Such antecedents and such facilities made intervention sooner or later inevitable. Domination was the implicit aim, whatever might be the language or event or thoughts of individuals. William James had not lost his country; his country was in good health and just reaching the age of puberty. He had merely lost his way in its physiological history."

Santayana here mirrors the attitude of many Europeans toward the Declaration. Wyndham Lewis, for instance, finds it filled with illusions, the most serious being that it injected "into the classical politics of the United States all that is unworldly, and, if you like, sentimental." Lewis errs, of course, when he says the Declaration injected this attitude into American politics. It was already there, and Jefferson merely extracted it from thoughts then in the air. He treads on more solid ground when he remarks: "It should be added that the theology, too, which, in the Declaration of Independence, is introduced to provide those 'rights' with a Divine Origin, conferred a further metaphysical complication upon this document."

Blame for this—if "blame" is the word—must fall on the Continental Congress, not Jefferson. Father Bruckberger finds this "metaphysical complication" a virtue. "The sentence inscribed on the wall by the French Convention as a preamble to the Declaration of the Rights of Man and of the Citizen—'The citizen is born, lives, and dies for his country'—is blasphemy; it is a profession of idolatry in the sense that it endows something created and created by man—the nation—with divine right over the individual. The American Declaration of Independence is at the other extreme from such idolatry. According to this Declaration man is born, lives, and dies free, created by God for happiness; he lives and dies under God's Providence, awaiting His judgment."

The danger in all this is the implication that God takes sides. The North and South both drew on the Declaration before and during the Civil War, and each spent much energy during the war telling their people God sided with them. (Only when the South lost did it decide God had been neutral and that material wealth, plus luck, had given the North victory.) Today a devout Congress has made sure that school children realize that the flag they pledge allegiance to represents one nation under God, and that the national government, which spends billions on armaments, has taken the added precaution of adding "In God We Trust" to the paper money. All this tends to further the American illusion that the Declaration expresses a sharp distinction between a virtuous United States and a tyrannical Europe.

Part and parcel of this illusion is the simplistic notion of evil in the Declaration. A tyrant, combining with a few others, had caused all the trouble. Remove him from the scene and all would go well. The evil had been imposed on America from outside by a few. Jefferson drew on a tradition for his Declaration that rejected "the Christian idea of the ambiguity of human virtue," to use Reinhold Niebuhr's words. "In the liberal world the evils in human nature and history were ascribed to social institutions or to ignorance or some other manageable defect in human nature or environment." This explanation of why society malfunctions —one that John Adams so vehemently rejected—has been perpetuated by every reform group in American history, with nearly all of them drawing on the Declaration for inspiration. The abolitionists were certain the Negro's problems could be solved simply by freedom. The Progressives were convinced that after tinkering with the nation's political machinery all would soon be right again with America.

The dilemma Jefferson led the United States into was, as we have seen, one hard for him to avoid. His job, among other things, had been to rouse the people, and to do this he had had to picture the enemy as the personification of evil. Unfortunately, he carried out the assignment so well that his argument became a fixed part of American ideology. The people are taught that all great political decisions are based on principles and that when conflict occurs it is between good and evil, two moral absolutes. No hint is given that there can be honest differences between men and governments in which neither side has a monopoly on good. In the 1952 Republican convention, a disagreement developed between the Eisenhower and Taft forces over the seating of certain delegates. Taft wanted the issue settled behind closed doors on the merits of the case. Eisenhower's people determined to reduce the difference to a moral issue and to picture it before the public as a battle between good and evil. They did this, and Taft, in the role of conniver, lost the battle.

The illusion perpetrated in the Declaration, that politics is an endless drama between forces of good and evil, Jefferson knew, if only from the debates on independence, to be nonsensical in 1776, but he never ceased moralizing on great political issues. Woodrow Wilson, for one, saw this flaw in Jefferson's writings. He thought they lacked "hard and practical sense," that they were "un-American in being abstract, sentimental, rationalistic, rather than practical." And yet Wilson often lifted Jefferson's words for his own speeches, and he adopted the same double-image used by Jefferson and most American leaders—on the one hand he was the great idealist to the public who took his stand on moral principles; on the other he was the politician who behind the scenes viewed foreign and domestic affairs with a sharp, practical judgment. The result of this double approach to politics was that the people were carried into World War I on false assumptions which, when their true nature was revealed, led to a cynical and bitter rejection of Wilson and much of what he stood for.

Wilson, of course, should not be censured unduly; no President, unless it was Lincoln, has done much to reduce the gap between the real and ostensible motives for American actions. "In foreign affairs," Abraham Kaplan has written, "we picture ourselves as actuated only by moral considerations, while other nations go whoring after the false gods of their own self-interest." Ours is a morality of words to Kaplan. "What is objectionable in a verbalistic morality is that its symbols function not as ideals but as utopias. They do not guide moral action, but substitute for it."

Another illusion implicit in the Declaration is that Americans are God's chosen people. John Adams, for all his Puritan roots, would have none of this. "We may boast that *we* are the chosen people," he said in 1814; "we may even thank God that we are not like other men; but, after all, it will be but flattery, and the delusion, the self-deceit of the Pharisee." Adams also decried the belief that the American view of life could and should be projected onto the world scene. Father Bruckberger has advanced the latest version of this missionary duty of America. "Now, America, your task is to extend the Declaration of Independence to the whole world, to all nations and races," he writes in *Image of America*. "If you are to remain worthy of your heritage, you must now help solve the social problems between white and colored peoples." Father Bruckberger believes one world not only possible but necessary, and it must be under American auspices. Reinhold Niebuhr, on the other hand, sees this as one more illusion stemming from the Declaration. He believes that "our success in world politics necessitates a disavowal of the pretentious elements in our original dream, and a recognition of the values and virtues which enter into history in unpredictable ways and which defy the logic which either liberal or Marxist planners had conceived for it."

It is hard to believe, to judge by the number of still thriving illusions in the Declaration, that the document any longer serves as a valuable part of the real American tradition. What, then, if anything, in the Declaration remains a living force that justifies its high position in the American tradition?

First, it should be remembered that the Declaration puts human rights above property rights. "From Americans we learned that it is *only* human beings that are important," a Manus islander once told Margaret Mead, revealing a view toward life that Jefferson and his Declaration helped to impose on the United States. And in putting human rights over property rights the Declaration also serves to check the state's power. The absolutes it sets up have nothing superior above them, not even the nation. "The State always discovers excellent excuses for depriving the individual of his rights or for narrowing his exercise of them," Father Bruckberger remarks. "One of the most persuasive excuses is the claim to be acting for the common good and for national unity. The founders of the American republic believed that the best way to safeguard the common good and national unity was to entrust them as far as possible to the private initiative of free individuals. In this they were truly original."

The Declaration also remains that still small voice constantly pricking the American conscience. "There have been lapses," says Roger Burlingame, thinking of the American attitude toward the Negro, "but these lapses have always been accompanied by loud whispers of conscience." All men may not, by any test of logic, be created equal, but, says Burlingame, "however false we denote it, we cannot forget it . . . it keeps shaming us into reforming legislation, to stir us, to war against those who exploit the inequalities of man."

The assumptions of the Declaration in a strictly logical sense are wrong. There are no rights of men that originate in nature, there are, indeed, no purely absolute rights at all. What is involved here, however, is an attitude, to borrow an insight from Charles L. Black, Jr. Men who regard these rights as absolute will work with more determination to realize them than men who regard them as relative to time and place. By calling these rights natural or absolute we only "express our determination not to *allow* their alienation." But there is a danger here that the Declaration obscures. Natural rights, as Abraham Kaplan states, "are an achievement, not a heritage. It is the blunting of this point in the attempt to justify these values by referring them to a basis in 'nature' which is a danger to democratic values."

One of the striking things about the Declaration is that throughout its life, regardless of who has used it, it has rarely served to promote the status quo or to defend vested interests. (An exception to this occurred in the late nineteenth and early twentieth centuries when the courts emphasized the word "liberty" in order to promote the "liberty of contract" concept, which favored business over labor and generally operated against the welfare of the people at large.) Jefferson's ideas originated in the liberal tradition of Europe and America, and that tradition has never feared change.

Near the end of a long life, Alfred North Whitehead told a friend that "no period of history has ever been great or ever can be that does not act on some sort of high, idealistic motives, and idealism in our time has been shoved aside, and we are paying the penalty for it." What idealism does survive in our times stems in some measure from the high purposes Jefferson set forth in the Declaration. This idealism has at times made America appear self-righteous in the eyes of others, but it has also prevented any gross abuse of its power. No nation in history has been more generous with its abundance nor asked for less in return. Surely, some of this—a nobility of action, not just of thought—has rubbed off from the Declaration.

Bibliographical Essay

This book grew out of an earlier work, *In the Midst of a Revolution* (1961), which dealt with an upheaval in Pennsylvania politics in mid-1776. Though that volume centered on Pennsylvania, the presence of Congress in Philadelphia caused local and continental affairs sometimes to intermesh, particularly during the months when Congress approached a declaration of independence. Despite occasional over-lapping in the two stories they have been fairly easy to keep separate. The earlier account concerned itself mainly with political events. This one is essentially a history of ideas and concerned with politics only to the extent activity in that sphere illuminates or clarifies the ideas of eighteenth century American leaders.

Temerity blended with trepidation is required to launch one more book on the Declaration of Independence. The work done has been, of course, enormous. Much of it is jejune, much repetitive; some, like J. H. Hazelton's, is exhaustive; and some, like Carl Becker's and Julian Boyd's, ranks among the best writing done by American historians. I am under no illusion that in this new re-telling the story has been told once and for all. I will be satisfied if, to use the words of another, this book gives a glimpse of the ingredients which went to make up the thought patterns of Americans in the late eighteenth century.

All quotations are reproduced as they appear in the sources used. I have up-dated spelling and punctuation only where the editors of the sources have done so. I have avoided "a paroxysm of citations," hoping that the bibliographical comments for each chapter will satisfy those who wish to follow up a particular aspect of the story.

A final word. Let me thank those friends at Pace College who read this work in manuscript—Benjamin Ford, John Flaherty, and John Walsh. Let me thank especially two other friends—Merle Curti for encouragement, and Ruth Ann Lief, my first and possibly my best reader.

Chapter 1: THE COURSE OF EVENTS

The Journals of the Continental Congress, 1774–1789 (34 vols., 1904–1937), edited by Worthington C. Ford and others, provided the foundation for events that occurred on the day of Jefferson's return. Equally helpful was the Fourth Series (1774–1776) of *The American Archives ...a Documentary History of...the North American Colonies* (6 vols., 1837–1846), edited by Peter Force. Volume six has the letters from Washington and Schuyler read aloud by Hancock.

Anyone who wishes to know something of the tension and confusion that dominated Congress from 1775 to mid-1776 must turn to the writings of John Adams. For this chapter I drew particularly on *The Life and Works of John Adams* (10 vols., 1850–1856), and *The Familiar Letters of John Adams and his Wife Abigail* (1876), both edited by his grandson Charles Francis Adams. (All previous published versions of John Adams's writings are being superseded by the magnificent new edition, six volumes of which have thus far appeared, edited by Lyman Butterfield and others. All my quotations come from the earlier editions, some of which transcribe his writings literally, others of which modernize his spelling and punctuation.)

This chapter draws much from the diary of Richard Smith, which appeared in the *American Historical Review*, 1 (1896–1897), 288–310, 493–516. Smith's abbreviated daily account of happenings in Congress often fills gaps left by Adams, whose multitude of committee duties left him by 1776 little energy or time to keep up his own diary. Whatever lacunae still exist can be filled from Edmund Cody Burnett's superb collection of *Letters of the Members of the Continental Congress* (8 vols., 1921–1938). Volume one offered the most for this chapter.

Burnett's *Letters* provided the raw material for one of the most satisfactory secondary accounts of Congress, his *The Continental Congress* (1941). The chronological arrangement makes it possible to follow events day by day. A more popular account but nonetheless able and accurate is Lynn Montross's *The Reluctant Rebels* (1950). Montross's title reflects a sounder judgment on the delegates than Cornelia Meigs's *The Violent Men* (1949). Miss Meigs's subtitle—*A Study of Human Relations in the First American Congress*—points up her particular approach to the subject.

While Curtis Nettels's *George Washington and the American Revolution* (1951) pushes Congress off center-stage, his book is indispensable for understanding the period. Nettels's thesis, that in the main it was George Washington and not Congress who led America toward independence, must be taken with salt, but the book as a whole is one of the ablest to emerge in recent years on the period. I qualify that remark only enough to make room for a slim but excellent volume by Edmund S. Morgan, *The Birth of the Republic 1763-1789* (1956). Morgan has managed with a succinctness that never sacrifices relevant detail to catch the feeling of the era and yet remain always accurate in emphasis and content.

For a fuller account of the ground covered by Nettels and Morgan, turn to John C. Miller's two well-written books—*Origins of the American Revolution* (1943) and *Triumph of Freedom* (1948). Miller sees the Declaration as a victory for the radical wing of the Whig Party, a false conclusion it seems to me but one that only slightly mars his excellent panoramic picture of the war and politics of the period. The early part of Allan Nevins's *The American States During and After the Revolution 1775-1789* (1924) remains important for anyone who wants to dig deeply into the period, but the plodding style makes it heavy going for all but the most interested. Harold Donaldson Eberlein and Cortlandt Van Dyke Hubbard have provided a reliable account of the State House's history, interlarded with excerpts from original sources, in their *Diary of Independence Hall* (1948).

The confidence Americans expressed on the eve of independence turns up everywhere. Even Anglophiles like Daniel Leonard, writing as Massachusettensis in 1775, and Charles Inglis in *The True Interest of America Impartially Stated* (1776), shared it. Franklin's remark appears in a 1760 letter to Lord Kames. Adams's remark, which he later called "my declaration of independence of 1755," turns up in a letter to Nathan Webb, October 12, 1755. Jefferson's comments occur in a letter to William Randolph, written in either late May or early June of 1776, found in Volume one of Julian Boyd, ed., *The Papers of Thomas Jefferson* (fifteen vols. thus far, 1950-1964). Aaron Leaming's diary is located at the Historical Society of Pennsylvania, Philadelphia. Lee McCardell, *Ill-Starred General: Braddock of the Coldstream Guards* (1958), gives an idea how Braddock's defeat helped bolster American self-confidence as early as 1755. Alexander Hamilton's remarks are found most conveniently in Richard B. Morris, ed., *The Basic Ideas of Alexander Hamilton* (1957).

The influence on independence of the news that Hessian troops would be used in America has never been fully developed by historians, though comments on the event pervade writings of the day. Arthur M. Schlesinger, Sr. in *The Colonial Merchants and the American Revolution 1763-1776* (1918), quotes a British officer that it was "above all, the hiring of foreign troops to desolate their country" that made America "fierce, frantic and invincible." Reactions of delegates in Congress are found scattered throughout Volume two of Burnett's *Letters*.

William Bradford, Jr.'s letters to James Madison, 1774–1775, give a picture of Philadelphia and Congress of that period not found elsewhere. These letters, recently available only in manuscript at the Historical Society of Pennsylvania, now appear in the first volume of the Madison papers edited by William T. Hutchinson and William M. E. Rachal and others (2 vols. thus far, 1962).

The most succinct and clearest accounts of the prisoner-of-war isssue Washington talks of and also the troublesome problem of Dr. Church are found in Nettels's *Washington*. Miller's *Triumph of Freedom* and Carl Van Doren's *Benjamin Franklin* (1938) give adequate accounts of the Canadian fiasco, with Van Doren, of course, emphasizing Franklin's role.

The remark about a General Quillman being good for little comes from *The Autobiography of Benjamin Rush* (1948), edited by George W. Corner. Rush is quoting Stephen Hopkins of Rhode Island. Alexander Graydon's *Memoirs of His Own Times with Reminiscences of the Men and Events of the Revolution* (1846 edition) is the source for the quotation about the Pennsylvanian who loved his ease and Madeira more than liberty. Dr. James Clitherall's diary, extracted in the *Pennsylvania Magazine of History and Biography*, 22 (1898), 468–474, gives the early prediction of Washington's future reputation. The *Journal . . . 1789–1791* of William Maclay (1927 edition) provided the fact that Jefferson normally slumped in a seat.

Chapter 2: A Mind in the Making

Merrill D. Petersen's excellent *The Jefferson Image in the American Mind* (1960) devotes sixty-three closely printed pages to bibliographical information about Jefferson. Even that compendium fails to cover the material available. All that is possible here is a comment on reading that has in some way enlightened my own understanding of Jefferson. For more elaborate and perhaps more balanced listings see Petersen or the third volume of the *Literary History of the United States* (3 vols., 1948; supplement to Volume three, 1960).

The first volume of Julian Boyd's meticulous and brilliant edition of the *Jefferson Papers* was, of course, indispensable. As those who have used this edition know, the introductory essays to the more important papers, like *A Summary View*, Jefferson's Constitution for Virginia, or the Declaration, are major aids to understanding the man and the period. A brief but reliable collection for those less fully concerned with Jefferson is the Modern Library edition (1944) of his writings edited by Adrienne Koch and William Peden. Francis Coleman Rosenberger's *The Jefferson Reader* (1953) is a sensible collection of useful secondary and original accounts. The fascinating recollections of Edmund Bacon, Jefferson's overseer, and Isaac Jefferson, one of his slaves, can be read in excerpt in Rosenberger or in full in Hamilton W. Pierson, *Jefferson at Monticello; The Private Life of Thomas Jefferson; From Entirely New Materials* (1862), and Rayford W. Logan, ed., *Memoirs of a Monticello Slave: As Dictated to Charles Campbell in the 1840's by Isaac, One of Thomas Jefferson's Slaves* (1951).

Among the multitude of essays on Jefferson I mention only three I profited from reading. John Dos Passos's in *The Ground We Stand On* (1940); Carl Becker's "Thomas Jefferson" in the *Encyclopedia of Social Sciences* (15 vols., 1930–1934); and Esmond Wright, "Thomas Jefferson and the Jeffersonian Idea" in H. C. Allen and C. P. Hill, eds., *British Essays in American History* (1957).

A personal judgment of the most appealing biographies would include James Parton's *Life of Thomas Jefferson* (1899), and also Albert Jay Nock's *Thomas Jefferson* (1926), by far the best written work on Jefferson and in the early parts flawless. I found John Dos Passos's *The Head and Heart of Thomas Jefferson* (1954) curiously disappointing. Dos Passos knows the period and the man and can depict it as well as Nock, but he becomes so interested in Jefferson's surroundings that his main character gets lost in the landscape.

The monument in Jeffersonian biography is Henry S. Randall's *The Life of Thomas Jefferson* (3 vols., 1858). It has yet to be replaced. The next distinguished biography in point of time is Gilbert Chinard, *Thomas Jefferson, Apostle of Americanism* (1929). Chinard was among the first to tone down the emphasis on Locke and point up the importance of the classics and law in shaping Jefferson's mind. He exaggerates to my way of thinking the influence of law and makes Jefferson out to be more conservative and backward-looking than the facts warrant. I have less enthusiasm for Marie Kimball's *Road to Glory* (1943), the most relevant of her three volumes on Jefferson to my work. A pietistic quality detracts from her account. I think she exaggerates Peter Jefferson's aristocratic background, but her remarks on Jefferson's civilized youth do much to correct an old impression he was a child of the frontier. She is excellent on Jefferson as a lawyer, and I depended heavily on her account of Monticello and the sources Jefferson drew on for his ideas.

Dumas Malone has made the latest effort at a definitive biography of Jefferson. Of the three volumes that have thus far appeared, the first, *Thomas Jefferson and the Rights of Man* (1948), deals with Jefferson through the Revolution. Malone is judicious, thorough, and accurate. His study is the most reliable available, but it should be supplemented by Nock and Parton, both of whom for me do a better job of capturing Jefferson's personality on paper.

Anyone concerned with Jefferson's ideas must depend extensively on Adrienne Koch's *Philosophy of Thomas Jefferson* (1943), as well as the relevant pages in her *Power, Morals, and the Founding Fathers* (1961), a collection in paperback of several essays on eighteenth century luminaries. Miss Koch emphasizes the importance of the classics in shaping Jefferson's thought and argues, effectively to my mind, against Chinard's view that his outlook was essentially conservative and legal. Charles M. Wiltse's *The Jeffersonian Tradition n American Democracy* (1935) proved of less value for me and too much influenced by the New Deal environment in which it was written. One of Wiltse's central ideas, as well as Chinard's, makes Jefferson a practical thinker little concerned with unworkable abstractions, and this I accept heartily. A book worth a glance for its trenchant comments on Jefferson is Wyndham Lewis's *America and Cosmic Man* (1948). Ursula M. von Eckardt in *The Pursuit of Happiness in the Democratic Creed* (1959) has many sound comments about Jefferson's ideas and the books that shaped them, but she has, it seems to me, given the reader more the raw material of her research rather than the results.

Henry Bamford Parkes's *The American Experience* (1947) is a remarkable book that deserves a wider audience than it has received up to now. It was of use here for its enlightening account of the agrarian mind and of the Virginia in which Jefferson grew up. Charles Beard also gives a general picture of the agrarian environment in *The Economic Origins of Jeffersonian Democracy* (1915). Colonial Virginia has been lucky in attracting the interest of some of America's best historians. Carl Bridenbaugh's *Seat of Empire, the Political Role of Eighteenth Century Williamsburg* (1950), and *Myths and Realities* (1952), present the Virginia planters as hard-working men who "led a gracious but not a cultural life." John David Mays, *Edmund Pendleton, 1721–1803* (2 vols., 1952) is more than a biography; it deals with Virginia and Revolutionary politics, the legal profession, and in passing presents graphic pictures of such sidelights as a Virginia court day. A succinct, perceptive general account of colonial Virginia can be found in Thomas P. Abernethy, *Three Virginia Frontiers* (1940). On the fluidity of Virginia society see Louis Wright, *First Gentleman of Virginia; Intellectual Qualities of the Early Colonial Ruling Class* (1940). Wright finds more learning among the aristocracy than Bridenbaugh.

I drew on Randall, Kimball, and Malone for my picture of Peter Jefferson, and also on Jefferson's *Autobiography*. Malone and Bridenbaugh give the best summary of Williamsburg in the eighteenth century. Malone's remarks in his biography can be supplemented by his later article, "Thomas Jefferson Goes to School in Williamsburg," in the *Virginia Quarterly Review, 33* (1957), 481–496. On Dr. Small see, in addition to Malone's remarks and Jefferson's *Autobiography*, Herbert L. Ganter, "William Small, Jefferson's Beloved Teacher," *William and Mary Quarterly*, 3rd series, 4 (1947), 505–511; James G. Crowther, *Famous American Men of Science* (1937); L. C. Tyler, "Virginia's Contribution to Science," in American Antiquarian Society, *Proceedings*, new series, 25 (1915), 363–364; and Theodore Hornberger, *Scientific Thought in the American Colleges, 1638–1800* (1945).

A good start for the general cultural picture of the America of Jefferson's youth is Michael Kraus, *The Atlantic Civilization: Eighteenth Century Origins* (1949). More recent, more relevant, and exceedingly provocative is Daniel Boorstin's *The Americans: The Colonial Experience* (1958). This is perhaps the spot to mention an excellent essay that concerns itself with "the nature of the relationship between Enlightenment ideas and early American political experience"—Bernard Bailyn, "Political Experience and Enlightenment Ideas in Eighteenth Century America," *American Historical Review, 67* (1962), 339–351.

An essay of only tangential use for my purposes but well worth mentioning for its excellence is: Frederick E. Brasch, "The Newtonian Epoch in the American Colonies, 1680–1783," American Antiquarian Society, *Proceedings,* new series, 49 (1939), 314–332. Brooke Hindle reprints two interesting letters in "Witherspoon, Rittenhouse, and Sir Isaac Newton [1776]," *William and Mary Quarterly*, 3rd series, 15 (1958), 365–372. I found I. Bernard Cohen's *Franklin and Newton* (1956) heavy going but of great use. Also helpful in clarifying Newton's ideas were John Maynard Keynes's "Newton, the Man," in *Essays and Sketches in Biography* (1956), 280–290, and E. N. da C. Andrade, *Sir Isaac Newton* (1954). The second volume of A. C. Crombie, *Medieval and Early Modern Science* (2 vols., 1959), and A. R. Hall, *The Scientific Revolution 1500–1800* (1954), proved to be excellent surveys for my purposes. The religious adjustment to science is well handled in Basil Willey's *The Seventeenth Century Background* (1956). The relationship between natural law and natural philosophy is discussed in Willey's *Eighteenth Century Background* (1940), in Alfred North Whitehead's *Science and the Modern World* (reprint, 1948), and *Adventures in Ideas* (1933). The sources of many of Jefferson's scientific views are discussed in Charles A. Browne's *Thomas Jefferson and the Scientific Trends of His Time* (1944). Edwin T. Martin explores this aspect of Jefferson in more detail in *Thomas Jefferson, Scientist* (1952).

Locke's writings are available in a multitude of editions. One of the most accessible is Isaiah Berlin, editor, *The Age of Enlightenment* (reprint, 1956). The most recent and authoritative biography is Maurice Cranston, *John Locke—A Biography* (1957). The reader interested in a succinct summary of Locke's ideas should also see Cranston's "John Locke," *Encounter*, 7 (December, 1956), 46–54. In "John Locke and the Spirit of '76," *Political Science Quarterly*, 73 (1958), 413–425, Bernard Wishy finds little support for "the radically individualistic political theory said to be implicit in the Declaration." Wishy has high praise for Willmoore Kendall's *John Locke and the Doctrine of Majority Rule* (1941). For one of the most incisive treatments of Locke's philosophy and its implications for the twentieth century, see Leo Strauss, *Natural Rights and History* (1953), and also his "Locke's Doctrine of Natural Law," *American Political Science Review*, 52 (June, 1958), 490–501. My own belief is that if Professor Strauss had read Jefferson's *Literary Bible* (1928), and *Commonplace Book* (1926), as edited by Gilbert Chinard, he would have seen that Jefferson interpreted the natural rights doctrine in the classical sense. The most competent historical study of how the doctrine was used in America is Benjamin F. Wright, *American Interpretations of Natural Law; a Study in the Historical Process of Political Thought* (1931). H. Trevor Colbourn's "Thomas Jefferson's Use of the Past," *William and Mary Quarterly, 3rd series*, 15 (1958), 56–70, presents a balanced judgment of a subject Chinard first commented on.

Kimball presents a detailed picture of Jefferson as a lawyer. John W. Davis's excellent remarks on the subject are most available in Rosenberger's *Jefferson Reader*, 117–130. Kimball gives several of Jefferson's book lists but the full titles of those books were culled from E. Millicent Sowerby's *Catalogue of the Library of Thomas Jefferson* (5 vols., 1952–59). Peter Quennell's *Hogarth's Progress* (1956), gives the story of the satire on Palladian architecture. The quotation from Shenstone about Polydore comes from Kimball. More detailed comments on Monticello are found in Fiske Kimball's *Thomas Jefferson, Architect* (1916) and Lewis Mumford, *The South in Architecture* (1941). The historian who found Monticello chilly is Henry Bamford Parkes.

There is nothing superior in the field on Virginians' political habits to Charles S. Syndor's slim and delightful volume, *Gentlemen Freeholder—Political Practices in Washington's Virginia* (1952). Syndor provides the dialogue between voter and candidate and also the explanation to Jefferson's judgment that half the colony's white males were disenfranchised by the voting requirements.

On Richard Bland, see Wright's *American Interpretations of Natural Law* for his spot in the general picture. Clinton L. Rossiter has written a full-length essay on Bland in *Seedtime of the Republic; the Origin of the American Tradition of Political Liberty* (1953). An earlier essay still worth a look is James E. Pate, "Richard Bland's Inquiry into the Rights of the British Colonies," *William and Mary Quarterly, 2nd series, 11* (1931) 20–28. Bland's pamphlet is not available in any modern reprint.

Jefferson's *A Summary View* is available in almost any collection of his writings, but the best, for its textual notes and comments, appears in the first volume of the *Jefferson Papers*, edited by Boyd. See, too, Anthony M. Lewis's provocative "Jefferson's *Summary View* as a Chart of Political Union," *William and Mary Quarterly, 3rd series, 5* (1948), 34–51.

Philadelphia during Jefferson's and Adams's stay through the spring and summer of 1776 is discussed fully in my *In the Midst of a Revolution*. The articles of Elector and others can be found in all Philadelphia papers throughout the period. Comment about Jefferson's constitution of 1776 has appeared off and on in historical journals for over three-quarters of a century. Worthington C. Ford in *Nation*, 51 (1890), 107–109, found the document conservative in nature; D. R. Anderson in the *American Historical Review*, 21 (1916), 750–754, saw it as radically democratic. Charles Beard in *Economic Origins of Jeffersonian Democracy* judged it conservative. Julian Boyd's essay in the *Jefferson Papers* favors the democratic interpretation. Edmund Randolph in the *Virginia Magazine of History and Biography, 44* (1936), *43*, has some contemporary comments about Jefferson's ideas on ratification of the constitution. Incidentally, Randolph's "Essay on the History of Virginia, 1774–1782," which is spread through Volumes forty-three, forty-four, and forty-five of the *Virginia Magazine*, offers first-rate reading for anyone interested in Virginia politics of the period. Randolph wrote unusually well and had a fine gift for characterization. If he had been given time to put his work in shape—much of it is little more than rough notes—it might have become a classic of American literature.

The rumor that both Franklin and Bland were spies turns up in a letter of William Bradford, Jr., to James Madison in 1775. Jefferson's activity on the floor of Congress appears in Richard Smith's *Diary*. The comment on Louis XIV's height comes from *The Splendid Century* (1953), by W. H. Lewis.

Chapter 3: THE COLOSSUS OF INDEPENDENCE

Albert Jay Nock paused in his biography of Jefferson to remark that "the figure of Adams is perhaps the most congenial—one may say perhaps the most lovable—of any made on the page of history by an

American of his period." Nearly everyone who takes the time to know Adams through his writings comes away with a similar feeling about the man. And yet only in recent years has much interest been given Adams's career. The bibliography on him is slim compared to that on Jefferson, despite the fact that a great mass of his writing has long been available. The previously mentioned ten-volume *Works* edited by Charles Francis Adams contains his diary, all important essays, his autobiography, and a great number of personal letters. The *Works* is supplemented by the wonderful *Familiar Letters,* wherein the more "lovable" side of Adams is exposed most fully. Adams's career in Congress is filled out further in "The Correspondence between John Adams and Professor John Winthrop," in the *Massachusetts Historical Society Collections,* 5th series, Volume four, (1878), 289–313. *The Warren-Adams Letters,* published by the Massachusetts Historical Society (2 vols., 1917 and 1925) are a valuable source for John Adams's political views, his hopes for the future, and his activities in general during this period; Sam Adams, to a lesser extent, exposes his views in this collection.

Adams reminisced about the Revolution the rest of his life. One excellent source of his recollections is *The Adams-Jefferson Letters* (2 vols., 1959), edited by Lester J. Cappon. Another is Worthington C. Ford's edition of *Statesman and Friend—Correspondence with Benjamin Waterhouse 1784-1822* (1927). It was to Dr. Waterhouse that Adams gave his magnificent denunciation of the Age of Paine. A book often difficult to locate even in large libraries but well worth the trouble when found is *Old Family Letters: Copied from the Originals for Alexander Biddle, Series A* (1892). Here Benjamin Rush and Adams ruminate at length about the past, the present, and the future of the American experience. Rush's side of the correspondence is more available in the two-volume edition of his letters edited by Lyman Butterfield (1951).

Only two brief collections of Adams's writings are available, but each is highly satisfactory and well edited: George A. Peek's *The Political Writings of John Adams: Representative Selections* (1954), and *The Selected Writings of John and John Quincy Adams,* edited by Adrienne Koch and William Peden (1946).

Much of the little that has been written on Adams is excellent. Benjamin Rush's moving sketch of his old friend can be found in Rush's *Autobiography.* Vernon L. Parrington's essay in the first volume of his *Main Currents in American Thought* (1927) is to my mind one of the finest brief essays on Adams. Equally incisive are the several essays scattered through Zoltán Haraszti's *John Adams and the Prophets of Progress* (1952). Mr. Haraszti considers Adams one of America's greatest political thinkers and concerns himself primarily with this side of his thought. Gilbert Chinard, author of the first modern full-length biography of Adams, reaches a similar conclusion in *Honest John Adams* (1933). He judges Adams "the most realistic statesman of his age." Catherine Drinker Bowen's *John Adams and the American Revolution* (1950) catches the spirit of Adams the man and of colonial Boston and Philadelphia but fails to deal adequately with Adams's ideas. I have not read the latest widely praised biography by Page Smith (2 vols., 1962). The interest now being shown in the man and his ideas suggests that he perhaps even more than Jefferson has something to say to twentieth century America, now so aware of the role of force and power in national life.

Adams's ideas on power and politics are most intelligently discussed in Stephen Kurtz's *The Presidency of John Adams; the Collapse of Federalism, 1795–1800* (1957). I also found Chapters three ("The Political Theories of John Adams") and four ("The Economic Ideas of John Adams") in Manning J. Dauer, *The Adams Federalists* (1953), useful summaries. The most detailed study of Adams's ideas on politics is Correa M. Walsh, *The Political Science of John Adams* (1915). Further studies are: Anson D. Morse, "The Politics of John Adams," *American Historical Review*, 4 (1899), 292–312; Francis N. Thorpe, "The Political Ideas of John Adams," *Pennsylvania Magazine of History and Biography*, *44* (1920) 1–46; Charles Warren, "John Adams and American Constitutions," Kentucky State Bar Association, *Proceedings*, twenty-seventh annual meeting. Chapter eleven in Beard's *Economic Origins of Jeffersonian Democracy* has some relevant remarks.

The best discussion by Adams of his political ideas in 1776 occurs in a letter to James Sullivan on May 26, and in the letter-pamphlet *Thoughts on Government*. The Sullivan letter contains a reference to James Harrington, the seventeenth century author of *Oceana*, a book generally accepted to have helped clarify Adams's political and economic ideas. I side-stepped the complexity of Harrington's thought in my essay in order to give more space to explaining Adams's ideas rather than their intellectual source. Perhaps I erred. If so, the interested reader may explore the matter in Caroline Robbins's *The Eighteenth-Century Commonwealthman* (1959). About the only other book available on Harrington's influence in America is a superficial, exaggerated study by H. F. Russell Smith, *Harrington and his Oceana; a Study of a Seventeenth Century Utopia and its Influence in America* (1914). Harrington's turgid prose is most accessible in Charles Blitzer, *The Political Writings of James Harrington—Representative Selections* (1953).

The picture of Boston in Adams's years there prior to the Revolution is drawn mainly from Carl Bridenbaugh, *Cities in Revolt* (1955). William Shippen's letter of July 27, 1776, about beginning new governments *de novo* can be found in the manuscript collection of the Historical Society of Pennsylvania.

Chapter 4: IN THE VERY MIDST OF A REVOLUTION

The early part of this chapter that relates to Pennsylvania politics has been adapted from my *In the Midst of a Revolution,* wherein the sources used are listed and discussed in full. The debate of May 15 was one of the few Adams took the time to report in some detail, and nearly all the quotations are drawn from his *Works.* Caesar Rodney's comments can be found in George H. Ryden, *Letters to and from Caesar Rodney 1756–1784* (1933). Rutledge's letter is in Burnett's *Letters,* as is Carter Braxton's.

An admitted flaw in this chapter has been to exaggerate the part John Adams played. In a sense John was a "front man" for his cousin Sam, who stood behind the scenes directing every move. "His...character...," John once remarked, "will never be accurately known to posterity, as it never was sufficiently known to its own age: his merit in the Revolution, if there was any merit in it, was and is beyond all calculation." Sam Adams's part, however, can only be deduced from what others say; he left few writings or comments of his own that permit the historian to "fatten up" his role. Those interested in following up his activities might explore the *Warren-Adams Letters* already mentioned, and his *Writings,* which have been edited by H. A. Cushing (4 vols., 1904–1908). Carl Becker's essay "Sam Adams" in the *Encyclopedia of Social Sciences* and John C. Miller's *Sam Adams* (1935) are the best accounts of his life.

J. H. Hazelton's *The Declaration of Independence* (1906) gives the fullest day-by-day account of the period covered in this chapter. Jefferson's notes on the June debate appear with full annotation in the first volume of Boyd's *Jefferson Papers.* A later account by Jefferson of these days occurs in his letter to the editor of *Journal de Paris,* August 29, 1787, which appears in Volume twelve of the *Papers.*

Much of the material discussed under Chapter one is also relevant here. Dickinson's part in these events is covered in Charles J. Stillé, *The Life and Times of John Dickinson 1732–1808* (2 vols., 1891) and in the same author's "Pennsylvania and the Declaration of Independence," *Pennsylvania Magazine of History and Biography,* 13 (1889), 385–429. A perceptive essay that does much to clarify Dickinson's ideas is H. Trevor Colbourn, "John Dickinson, Historical Revolutionary," *Penn-*

sylvania Magazine of History and Biography, 83 (1959), 271–292. Charles Page Smith's *James Wilson, Founding Father, 1742–1798* (1956), is the best biography available but does not handle Wilson's part in the events of 1776 adequately. Wilson's defense is in the United States Revolution Papers, Library of Congress, from where Hampton L. Carson ferreted it out. An off-print of his copy is available at the Historical Society of Pennsylvania. Though Sherman has received full treatment in Roger Sherman Boardman, *Roger Sherman, Signer and Statesman* (1938), I prefer Julian Boyd's accounts in "Portrait of a Cordwainer Statesman," *New England Quarterly*, 5 (1932), 221–236, and in the *Dictionary of American Biography*. The early pages of George Dangerfield's *Chancellor Robert R. Livingston of New York, 1746–1813* (1960), illuminate the character and ideas of one who embraced independence most reluctantly. Richard Henry Lee's decision to return to Virginia as soon as his relief arrived can be found in his *Letters* (2 vols., 1911 and 1914), edited by J. C. Ballagh.

Ford's edition of the *Journals* was again useful. Dr. Clitherall provided the quotation about the poll of the city troops. Robert Penn Warren's remarks on the Revolution appear in his *The Legacy of the Civil War* (1961), 82–83.

Chapter 5: THE SKIFF CONSTRUCTED

Anyone who ventures to analyze the Declaration must end deeply indebted to the works of three men—Becker, Boyd, and Hazelton— each of whom adds to our knowledge of the document in his own way. Hazelton provides information, Becker interpretation, and Boyd textual analysis. In addition to the three books by these gentlemen mentioned earlier the reader should also consult Becker's "The Declaration of Independence" in the *Encyclopedia of Social Sciences*, Boyd's "New Light on Jefferson and His Great Task," *The New York Times*, April 13, 1947, and above all the scrupulously edited drafts of the Declaration in Volume one of the Boyd edition of the *Papers*.

A great deal of effort has gone into tracing the historical origins of many of Jefferson's phrases, a subject that holds only slight interest for me. For those attracted to this problem the most authoritative work is Edward Dumbauld, *The Declaration and What It Means Today* (1950). Also pertinent are: James Sullivan, "The Antecedents of the Declaration of Independence," *Annual Report of the American Historical Association for 1902*, I, 67–85; H. L. Ganter, "Jefferson's 'Pursuit of Happiness' and Some Forgotten Men," *William and Mary Quarterly*, 2nd series 16 (1936), 422–434, 558–585; and Miss Eckardt's *Pursuit of Happiness*. To my mind Hannah Arendt's *On Revolutions* (1963) succeeds where Miss Eckardt's book fails. It will always sadden me that I read Miss

Arendt's work only as my own was about to head toward the printer. She and I diverge at several points over the interpretation of certain words and phrases in the Declaration. Nonetheless, there is hardly a paragraph in this chapter that would not have benefited from her perceptions and profound learning.

Even more effort has gone into attempting to prove Jefferson plagiarized much of his paper. This charge originated in Jefferson's lifetime and has yet to die. Judge Drayton's charge to a South Carolina jury is one reputed source; it can be found in Hezekiah Niles, *Principles and Acts of the Revolution in America* (1822), 327. Another supposed source are two articles by "Hampden" that appear in the *Virginia Gazette* (Dixon & Hunter), April 20 and 27, 1776. *The New Yorker's* Anthony West finds that "the second sentence of the Declaration of Independence comes, almost entire, from pages 3 and 4 of Overton's 'An Arrow Against All Tyrants,' of 1646, along with the doctrine of the derivation of just powers from the consent of the governed." My own additions to this list would include a letter dated June 14, 1776, from Mechanicks-Hall that appeared in the New York press, and a list of charges against the King that appeared in the *Pennsylvania Evening Post* for May 14, 1776.

I doubt if Jefferson consciously lifted from any of these sources, if only because he was too busy re-working his own earlier writings. However, it does seem incontrovertible that Jefferson depended on Mason's phrasing in the Virginia Declaration of Rights. Kate Mason Rowland agrees in her *Life of George Mason 1725-1792* (2 vols., 1892), and so does the more detached William F. Dana in "The Declaration of Independence as Justification for Revolution," *Harvard Law Review, 13* (1900), 319-343. Boyd holds "that he was directly influenced by the Mason Declaration is not yet proved and must in all probability remain a matter of opinion."

The point that it was part of Jefferson's task to make clear that the American Revolution was not against authority in general is one made by Walter Lippmann in his *The Public Philosophy* (1955), and also in the Dana article mentioned above. Wilbur Samuel Howell, "The Declaration of Independence and Eighteenth-Century Logic," *William and Mary Quarterly*, 3rd series, 18 (1961), 463-484, shows that Jefferson's ideas "were given added persuasive power by their adherence to the best contemporary standards of mathematical and scientific demonstration and to what the best contemporary thinkers expected of proof before it could claim to convince the reason."

Alonzo Myers in *Are Men Equal?* (1945) did much to enlighten me on Jefferson's use of the word "equal." I. Bernard Cohen's essay in

Benjamin Franklin (1953), mentions the substitution of "self-evident" for "sacred & undeniable." I hold with Boyd that it was Jefferson not Franklin who made the change, but Cohen's point nonetheless remains valid. Louis Hartz, *The Liberal Tradition in America; an Interpretation of American Political Thought Since the Revolution* (1955) develops further the meaning of "self-evident" for Americans of the day and why the word was so appropriate in the Declaration.

The interpretation in this chapter on the omission of the word "property" is only one more added to the many that historians have enjoyed making for well over a century. Myers suggests Jefferson left it out because it is "the most ambiguous of all the so-called natural rights." Wiltse and Chinard argue it is not a natural right at all, but a right of compact, and thus had no business in the preamble in the first place. Adrienne Koch in *Jefferson and Madison* (1950), discusses several practical reasons for the omission. My own belief is that agitation in Philadelphia and elsewhere to lower suffrage qualifications helped persuade Jefferson to drop the word. This, of course, remains a matter of opinion, as I have tried to make clear in the text. However, Chinard is most surely wrong in denying that property was not something Jefferson included among the natural rights.

"Pursuit of Happiness" is discussed in detail by Miss Eckardt, ably by Miss Koch in *The Philosophy of Thomas Jefferson,* and succinctly by Wiltse. Hannah Arendt's remarks are the most enlightening, especially in pointing up the eighteenth century distinction between private and public happiness and how Jefferson tended to obscure this distinction in his felicitous phrase. Howard Mumford Jones writes of what the phrase has meant since 1776 to Americans in *The Pursuit of Happiness* (1953).

The changes made by Jefferson, his committee, and Franklin are discussed in detail by Becker and Boyd. With hardly an exception I have followed Boyd's conclusions, most notably when he attributes "self-evident" to Jefferson, not Franklin as has generally been done.

I have skipped lightly over the twenty-eight charges in the Declaration. For those interested in knowing more about them see Sydney George Fisher, "The Twenty-Eight Charges Against the King in the Declaration of Independence," *Pennsylvania Magazine of History and Biography,* 31 (1907), 257–303, Herbert Friedenwald, *The Declaration of Independence* (1905), and especially Edward Dumbauld's *The Declaration of Independence and What it Means Today,* the latest and most authoritative account.

Divergent views on what Jefferson had done in the Declaration can be found in F. S. C. Northrop, *The Meeting of East and West. An*

Inquiry Concerning World Understanding (1947), especially Chapter three, and Ralph Barton Perry, *Puritanism and Democracy* (1944), Chapters six and seven. Two additional essays not to be missed are Carl Becker's "What Is Still Living in the Political Philosophy of Thomas Jefferson," *American Historical Review, 48* (1943), 691–706, and Moses Coit Tyler's in the first volume of his *Literary History of the American Revolution* (2 vols., 1897). Henry Bamford Parkes has an excellent essay in his *The Pragmatic Test* (1941) on Jefferson's ideas and why they were effective in eighteenth century America.

The interpretation in this chapter of the Declaration as a liberal document is one not currently popular. Vernon L. Parrington, whose reputation is at a low point, comes closest to the view I elaborate here. Parrington wrote in *Main Currents in American Thought:* "Samuel Adams and other followers of Locke had been content with the classical enumeration of life, liberty, and property; but in Jefferson's hands the English doctrine was given a revolutionary shift. The substitution of 'pursuit of happiness' for 'property' marks a complete break with the Whiggish doctrine of property rights that Locke had bequeathed to the English middle class, and the substitution of a broader sociological conception...." The opposite view is best expressed by Bernard Wishy's earlier mentioned article and by Robert R. Palmer in his "Notes on the Use of the Word 'Democracy' 1789–1799," *Political Science Quarterly, 68* (1953), 203–226; "The Dubious Democrat: Thomas Jefferson in Bourbon France," *Political Science Quarterly, 72* (1957) 388–404; and in his précis of Otto Vossler's *American Revolutionary Ideals in Their Relation to the European: A Study of Thomas Jefferson* which appeared in the *William and Mary Quarterly*, 3rd series, *12* (1955) 462–471. The reader is urged to see also Merrill Jensen, "Democracy and the American Revolution," *Huntington Library Quarterly*, August, 1957, and Roy N. Lokken, "The Concept of Democracy in Colonial Political Thought," *William and Mary Quarterly*, 3rd series, 16 (1959), 568–580.

Details about Jefferson's apartment in Philadelphia came from Thomas Donaldson, *The House in Which Thomas Jefferson Wrote the Declaration of Independence* (1898). Wright Morris's remarks at the head of this chapter are from *The Territory Ahead* (1958).

Chapter 6: A LEAP IN THE DARK

The title for this chapter comes from an essay in the *Pennsylvania Gazette* of May 1, 1776, where independence was regarded as a visionary scheme, "a leap in the dark." Leonard W. Labaree's *Conservatism in Early American History* (1948) directed my attention to this article.

My reconstruction of the debate in Congress July 1 and 2 draws heavily on Hazelton, on Boyd's *Jefferson Papers*, Volume one, Jefferson's letter to the editor of *Journal de Paris* in Volume twelve, and on John H. Powell's "The Debate on American Independence, July 1, 1776," *Delaware Notes, 23* (1950), 37–62. My account diverges at several points with Powell's and Hazelton's. We simply interpret the available material differently. Powell's essay seeks to understand Dickinson's action on the question of independence. It succeeds admirably in making the point, to use Powell's words, that "there was nothing timid or hesitant about Dickinson's program."

Powell's editing of "The Speech of John Dickinson Opposing the Declaration of Independence, 1 July 1776," in the *Pennsylvania Magazine of History and Biography, 65* (1941), 458–481, has been slightly modified here. Also the tense in Adams's recollection of his speech in answer to Dickinson has been altered. The account of Rodney's arrival comes mainly from a letter of Thomas McKean to Caesar Rodney, September 22, 1813, in Ryden, *Rodney Letters*. Edmund Randolph's remarks about the debate over "equal" in the Virginia Convention and his sketch of Robert Carter Nicholas are found in the *Virginia Magazine of History and Biography, 44* (1936), *45*, and *43* (1935), 125.

Abraham Clark's letter of July 4 is found in Burnett's *Letters*.

Chapter 7: THE SKIFF SETS SAIL

The account of the reading of the Declaration on July 8 is drawn principally from William Duane, Jr.'s *Passages from the Remembrancer of Christopher Marshall* (1839), from Burnett's *Letters*, and from Eberlein and Hubbard, *Diary of Independence Hall*. A biographical sketch by E. H. Hart of John Nixon, who read the Declaration that day, appears in the *Pennsylvania Magazine of History and Biography, 1* (1877), 188–202. John H. Powell in *The Books of a New Nation* (1957) lists the surviving copies of the Dunlap edition as fifteen. J. Michael Walsh, "Contemporary Broadside Editions of the Declaration of Independence, *Harvard Library Bulletin, 3* (1949), 31–43, puts the number at fourteen.

For contemporary comment on the reception of the Declaration see Hazelton. What Hazelton fails to do—perhaps it cannot be done—is to distinguish between the reaction to the act of declaring independence and the paper that announced that act. Did Jefferson's Declaration affect the minds and hearts of Americans then or were these noble sentiments forgotten until another day?

"How the First Anniversary of the Declaration of Independence was Celebrated in Philadelphia," *Pennsylvania Magazine of History and Biography*, 35 (1911), 372–373, provided the basis for the description of July 4, 1777. A letter from George Bryan to his wife in the same magazine, 41 (1917), 382–383, additional letters in Burnett's *Letters*, and a note of the Executive Council in the *Pennsylvania Archives: First Series* (12 vols., 1852–1856) in Volume five, 411–412, rounded out the picture.

Much of the bibliography in earlier sections of this essay dealing with Jefferson and Adams applies here. Most of the quotations that expose the thoughts and feelings of these men as they moved into old age are drawn from Cappon's edition of the Jefferson-Adams correspondence. My limited objective in this chapter has, of course, obviated any attempt to exhaust the differences between the two men.

Epilogue: A SALAD OF ILLUSIONS?

Curiously, there has been no full-length study of how Americans have used the Declaration of Independence. What Merrill D. Petersen has done for the Jefferson image in the American mind should some day be done for Jefferson's Declaration. The final chapter of Becker's *Declaration* provides a brilliant illustration of the possibilities in any such approach to the American past. I have done little more than lightly explore areas that Becker passed over. The best single essay I have seen on this subject, which appeared after this chapter was completed, is Philip F. Detweiler, "The Changing Reputation of the Declaration of Independence: The First Fifty Years," *William and Mary Quarterly*, 3rd series, *19* (1962), 557–574.

Niles' Register for 1826 is packed with material on the death of Adams and Jefferson, with the latter receiving much the most space. Samuel Eliot Morison's "John Adams and Thomas Jefferson" in *By Land and Sea* (1953), 219–230, gives a moving account. The event is discussed more fully in Lyman Butterfield, "The Jubilee of Independence, July 4, 1826," *Virginia Magazine of History and Biography*, *51* (1953), 119–140.

John C. Fitzpatrick, *The Spirit of Revolution* (1924), deals prosaically, compared to Becker, with the Declaration's history in the nineteenth century. The late eighteenth century's relative lack of interest in it appears in two of the early histories of the Revolution: David Ramsay's (1789), and William Gordon's (1788). Howard Mumford Jones, *The Pursuit of Happiness*, discusses the slow acceptance of the preamble in state constitutions. Philip F. Detweiler, "Congressional Debate on Slavery and the Declaration of Independence, 1819–21," *American Historical Review*, 63 (1958), 598–616, deals thoroughly with the first time the preamble "was examined and analyzed, praised or criticized, in large-scale fashion." Wesley Frank Craven, *The Legend of the Founding Fathers* (1956), and Merle Curti, *The Roots of American Loyalty* (1946), have something to say about the early use or lack of use of the Declaration in relation to the celebration of Independence Day. Craven makes the point that the document was in its early days used mainly to promote the union. Scattered references in Merrill Jensen, *The New Nation* (1951), suggest it was also being used to advertise America's purity and its mission to improve mankind.

With the onset of the French Revolution others besides John Adams directed their fury at the Declaration. Explore the writings of any Federalist and you come upon denunciations. A speech that Noah Webster or Fisher Ames might have made is David Daggett's 1799 Independence Day oration, *Sunbeams may be extracted from cucumbers, but the process is tedious*, reprinted in *The Magazine of History* (1922), extra number, No. 76. Daggett's Founding Fathers are not the Signers or those who made the Constitution but the early settlers of New England, and in praising them he manages to avoid all mention of the Declaration.

Margaret B. Smith, *The First Forty Years of Washington Society* (1906), 382–383, pictures Monticello thirteen years after Jefferson's death. Jarvis Gregg's attack on the Declaration appears in *American Quarterly Observer*, 2 (1834), 48–89. A marvelous summary of the natural rights doctrine in the midst of the slavery controversy occurs in John Quincy Adams, "An Oration Delivered Before the Cincinnati Astronomical Society" (1843), reprinted in the Koch-Peden edition of his writings, 397–407.

By the 1840's the Declaration is in low repute. Rufus Griswold in *Prose Writers* (1846) does not bother to mention it among Jefferson's writings that have any "claims to consideration." Richard Ely Selden, *Criticism of the Declaration of Independence as a Literary Document* (1846), speaks of "the unintelligible generalities at the beginning,... the sounding nonsense at the end." Rufus Choate's remark about "glittering generalities" turns up in "Letter of Rufus Choate to the Whigs of Maine, 1856," which can be found in Samuel G. Brown, *Works of Rufus Choate with a Memoir of His Life* (2 vols., 1862).

The comments of Lincoln and Douglas can be found in any collection of their debates of 1858. I used Paul M. Angle's edition, *Created Equal?*

The Complete Lincoln-Douglas Debates of 1858 (1958). *The Collected Works of Abraham Lincoln* (9 vols., 1953), edited by Roy P. Basler, lists over sixty references to the Declaration in its index. Harry V. Jaffa's *Crisis of the House Divided—An Interpretation of the Issues in the Lincoln-Douglas Debates* (1959), one of the outstanding books on Lincoln in recent years, pays particular attention to Lincoln's use of the Declaration.

After the Civil War, interest in the Declaration diversifies. Charles Francis Adams draws on the document in a way that would have horrified his grandfather in *"The Progress of Liberty in a Hundred Years, an Oration Delivered before the Citizens of Taunton 4th July 1876* (1876). George W. Cable's views can be found in Arlin Turner's edition of his writings on *The Negro Question* (1958). William Graham Sumner, who by the 1880's saw the doctrine of equality "being gradually dropped, for its inherent absurdity," can best be read in *Sumner Today* (1940), edited by M. R. Davie. Ames K. Fiske's attack on equality appears in "Some Consecrated Fallacies," *North American, 169* (December, 1899), 821–828.

The Populist-Progressive period saw a revival of favorable interest in the Declaration. Samuel C. Parks wrote "A Defense of the Declaration of Independence" for *Arena, 30* (August, 1903), 152–158, and in an earlier issue that magazine's editor, B. O. Flower, included "Jefferson's Service to Civilization During the Founding of the Republic," *29* (May, 1903), 500–518. Woodrow Wilson's defense of the document as "intensely practical, even upon the question of liberty," appears in his *Constitutional Government in the United States* (1908), 4.

The warmest defender of the Declaration in the 1920's was Vernon L. Parrington, whose two completed volumes of *Main Currents in American Thought* are an oblique defense of Jefferson's ideas as exemplified by the Declaration. Gunnar Myrdal summarizes in his Introduction to *An American Dilemma* (1944) that emerged out of the Declaration. Wyndham Lewis's views on Jefferson and his paper are scattered throughout his *America and Cosmic Man* (1948). Santayana speaks of "a salad of illusion," in *The Middle Span* (1945), 169. The remarks of Reinhold Niebuhr used in this chapter are scattered through *The Irony of American History* (1952). Seymour Martin Lipset defines equality in "Equal or Better in America," *Columbia University Forum, 4* (Spring, 1961), 17. Charles L. Black, Jr.'s remarks about absolutes regarded as an atttiude appeared in *Harper's Magazine*, February, 1961. Abraham Kaplan's closely reasoned defense of relativism is entitled "American Ethics and Public Policy," and appears in Elting E. Morison, ed., *The American Style—Essays in Value and Performance* (1958).

Index